The other volume in this series is:

Equality and Diversity in Education 2: National and International Contexts
Edited by *Patricia Potts, Felicity Armstrong and Mary Masterton*

This Reader is part of an Open University integrated teaching system. It is designed to evoke the critical understanding of students.

If you would like to study this course, please write to the Central Enquiries Office, The Open University, Walton Hall, Milton Keynes MK7 6AA, for a prospectus and application form. For more specific information write to the Higher Degrees Office at the same address.

Equality and Diversity in Education 1: Learning, Teaching and Managing in Schools

On what grounds are students included in or excluded from the educational mainstream? How can appropriate support be guaranteed for children, young people and adults who experience difficulties in learning, who are disabled or who experience social or other kinds of difficulty? This volume explores experiences of learning, attempts to develop inclusive curricula and the management of school-based provision. Each of the three parts is designed to bring alive and critically discuss for readers the personal experience of other people, the detail of innovative curriculum developments and the complexity of issues facing educational providers in the 1990s. Part I contains a range of personal and professional experiences; Part II turns to curricular issues; and Part III focuses on the problems facing teachers and governors in schools.

This volume and her sister, *Equality and Diversity 2: National and International Contexts*, are Readers for the Open University Course 'Developing Inclusive Curricula: Equality and Diversity in Education' (E829). The majority of the chapters are published here for the first time, reflecting a wide range of perspectives and interests on educational issues, and including both experienced and first-time writers. The two books in the series will appeal to teachers, non-teaching assistants and other school-based staff, parents, disabled people and those who have experienced difficulties in learning, social and health workers, and those working for voluntary organizations.

Equality and Diversity in Education 1: Learning, Teaching and Managing in Schools

Edited by
Patricia Potts, Felicity Armstrong
and Mary Masterton

London and New York
in association with
The Open University

Contents

Part III Managing education in the 1990s

Preface

This volume and her sister, *Equality and Diversity in Education 2: National and International Contexts for Practice and Research*, are the Readers for the Open University course 'Developing Inclusive Curricula: Equality and Diversity in Education' (E829), which is a module within the MA in Education Programme and also the postgraduate component of the Advanced Diploma in Special Needs in Education (D06). The course extends and complements our undergraduate course 'Learning for All' (E242).

The legislation of the late 1980s and early 1990s has transformed the education system in the UK, particularly in England and Wales. Centralization of control over the curriculum and assessment and decentralization of funding and management have affected the experience of all learners, from pre-school children to adults. Nurseries, schools, colleges, governing bodies, local education authorities, professional associations, voluntary organizations and parents' groups are all having to re-think their approach in response to the government's measures.

Competition between educational institutions in a commercial market place raises questions about the selection and classification of students. What grounds are accepted for their inclusion and exclusion? How can appropriate support be guaranteed for children, young people and adults who experience difficulties in learning, who are disabled or who experience social or other kinds of difficulty?

We expect our students to pursue their own lines of critical enquiry into these policies and practices and we have tried to reflect the diversity of their own interests in the course materials. We are also concerned to develop an awareness of those features of an education system which promote equality of value and opportunity for each student, whatever his or her ability or attainments. These commitments have determined our approach to shaping the contents of these Readers, which therefore include:

- Discussions of working towards equality in education;
- Illustrations of the range of perspectives and interests which exist on

educational issues, including parents' and consumers' views;
- Encouragement to develop a personal voice and a critical viewpoint, which includes reflecting on educational language and terminology;
- Reflections on the process of making enquiries;
- Comparative material from around the UK, Europe and beyond;
- Discussions of policy and practice in nursery, primary, secondary, tertiary and segregated specialized provision;
- Interdisciplinary and interagency material.

Students following the course actively investigate aspects of the education system, on their own or in collaboration. They all undertake three small-scale research projects: one on pupil perspectives, one on curriculum analysis and design and one on policy, decision-making and power. Each Reader contains material to support the stages of each project: to help students work out their research questions, to decide what methods of enquiry are appropriate and to evaluate their findings.

This volume focuses on experiences of learning and teaching and developments which concern individual schools. Reader 2 examines wider national and international contexts and discusses a range of practical, ethical and political issues relevant to the process of doing research.

Forty of the fifty-one contributions have been specially written for these books. The authors are not all white, not all able-bodied, not all men, not all professionals, not all teachers, not all educationally successful. They include both experienced and first-time writers.

Students following 'Developing inclusive Curricula: Equality and Diversity in Education' will include teachers, non-teaching assistants and other school-based staff, parents, disabled people and those who have experienced difficulties in learning, social workers, health workers and those working for voluntary organizations.

Patricia Potts

Introduction

Patricia Potts

This volume is concerned with experiences of learning, attempts to develop inclusive curricula and the management of school-based provision. The three parts of the book represent a sample of all the possible contributions that we could have commissioned or reproduced from other sources. They are designed to bring alive and critically discuss for readers the personal experience of other people, the detail of innovative curriculum developments and the complexity of issues facing educational providers in the 1990s.

Part I contains a range of personal and professional experiences. Corinne Grant's eldest daughter was experiencing difficulties in communication in her infant school. The subsequent assessment of Kelly's educational needs was painful for Corinne because it brought back memories of her own difficulties as a child. Telling her own story and linking it to what is happening to Kelly now has released Corinne to be more confident and articulate.

David Myrie, Anya Souza and Claire Debenham reflect back on their school and college days, commenting on their growing awareness of their difference and how they perceived this at the time. David links his own experience to that of the black students with whom he works, Anya remembers being treated as an alien being and Claire argues that her education has reinforced her sense of herself as working class. Past and present pupils in residential special schools then vividly describe the intensity of their damaging and restorative experiences and the section concludes with a collaborative chapter on experiences of being in care and of being a foster mother.

Part II turns to curricular issues and begins with a discussion by Judy Sebba of what teaching history means in the context of working with students who may be seen to have very little understanding of place, space and time. Christine Howe draws on psychological research into cognitive development to investigate her expectation that mixed-ability group work can enable children to make sense of physics and Caroline Haycock explores the benefits of using drama with junior pupils who experience difficulties with reading and writing.

The area of personal, social and sex education has become a priority in the mid-1990s. Inge Hempstead recorded and transcribed for us two conversations she had on these subjects with teenagers in Hounslow, where there is no longer any segregated provision for physically disabled students, and Karen Muskett reflects back on her years of teaching sex education in a special school for children and young people who experienced severe difficulties in communication. She discovered that they literally had no way of conversing about sex and that they had to create their own signs.

Marian Ellis describes how an inclusive approach is an extension of her nursery school's commitment to the LEA entitlement curriculum and the values of educational equality. She tells a graphic story of daily life in the nursery and details the activities of a group of children who are seen to have 'special educational needs'.

June Statham and Sian Wyn Siencyn report on how far Wales's policy of encouraging a bilingual approach can include disabled children and young people and those who experience difficulties in learning, and Felicity Armstrong presents a case study of a secondary school in north London where the fact that English is not the mother tongue of the majority of the students has been recognized and responded to. For example, worksheets for a technology course are available in Somali and Arabic as well as English.

Petra Pryke is an artist-turned-teacher working with young people on a visual arts youth training scheme. She describes the process by which her students are categorized as A, B or C types of learner and how the work they go on to do fails to match these negative expectations. This section concludes with a discussion of how far it is possible to develop an inclusive approach to the education of teachers.

Part III focuses on the problems facing senior teachers and governors in schools. Jim Conway and Mary Lawrence argue that it is possible to fulfil their twin aims of raising educational standards and of developing an inclusive approach which values all students equally. Felicity Fletcher-Campbell introduces the new inspection arrangements and discusses the implications for provision for disabled children and young people and those who experience difficulties in learning.

Next, Tim Silvester discusses the problems he faces in the 1990s as the headteacher of a non-maintained special school which provides for students what hardly any ordinary schools do, namely, an appropriate linguistic and cultural environment for deaf students. Geraldine Bunting and David McConnell then provide a Northern Ireland perspective on the education of children and young people who experience emotional and behavioural difficulties. What does it mean to be 'disruptive' in Belfast?

Margaret Bethell discusses issues for governors of secondary schools from her varying position as a governor and governor trainer who sometimes uses her wheelchair and sometimes does not.

The final two chapters describe and discuss ways of providing a mainstream post-16 curriculum for students whose educational requirements nearly always preclude their membership of ordinary communities. Liz and David Arrondelle have been tenacious in securing the kind of education that they want for their daughter Kirsty and Richard Westergreen-Thorne, a deputy head at Kirsty's school, sets her experience in the context of the school as a whole and its local consortium partners.

Part I

Experiences of learning

Chapter 1

'Unless I chose to tell you, you wouldn't know'

Corinne Grant

Corinne was prompted to reflect on her own schooldays when she and her husband became involved in the assessment of their daughter's difficulties in learning. Telling her own story has been both painful and rewarding.

Unless I chose to tell you, you wouldn't know – so I hope you will read this.

Just having to rely on someone to help with spelling, filling out forms, not really knowing what it would be like to have to go through life not having to ask 'is this filled out right?', 'did I spell that right?', and sometimes just not having enough confidence to ask people is the hardest thing for me. I know it may sound silly to someone else, but it's been my biggest hurdle in life.

When I was 8 years old I started at a school for children with special needs. My needs really being very basic reading, writing, maths and spelling. All the things that other people seem to find easy I seem to have to struggle with.

Thicko, spastic, nurd, stupid. All of these names have been applied to me over the last fifteen years, at first by other children but some adults have also voiced this opinion. Some have not been brave enough to say it to my face, but there are a few that have. I wish sometimes people would stop and think or, as the saying goes, 'engage their brain before they open their mouths', maybe then I wouldn't feel such an outsider. Or maybe it's just me, or maybe that's how I have been made to feel.

I grew up in a small village and went to the local school where my life consisted of being picked on, mostly by other children but sometimes the teachers would also have their say.

I remember being sat in assembly on my sixth birthday and being asked how old I was, I was so nervous I couldn't say a word. In the end they gave up and asked my brother. When I got back to class the teacher turned round on me and asked if I was an idiot. I asked if I could go to the loo. When she said yes I left the class like my feet were on fire. Now it's just a part of my life I would like to forget but if memories were that easy to forget I guess a lot of my life would have been erased.

I was born in 1969 and my mother had a nervous breakdown when I was 6, so I had to grow up very fast. I think it must have taken its toll on me somewhere along the line but I don't think it affected my education in any way. I know when Mum came home from hospital there were some days I didn't want to go to school in case she wasn't there when I came home from school but with time that feeling disappeared.

It's always seemed important to get my Dad's approval but in most cases I didn't succeed because I don't think he really understood about my problems. He always seemed to have time for my brother. When it came to me it was a case of 'in a minute'. Unfortunately, 'in a minute' seemed to come and go just like that. Now my Dad has remarried I don't see much of him so in a way the problem has sorted itself out. Now I have no expectations of him so therefore he doesn't have to have any of me. Deep down I know he loves me and maybe it would have been different if I'd not had any problems. It may have been easier for him to accept me.

My Mum was and still is there for me. That's not to say we didn't have our ups and downs because we did and still do. Mum spent most of her life sticking up for me. The family were always saying they couldn't understand why she sent me to special school because in their eyes there was nothing wrong with me. One thing it didn't stop her doing was talking for me when other people asked me questions. Mum would always speak for me. Sometimes I wish I'd had the guts to look up and say I can speak for myself, but I never did.

My big brother was always there to stick up for me, although we used to fight like cats and dogs when we got in from school. He only ever called me thick once. I told him if he did it again I was sure I could fix it so that he'd have to take a quick trip to the dentist. Of course we get on a lot better now, but sometimes if he steps out of place I just tell him he's not so perfect, which usually has the desired effect.

I wouldn't want you to think I was the best-behaved person in the world, I could kick and scream along with the best of them and sometimes that's just what I did.

I've always had one very important person in my life who had a very big influence on me, she was a teacher who was there to talk to me whenever I felt things were getting too much for me. With her help and understanding I began to see life a bit differently. We still keep in touch and when she can she comes to see us.

KELLY

Now it's about-turn for me because I have a child with special needs. Her main problems are speech and concentration.

How do you love a child with special needs? The answer is it's very hard. At times I really hated her for being the way she was, maybe you would have cause to reproach me. I think it was my way of coping with the situation. I felt that if I ignored her the problem would go away, but of course it didn't.

I think the worst thing from my point of view was that I felt I'd let her down and at the time it was easier to hate her than to love her. The biggest step for me was facing up to the fact she had a problem. When I did, it made life a lot easier for both of us. Now I wouldn't be without her.

You see, when it came to it I didn't want for my daughter what I've had to cope with most of my life.

It's really hard to know what my daughter feels. Sometimes it's written all over her face. On another day it's like a game of twenty questions. She's only 5. We have noticed that when something really scares her she will say 'don't frighten me'. When she feels frustrated she has a temper tantrum which can last 10 to 20 minutes. Most of all it's lots of cuddles when someone or something upsets her.

My biggest worry was maybe it was something I hadn't done, but I have been put in my place and told it is not my fault. Just knowing that has made all the hard work we have done all worth while.

The portage worker came to our home once a week and did one-to-one play with our daughter; things like colour matching, sound lotto, etc. The opportunity group is a playgroup for children with special needs. They also do one-to-one play with the children. They have speech therapy and music therapy. Without all these people I think we would have still been going around in the dark. If it was not for the wonderful work and dedicated help put in by the portage worker and the opportunity group our daughter would not have come as far as she has.

It hasn't all been plain sailing. Someone said to me the other day, 'you're not going to send your little girl to special school are you? She's such a pretty child'. I had to point out that my daughter's looks would not get her through the rest of her life and we would do what was best for her.

Another thing I remember very well was when I took my daughter to be assessed. At the time I was asked if I would mind if she went to special school. My reply was 'yes I would'. I wanted her to have a chance in mainstream school first. When asked why I was so against going I said 'I went to special school'. The reply from the doctor was 'so you have something against other children with a disability?'. I said no, I didn't. My memory was to stand tall and count to ten before I turned round and told the doctor I used to go and help with some of the disabled children because I enjoyed it and all I wanted was for my little girl to at least have a chance to go to her local school.

My little girl began at the local school three days a week and was doing very well. Now, however, it has been decided that our daughter needs a lot more help so we sat down with the educational psychologist and said we would agree to her going to special school. She is now a much happier child. The class she's in is smaller, she goes swimming, for walks and horse riding. She has also started to learn to read and write. We've said alright, because we know we've done all we can and she had a chance in mainstream school.

The thing that really makes me mad about the whole situation is that there is still not enough money to help children with special needs that go into mainstream school. So if you don't have the money it seems like a case of out of sight out of mind. So I guess not an awful lot changes.

SOCIETY

Society as far as I can see fits into two groups. Those who can and those who can't. I'm sure we all know a lot of those who can go through life and get out of it what they can. I'm not saying that they don't work hard to get there because I'm sure a lot do, but it seems to me that society is geared for people who have got it 'all up top' as I would say.

We are people in our own right if you gave us a chance. We can do it so why not give us a go. I know there would have been times I would have willingly got down on my knees and begged for a job. I shouldn't have to do that, I know, but in most cases that's how it goes. When you have had enough nerve to look up and say well I don't have any excuses but I could do that job just give me a go, you can see their faces drop a mile.

At last, with the help of my husband, I'm learning I'm as good as the rest. It's really just a shame it's taken me fifteen years to find that out. It would be easier if my family had not always treated me as if I were a child.

Sometimes I feel like saying, 'This is me, what you see is what you get', but I realize I don't have to prove myself to people although, in the back of my mind, I still feel I have to prove that I am as good as they are. I put that down to it being me, then it's that same question, 'is it me or is it the way I have been made to feel?'.

Things have got a lot better for children with special needs today. I'm not just talking from my point of view but, I hope, for all of the other people out there with an invisible disability. If the money is not there for the much-needed portage and opportunity groups and all the help they provide then most of the children with special needs will fall through the net. The money has to be found or else we risk losing all of this help and I know as a parent what it would have meant to my little girl: a very hard time at school and it may be her sitting here in twenty years' time doing the same as I'm doing now.

When I sat down to write this, I know what I wanted to say, but as I went along the need to prove myself to people came to the front again, so I put it down for a few days and then came back to it. I wouldn't want anyone to read this to think my school days came one bad day after another, because they didn't. I had fun, I like to learn and made some very special friendships. My education was very good. My need to learn, I think, could be classed as sometimes driving most sane folk up the wall. Now my solace is being able to pick up a book and read and, to be honest, maybe my way of hiding from the world, which at times I think we all feel the need to do. It's like my bridge over troubled waters, that's how I look at it.

At last I think I am getting there, although sometimes it only takes a little misunderstanding for my confidence to be knocked and back into my shell I go, but with the help of my husband, my children and some very good friends, I am getting there. My children being my biggest help from day to day, because at their young age, the world doesn't always seem so harsh to them.

In writing this it upset me and opened up a lot of old wounds. In doing so it also helped me to heal some of the wounds. Now at last I feel I can get on with living and maybe if one voice along with others can change things it's all for the good.

I would like to say thank you to my husband and also to Jane – you have both been a great help in the past few weeks. Thank you both for believing in me.

Now one last thing I would like to do is wish everyone who is doing this course the best of luck.

Chapter 2

Experiences of black students

David Myrie

---

*Born in England, in his teens David went with his family to Jamaica,
where he later trained as a teacher of English Literature. After teaching for
a few years, David returned to England, becoming an inner-city
Education Welfare Officer and an Open University student. This chapter
is based on the postgraduate project work that he completed for the Open
University Advanced Diploma in Special Needs in Education. David
accounts for the difficulties experienced by black students in his school in
terms of a clash of cultures.*

INTRODUCTION

My life started in the early 1960s in the quiet little town of Wellington
Telford, in the Midlands. In my mid-teens my parents decided to return to
their homeland of Jamaica. The family therefore uprooted to what was a new
but extremely exciting environment for me. I completed high school,
worked for a year then attended Teachers' College for three years, gradu-
ating with a Diploma in Secondary Education, specializing in English
Literature. I taught for a couple of years at Clarendon College (high school)
and was tutor to a Form 1 (= Year 7) group which included four pupils
whose parents resided in England but had sent their children to be educated
in Jamaica. It was at this school my interest in special needs developed, as I
also taught what was then termed a remedial group.

I returned to England in the late 1980s and worked at a regional assessment centre for three years, at which time I joined the swelling ranks of
Open University students trying to further their education and educational
careers. As an Open University student I felt part of a very progressive
university, but also felt detached and at times very alone owing to the sheer
lack of black students on the courses I opted for. This feeling heightened
whenever summer school came around. In fact if this aspect of my study was
not compulsory, I would certainly not have attended them. Despite this I
enjoyed this mode of studying, and to date have acquired an Advanced

Diploma in Special Needs in Education, and am looking forward to completing the master's degree in 1994.

AN EDUCATION WELFARE OFFICER IN THE MARKET PLACE

At the same time as taking up Open University studies I accepted the position of Education Welfare Officer at Windmere School. At the core of my remit was the enforcement of attendance, this being achieved through dialogue with schools, pupils and parents. Ultimately court action would be considered if the dialogue failed to effect the desired change. I further worked with staff and other professional agencies and groups to identify and assess the needs of pupils where there was concern over behaviour, general difficulties being experienced by the child in school, the need for improved home–school liaison, and/or material or social need. In addition I was involved in the statementing process – delivering the initial proposals to parents and explaining the process to them. I further contributed to the process by offering advice in the form of reports for the full assessment. I worked closely with the head of special needs department in Windmere, and was involved in annual statement reviews. I was also heavily consulted on various issues, child protection being a major one. I worked on a number of projects in Windmere, one such project investigated the underachievement of Afro-Caribbean pupils in school, which incidentally formed the base for my first project in the second part of the Open University Advanced Diploma in Special Needs in Education. Although I was based in the school I was employed by the local authority (the borough).

The local authority took over the running of education in 1990. Discussion with senior staff indicates that as early as this, clear shifts could be seen away from an emphasis on special educational needs (SEN) and multicultural education. The area is considered a very 'bright' borough which believes in and prides itself on its 'political correctness'. All government policies are implemented with great speed and enthusiasm. For example, zero poll tax was taken to its limit despite the pain and cuts being felt in education, other departments and services. The implementation of aspects of the 1988 Education Reform Act was greatly welcomed, with the borough expressing support for grant-maintained status. Out of nine secondary schools, two have been closed, four have gone grant maintained, and the remaining three are primed to introduce elements of selection. One of the three mentioned above has been redefined and renamed a City Technology College and its admission policy will be 100 per cent based on aptitude for technology. Of the other two, one will contain 40 per cent of places awarded on the basis of art, design and languages and the other will be a 50 per cent selective boys' school. The borough does not believe in comprehensives.

All schools in the borough which are not grant maintained will fall under the local management of schools scheme. The approach has two main strands: decentralization and increased competition. Schools funding from now on will be based on how many 'bums' they have on seats. Thus there is a financial incentive to attract pupils, to win against other schools: market forces in operation as schools will be forced to give parents what they want, the ideology that good schools will survive and bad schools will go out of business. The effect of all this will be that experienced and specialist staff will be deemed unaffordable and it will come as no surprise that the pupils most affected will be those seen to have special needs and those from ethnic minorities.

The above discussion raises a number of questions about the future of Statements of Special Educational Needs, learning support and the LEA itself. In a nutshell, the authority seems to have an unwritten policy of a reduction in the number of statements made, particularly if the provision could prove costly, i.e. placements in a boarding school or the independent sector. I was personally involved in a case where the special learning needs of the pupil were 'painfully' obvious, but the authority decided that it would not make a statement. The head of the pupil's special educational needs department wrote to the authority expressing concern and indicating that the parent had been given the number of Parents Concern and had been in contact with them. A swift response came back from the authority indicating to the head of special educational needs the appropriate behaviour of an LEA employee and that serious consequences could follow if employees openly put their employer into embarrassing situations. A clear indication of the direction of the LEA's special educational needs policy.

The present situation is one of permanent reviews. All off-site centres barring two have been closed, and there are plans to stop all sessional support at these centres. In future the centres will only cater for permanently excluded pupils. Within schools all peripatetic support has been stopped and only pupils with statements are catered for. The authority is presently discussing a formula to charge grant-maintained schools for this service. The borough's aim is to delegate as much as it can to schools, leaving a skeleton LEA to carry out statutory duties. This policy applies to most departments, the Education Welfare Service being no exception.

How has Windmere School itself fared? Since becoming grant maintained, streaming has been introduced in a number of subjects and the school is primed to introduce selection into its admission policy. This is justified on the basis that if they do not, this could end up being the 'sink' school of the borough. In a discussion with a deputy head of the school, he informed me that they are teachers not social workers. An indication of the future direction of the school?

The school was previously noted for its high exclusion rate, particularly of black males and SEN pupils. Figures collated by the school for 1991 showed a total of both fixed-term and permanent exclusions as 74, of whom 45 were black pupils. This formed the basis for a project I undertook, which looked at the school's attendance policy. The fact that black pupils regularly attend school is an indication that they want to achieve and they are looking to the school to reward this. Unfortunately as I have indicated, the reward is often exclusion, permanent in a number of cases. What has been the experience of these students?

BLACK STUDENTS IN A WHITE EDUCATION SYSTEM

Underachievement by Afro-Caribbean students has long been one of the most controversial areas of educational research. It has been suggested that race is a prime determinant of intelligence, as evaluated from IQ tests created by white psychologists and based on white middle-class norms and values. Since then, a plethora of research and empirical studies have been produced supporting and refuting various stances. The commonality amongst all these studies is the belief that Afro-Caribbean pupils are indeed underachieving in schools.

Quality Education Consultants analysed figures from six Metropolitan Authorities which showed that 85–90 per cent of pupils excluded from school were black and predominantly males (*Voice*, 18 June 1991). If these pupils are systematically excluded from school how are they expected to learn? In 1979 and 1982 the Inner London Education Authority carried out research into exam achievement according to ethnic background, involving over 80 per cent of schools. The findings indicated that the performance of Afro-Caribbean pupils was well below average. A major government study (Swann 1985) identified the percentage of Afro-Caribbean pupils achieving five plus CSE or O-levels grades A–C at 3 per cent in 1979 and 6 per cent in 1982. This compared extremely poorly with Asians who had 17 per cent in both 1979 and 1982. The English and Welsh group was 16 per cent in 1979 and 19 per cent in 1982.

On the evidence from my own school, the above trend seems to be continued. Figures published by the school in 1991 indicated that GCSE passes for Afro-Caribbeans were shockingly low in comparison to other groups of pupils. Of white students, 50 per cent achieved grades A–C, for Asians the figure was 56 per cent, for Afro-Caribbeans the figure was 14 per cent. The number of Asian pupils with no A–C was 2, for Afro-Caribbeans it was 18. In my project, I took the stance that the school was responsible for this unacceptable position and I set out to prove this.

My view was supported from findings by Eggleston *et al.* (1986) that the second largest group of pupils at further education college were Afro-Caribbean and that they were doing GCSE O- and A-levels. Eggleston further indicated that these students do achieve. For example, in 1974, 28–30 per cent of Afro-Caribbeans had succeeded in gaining some type of further education qualification since leaving school, compared to 22 per cent of whites. As a result of the above exam fiasco I set up a project involving black males from Years 9–11 to ascertain their views about this underachievement and what they and the school could do to correct both this situation and also the high level of exclusions. This project was accepted by the senior management of the school. It is important to point out that I had immeasurable support from the First Deputy Head, but as far as the headteacher and the other deputy heads were concerned, this work was only important in the sense that when questioned by 'inquisitive' governors about the plight of black students in the school, they could point to what I was doing, claiming to positively address the situation.

To counter the claim that if I used a student who failed in school I would receive a warped view of the school, I instead chose from the project group mentioned above a student who was in the lower sixth form and who had gained nine GCSE passes. He charted his experiences in the school, which proved extremely revealing.

John

According to John, by the end of Year 8 he was labelled as a troublemaker, 'aggressive, lippy' and was widely viewed by staff as of low ability. Prior to and after mock exams, his projected grades were Fs and Us and it took several uncomfortable trips up to the school by John's mother before he was entered for some subjects. John was also a member of a group of some black boys, who met and played at breaktimes and travelled to and from school together. This group quickly acquired an 'up to no good' label. John claimed that this view was reflected in crude references made to them in classes. They were also constantly brought before the headteacher for minor misdemeanours including the wearing of hats. According to Troyna (1987) this group formation in most cases is a reaction to poor relationships between Afro-Caribbean students and their teachers.

John claimed that on a daily basis he and other black students encountered negativity. Time was not spent expressing the importance of work, in fact, teachers, when not criticizing the group and himself were intimidated by them. This, he claimed, resulted in teachers accepting behaviour from them which they rejected and opposed from white students. John claimed teachers perceived black students as violent and ignorant; he also stated that he was in a 'white man's' world and thus did not expect to be treated fairly.

John claimed that things changed for him after mock exams when he saw the 'told you so' smiles on the faces of some teachers. He also thought 'these teachers would feel justified if I failed'. This he claimed made him determined to 'show' them. He claimed that at school his behaviour did not change, but out of school he spent every evening in the library followed by a couple of hours studying at home. He also joined the study group run by his local youth club and claimed that this was instrumental in him passing his exams. Following his GCSE passes, teachers who would not allow him to do their subjects at GCSE level, wanted him to do them at A level.

John indicated that he still feels bitter and angry with the school and claimed that there were many Afro-Caribbean students who were more talented than himself, but failed because they lost faith in the school and their ability to achieve. A number of these students were also permanently excluded.

John's Head of Year

To gain further insight and another perspective on John's views and experiences, I interviewed a number of school staff, but here will briefly concentrate on an interview with Mr Phillips, who was John's Head of Year for five years. This member of staff was Head of Year for the exam year 1991 mentioned earlier.

Mr Phillips opened the interview by saying (jokingly) that he is 'white, middle-aged and from Yorkshire and that the village I grew up in had only one black family'. He then stated that it was difficult to talk about a particular ethnic group as he had spent all his teaching life treating all students the same. Despite this he felt that the interaction between Afro-Caribbean pupils and staff was characterized by mistrust and confrontation. He further claimed that the cultural background of staff affected this interaction and that most staff came from a white middle-class background and aspired to middle-class values in direct conflict with Afro-Caribbean pupils. He claimed that more positive images of black people needed to be projected in the curriculum, but claimed that the National Curriculum and testing did not lend themselves to such innovations.

When questioned about John he claimed that John was lucky he was not permanently excluded from school. He further stated that John was representative of the Afro-Caribbean group in school who did little or no work and who were much more concerned with their appearance. He still expressed surprise at John's passes, stating that John must have spent most of his time after school doing course work. He also claimed that the school was obviously doing a better job than people thought. He concluded that the school's role in the underachievement of Afro-Caribbean students was to some extent exaggerated, and felt it was in fact the Afro-Caribbean community who at times had failed to support the school.

Thus the experience of Afro-Caribbean pupils in my school could be characterized by a rejection of pluralism and a culture clash which reinforced the negative stereotypical views held. According to Troyna and Carrington (1990) the black child's identity is denied daily in the classroom and he labours under three crucial handicaps: low expectation on his part about his likely performance in a white-controlled education system, low motivation to succeed because he feels the cards are stacked against him, and low teacher expectations, which affect the amount of effort expended on his behalf by the teacher which in turn affects his own image of himself and his ability. This can clearly be seen in the interviews with John and his Head of Year. John was a 'one-off case' of someone who tenaciously hung on despite the odds. He was strong enough to use the negativity to fuel his determination and was also lucky to have a network he could call on for support outside school. For many other Afro-Caribbean pupils this is not the case. Instead the negativity experienced acts as a self-fulfilling prophecy.

A FUTURE FOR BLACK STUDENTS?

Unfortunately, the future seems to offer little or no hope for the improvement of the lot of black students even with the introduction of the National Curriculum which it is deemed will improve the lot of all students. In fact this innovation along with its stablemates, grant-maintained schools, open enrolment, league tables and market forces, could prove detrimental to black students. The few LEAs which have made determined attempts to represent black communities and to control service delivery directly towards anti-racist ends have frequently been the object of media vilification and political attacks. On the other hand, when Sainsbury and Tesco's develop products and strategies to capture sections of the ethnic market, this is considered sound business practice by all.

The National Curriculum has put an end to attempts at multicultural and multiracial education. The very emphasis on 'national' in the National Curriculum, the centrality of a notion of national testing with all the cultural and linguistic bias which it implies, the failure to recognize languages other than Welsh and English as pupils' first languages and the omission in any of the consultative papers, let alone in the 1988 Education Refrom Act of any reference to the 1985 report of Lord Swann's committee of enquiry into the education of children from ethnic minority groups (*Education for All*), clearly indicate the future for black pupils.

The National Curriculum has to some extent eroded the vocationalist agenda which was developing in schools. In my school, for example, the majority of students engaged in the Technical Vocational Education Initiative are black – not surprising, as the school used this as a holding-ground for the less able pupils, those who it was deemed were failures academically. Black pupils in the school, because of the sheer level of their underachievement, were considered to be in this category. However, achieving in this area could still help in the lifting of self-esteem and self-confidence. Not so with the rise of a subject-based academic curriculum.

With the advent of league tables many schools, particularly grant-maintained ones, will be reluctant to admit black pupils and special needs pupils, as these groups are perceived to underachieve, thus affecting the school's statistics and standing in the league table. All schools will be competing for a particular group of pupils whose colour I fear will not be black.

Financial delegation and local management of schools will shift the balance of power and decision-making from LEAs to school governors. Funding will be largely based on school numbers and the age of pupils. The result will be to reward popular schools and remove funding from schools with falling rolls. The ability of LEAs to compensate for the effects on the curriculum of demographic change and falling rolls and to support and improve schools with problems will be highly constrained. The facts of racial disadvantage and the demography of race in Britain dictate that black pupils and their families will be over-represented in those schools which lose out in this process. There will also be a widening gap between LEA policy and schools' policy and practice on equal opportunities and race.

The introduction of market forces, I believe, has serious implications for black students, further affecting their experience of education and schooling. Brown and Lauder 1993) argue that the concept of market forces gives rise to the ideology of 'parentocracy', where the education a child receives must conform to the wealth and wishes of parents rather than the abilities and efforts of pupils. Therefore, the ideology of parentocracy is based on a different set of assumptions to those which have driven bureaucratic schooling. Bureaucratic schooling was developed partly as a means of ensuring that, through their abilities and efforts, students were given the opportunity to achieve in a meritocracy irrespective of their social circumstances. Thus in the market-led reform, where education is treated as a commodity, the economic power of parents or lack of it, becomes an increasingly important determinant of educational and life-chances. Afro-Caribbean families, positioned as they are at the bottom of the economic and social ladder, have little or no power and are therefore disadvantaged from the outset in these market-led educational reforms.

In educational terms, schools, credentials and the status attached to them are likely to become more sharply differentiated, creating elite schools for the rich and a gradation of less prestigious and less successful schools beneath them. It is not hard to perceive where Afro-Caribbean pupils will be placed. There is also the distinct possibility of racial segregation being created through grant-maintained status and open enrolment.

The will and motivation to develop an inclusive curriculum has evaporated. The agenda is now dominated by the requirements and demands of being grant maintained, the demands of the National Curriculum and the financial state of the school. Windmere's commitment to the education of all pupils seems to be over.

As for me, I will continue to exercise the power of the pen in writing and voting.

REFERENCES

Brown, P. and Lauder, H. (1993) *Education, Training and Employment*, E817 Summer School Booklet, Milton Keynes: Open University.

Eggleston, J., Dunn, D. and Anjali, M. (1986) *Education for Some. The Educational and Vocational Experiences of 15–18 Year-old Members of Minority Ethnic Groups*, Cheshire: Bemrose Press.

ILEA Research and Statistics Branch (1987) *Ethnic Background and Examinations Results 1985–1986*, London: ILEA.

Quality Education Consultants (1991) *Voice* newspaper, 18 January 1991.

Swann, W. (1985) *Education for All* (a brief guide to the main issues of the report), London: HMSO.

Troyna, B. (1987) *Racial Inequality in Education*, London: Tavistock Publications.

Troyna, B. and Carrington, B. (1990) *Education Racism and Reform*, Cornwall: TJ Press.

Chapter 3

My experiences of schooling

Anya Souza

Anya is employed by the organization Young People First to speak up as an advocate for people who have experienced negative discrimination at school because of their appearance or their assumed difficulties in learning.

I went to a special school called Holly Court in London. I was there for a term. One of the teachers did a stuffed fish and two bunny rabbits, but I took them home and I showed my mother, at that time I think I should of done them myself, in the end I ripped them up because I did not do them. Why do we need schools like that?

I went on to a primary mainstream school called Fitzjohn's School, I was there for eight years. For most people for seven years, but I had a year back to catch up because I have Down's Syndrome. I did very well. I went to Yorkshire and South Wales weekends. After that I went to my secondary school in London called Haverstock. I was there for five years. I should have been there for six years. I did my subjects in drama, housecraft, French, I loved it. Went to France five times. After five years the headmistress said to my mother behind my back, she said what is this Mongol person doing in my school? My mother went to High Court about this and we won. I left after that and I went on to a special school called College Park in London. I was there for a year and I was picked on because I have Down's Syndrome and one girl poured hot boiling custard down me. The school should not be on earth. The teachers and the headmistress should be banned from the school and the school should be closed down. They can't treat a person with Down's Syndrome. I left and I went on to college I went on to Paddington I did a clerical course in pre-vocational office work, typing, answering the phone, everything like that. Computers, duplicating and assignments, I did. After that I went on to Brixton College and Westminster College and I did food industry exams in catering, I was a chef and a waitress. I did an exam in food. I did continental foods, Czech, Italian, Spanish, German, French. I was at Brixton College for another year then I went on to work. I went to the Down's Syndrome Association, I was there for nine years and I was very popular at the beginning. I was on TV, I was on Channel 4 about a baby who had Down's Syndrome and she was slaughtered because she had Down's Syndrome. Loise Brown, we were in the paper and I was on radio too. After that we moved to south London and we were on TV again. Then I was there for nine years. When my mother died, she died of a heart attack in 1990, she was only 70 years old. They said to me they would help me and do this and do that with me. But I turned round, I said that they didn't do nothing for me, you are doing nothing to help me. I couldn't do anything at all, didn't even see my skills. Like answering a 'phone or a computer or using a typewriter. Nothing like that. I left on my own accord and I worked for a company called Camden Society for Learning Difficulties. I was their receptionist for two years then they said to me about Young People First and I had an interview and I said to my second mother, June Standing, why do I need this job. Because I can speak up for myself and when I want I do a lot for you People First we do conferences on aids and different things all the time, and workshops and meetings. I went to Barcelona to speak up to 600 people and doctors and researchers. They were saying about Down's Syndrome at an early age like animals. And the way they are treating us like that, we are not animals we are human beings.

Chapter 4

'Bloody uncomfortable!'
Reflections on class and education

Claire Debenham

Looking back on her own experiences of school, university and work, Claire reflects on the ways in which selection processes in schools, educational success and subsequent professional power are pre-determined by social class. Contrary to popular assumptions, she concludes that her lengthy education has done nothing to change her class membership, identity and allegiance.

I am silenced. Confusion, mind-buzzing. I can't explain it. I'm in a group of psychotherapists and social workers at a one-day conference, talking about why people do, or do not, respond to therapeutic groups. They all seem so confident, so condemning. They discuss the inadequates of this world who 'don't respond', don't get the best out of what they are offered in therapy, drop out, resist, deny, etc.

I am struggling, moving from anger to a sense of inarticulate inferiority. I came hoping, expecting to find like-minded people looking for radical solutions, and find myself overwhelmed by feelings of isolation, suddenly unable to formulate my thoughts. My questions evaporate.

The people they are talking about are being offered therapy by social work agencies. They are largely working class, many black, and many are women. Predictably, the lot I am with are largely middle class, all white, and many are male. Oh, how frustrated they all are with their ungrateful clients.

I eventually speak – in too high-pitched a tone. Could I suggest that the models they are applying may not feel very real, or comfortable to their clients, don't reflect their experiences? The theories are middle class and white in origin.

'Well I don't see what your argument is, you're middle class anyway' . . . well modulated, clipped tones rang out with petulance.

I am silenced. I argue back, but the utter irrelevance of the comment has confused me. I am trying to make the sense of it that others seem to have.

The discussion has moved swiftly on to new themes.

I remain impotent, confused, a sense of guilt, hurt, shame. Why? I can't concentrate for the rest of the afternoon. Why can't I express myself better, keep at it, get listened to? I hate myself, and them!

This incident happened a decade ago now. Walking home from the bus stop that night a thought slowly crystallized. 'I'm not middle class, I'm working class. I was always working class, so what's changed it? I lead a middle-class life, and frankly that's the bit that's bloody uncomfortable!' Relief came upon me with a rosy, cheerful glow.

My mind raced backwards and forwards over experiences, conversations. How many times had I experienced that others perceived me as middle class? A social worker, an educated person, done a qualification, been to university. This had become so like the truth I'd been believing it.

My Auntie Mary, an old family friend, brought up her own four children on her own. She helped Mum and Dad out with me, too, for a while. We met up again when I was with my sister. I was in my early twenties. In the course of conversation Auntie Mary swore about something, looked at me uncomfortably, apologized to me, and turned to my sister to say 'Does she swear?'. Auntie Mary was a figure of authority in my life, a very loved one. Why was she so distant now, putting me in judgement over her, treating me like a creature from outer space, okay with my sister but not with me? But I'd been to university, the only one in my family, and that had changed things. For my family too.

As a matter of fact I probably first gave my 'class' serious consideration at university. That was when I first felt what was working class about me in a conscious way, and saw it was a potential disadvantage. Before this I thought everyone was like me really – some were more or less well off, well dressed, well organized, but on the whole we all lived on the same estates, went to the same schools, had the same chances. Life was comfortable for the reasonably well-off working classes. They're nice people, normal. On arriving at university I became acutely affected by feelings of inferiority and reacted aggresssively, feeling up against it. To my amazement and horror the Federation of Conservative Students came into power in the students' union during my first year. I was a *fishwife* at the hustings. I became a screaming harridan surounded by 'toffs' calling themselves students. Surely the terms were incompatible? It was a cold dawn of realization which shifted my egocentric view of the world just a little.

Looking back I can see that the feelings of inferiority were there from the very beginning, of course. And intricately bound up with the shape of my education. All those streamed classes, and streaming within classes. In the infants' reception class my friend Sally was on the top table, I was on the second. Her Dad was a headteacher. We were very drawn to each other – giggly. Her Mum thought I was not particularly desirable as a friend for Sally, although she was nice to me. She encouraged other friendships. My mum thought she was a snob and I knew that. And we lived in very different areas.

In contrast, on leaving university and deciding on social work as a career, I met people every day across the duty desk who perceived me as thoroughly middle class. Of course, social work is an educated working-class girls' career (although I didn't know it then). But there was no sisterhood here – and rightly so. I had embraced the power of the middle classes.

What is this power? The power to consume, to own, to judge. The power to donate education. A basic assumption is that to be educated is to be middle class. Education belongs to the middle classes, doesn't it? Working-class oiks who benefit from its munificence are transformed, consumed, abandoning their origins and experiences. They *are* middle class themselves – and surely grateful for the benefit? 'You're middle class anyway.' All else is irrelevant, no further argument needed. If we are not careful we can barely recognize ourselves, or each other.

The complexity of origin is thus denied. Hence my confusion and silence. A potential rebellion squashed, strangled by conflicting values and experiences, which can't be fully explained to either side. Sadly, too many of us are trapped in a system established of values not of our origins, but which our 'life experience' fits us to operate effectively for others – teachers, social workers, the 'caring' professions. Looking after our own?

Sitting in a pub this weekend I saw an actor in a well-known comedy series sipping his gin and tonic. In the series he is an 'amusing' working-class character, with a nasal Midlands accent. In a Sussex pub his tones were refined – middle class to the core.

The friend I was with commented on his accent, saying 'here's another example of a middle-class actor making mileage out of a shallow stereotype of the working classes. No depth.' I couldn't help wondering if there was a different explanation. What if he were a working-class person, learnt to be middle class, now acting a shallow characterization of his origins. Who would share his perspective on the comedy? Could he tell it?

I think I know where I am in the class arena now, but it has taken far too long to work it out.

Chapter 5

Another world: experiences of residential special schooling. Then

Steve Humphries and Pamela Gordon

First published in S. Humphries and P. Gordon (eds), *Out of Sight: The Experience of Disability 1900–1950*, Plymouth, Northcote House Publishers, 1992.

Steve Humphries and Pamela Gordon draw on personal accounts to illustrate how fear, understaffing and the lack of appropriate resources compounded the difficulties faced by disabled children and young people in the first half of this century. These extracts cover four themes: admission to a residential institution, separation from parents, teaching and learning and systems of punishment.

In 1935, 12-year-old Mary Baker was sent to The Halliwick Home for Crippled Girls, a Church of England institution for physically and mentally disabled girls. She had a dislocated hip as a result of which she walked with a limp. Mary was the daughter of a Dorset agricultural labourer who was wounded during the First World War, and she had three brothers. When her mother died in 1933 the authorities decided that her father would be unable to bring up the children and they were sent to the workhouse at Wimborne Minster. From there she was separated from her brothers and despatched to Halliwick.

'When I first arrived at Halliwick the nurse took me into this bathroom and she stripped me off completely. She cut my hair short, right above the ears. And then I was deloused with powder of some description. Then they put me in a bath and scrubbed me down with carbolic soap. It was very degrading to me and I felt as though the end of the world had come and so I cried, I sat in the bath and cried my eyes out. At any rate they told me it was no good in crying and dried me down. They used such rough towels it felt like they were sandpapering me. Then I was dressed in the Halliwick uniform, navy blue socks, stockings and a gym slip and a serge jumper and I was taken up into the dormitory, a big huge room it seemed, with about ten beds in it. I went in there and lay down on my new bed, I felt awful and I thought that nobody cared for me. Anyway,

I don't think that I slept that night, I felt so lonely. I didn't know what to do, had no idea what I was going to do. But it was huge and it was lonely, the place. And I felt really lost and I thought, what am I going to do with no one to love me? I had entered a different life. My father was far back home and I thought that everyone had forsaken me. I think I cried most of the night. So this was my start. The next morning you were given a number and you had to remember it. My number was twenty-nine and when I got up and went to wash, my towel and flannel had my number on them. Twenty-nine was engraved on all my hairbrushes and things with a big hot poker-like thing. Everything I owned had a marking of twenty-nine on, so I can never forget that number. Our lockers in the playroom had the same number and our clothes were marked with our numbers, so we knew what we had. We were hardly ever called by our first names, only by the other girls. And if matron wanted you she called you by twenty-nine or whatever number you had. We never had names, we were just numbers there. It was all very disciplined. I couldn't make it out at first, why we should all have numbers and not names. I felt a bit low about it. I couldn't really put my feelings into an expression, only that I felt very lonely about it.'

In 1932, 5-year-old Hazel Boucher had to leave her family in Brigg, near Scunthorpe, to begin her first year living in at the Yorkshire Residential Institution for the Deaf in Doncaster.

'When I first came to the baby school, when I was 5, I came with my mother. We had a look around the school then suddenly my mother had gone – I didn't realize at first and then I started looking for her and couldn't find her, she'd disappeared and I started crying. I remember having a dummy in my mouth and I was crying and crying and missing my mother. And then for a few days I had to settle down and live with the other children and start to play with the toys there. On the next Saturday when my mother came to visit me I started to remember, oh that was my mother, it seemed a long time since I had seen her. She took me round the shops in Doncaster for the afternoon. And then I realized that I was coming back to school so I clung to a lamp post saying, 'No; no, I don't want to go back to school. I want to go home with you.' My mum was dragging me. She says, 'Come on, come on you've got to go back into school.' And anyway she brought me in, then she went off home and I was left there on my own again.'

Marjorie Jacques, born in Guildford in 1920, contracted polio when she was 11 months and as a result was unable to walk. She was sent to Chailey Heritage Craft Institution near Lewes in Sussex from the age of 3 to 10.

'We only had one visiting day a year all the time I was at Chailey. I used to miss my parents so much, I used to cry myself to sleep. The homesick-

Figure 5.1 A class of girls at The Halliwick Home in the 1950s

Source: The Children's Society

ness was really terrible and we were only allowed home in the Christmas and summer holidays which were marvellous. I remember that if I was naughty at home my mum used to say she would send me back to Chailey early. I would do anything rather than go back early, that was really like holding a gun to my head. The night before I had to go back, I used to cry myself to sleep. As soon as we arrived back at Chailey they took our own clothes away and parcelled them up and out came the dreaded uniforms.'

In 1928 5-year-old Jeanne Hollamby left her home in Beckenham, south London to go to Tite Street Children's Hospital, Chelsea to be treated for cerebral palsy. She was to remain there for five years.

'I was in hospital for five years and my mum used to visit me every week but she wasn't allowed into the ward, not once in all that time. She just looked in through the window in the ward door and waved at me like all the other parents. That was really upsetting, much more upsetting than if we'd have had proper visits. She used to leave me presents to have when she had gone home but of course it wasn't like seeing her properly. All year we looked forward to the garden fete in the summer so then we could be with our mums properly for an hour or so.'

The quality of schooling the children received varied greatly between different types of institution. Generally the best education was given to the blind for it was widely assumed that out of all children with disabilities they had the greatest learning potential. Victorian institutions for the blind had enjoyed some success in teaching pupils using the new method of Braille. There was even a kind of public school for the blind – Worcester College, opened in 1866 – which taught fee-paying, middle-class boys. All this enhanced the status of teaching the blind so that by the first decades of the century some institutions for the blind could attract trained and committed teaching staff. However the severely authoritarian teaching methods which were standard practice at the time often instilled a special fear in pupils without sight. This frequently reduced the effectiveness of the education that was provided for blind children, as Ted Williams remembers.

'I took to Braille very quickly after I lost my sight. When I was 9 and I'd only been there a year, I could read Braille books from the library – it came natural to me. And because I was good at it some of the teachers gave me a lot of help. I know I got special lessons from the headteacher. But they were very hard those teachers. Especially the music teacher. Now I desperately wanted to take music lessons and learn to play, but I was just too frightened. Because that music teacher had such a fearsome reputation, he punished the boys so much, I thought I can't do it. And I didn't. Now that was a great opportunity lost, all because the teacher was such a disciplinarian.'

Figure 5.2 The dining room at Elm Court Blind School in West Norwood in 1908. Discipline was strictly enforced at mealtimes when the children were expected to eat what was put in front of them in absolute silence.

Source: Greater London Photograph Library

There was a growing interest in educating deaf children from the late nineteenth century onwards which brought some advantages in terms of trained teachers and extended schooling. However in most institutions there was a narrow pursuit of the oral method of communication involving lip-reading and deaf aids which many children found extremely difficult. Signing – the natural language of the deaf – was often brutally repressed. Joyce Nicholson was a pupil at The Royal School for the Deaf and Dumb, in Birmingham, in the 1920s.

> 'We were never allowed to sign in class at school. They tried to make us speak and to lip-read which I really found difficult. We used to look forward to being out of the teacher's eye so we could sign. We used to sign behind their backs when they were writing on the blackboard with our hands under our desks. But if you were caught the teacher would be very angry. Sometimes we would get smacked on the hands and our arms would be tied by our sides for the morning or afternoon just to stop us from signing. One day my teacher caught me signing to my friend under the desk. She was angry and said that I shouldn't use sign. She said that I looked like a little monkey. That's what they used to call us whenever they caught us signing, little monkeys.'

Although this was an era when corporal punishment was widely used in schools, the punishment inflicted upon children with disabilities were of an altogether different order. The most brutal aspect of these punishments was that they often actively exploited the children's disabilities. A variety of mental and physical tortures were used in many institutions, designed to humiliate and terrify the most defiant young inmates. Ted Williams remembers the brutal punishments used at Manchester Road School of the Blind in the 1920s.

> 'One of the prevalent methods of caning was on the hand. Blind people, of course, are very dependent on their hands and fingers but I suffered a stroke hard across the fingers quite often. And believe you me it used to hurt. Well, that for quite a while left the hand really numb and dead and we used to have to wait before we could even think about looking at a Braille book, until the numbness wore off. One particular teacher used to delight in punishing us in the maths lesson. We all had little arithmetic frames with sharp points sticking up to denote certain numbers to us. Now, if the teacher was trying to instil a sum into our heads and we couldn't get it she would clamp her hands on the backs of our fingers on these points and press them down and say, 'Can't you feel? Can't you feel?'. And this again meant our fingers would be dead for a good time afterwards and any Braille reading was impossible.'

This kind of sensory deprivation was especially common in institutions which contained both blind and deaf children housed in separate wings. Disobedient blind children would be sent to the deaf section and vice versa. Cyril Hayward Jones was a pupil at The Mount School for the Deaf and the Blind near Stoke-on-Trent around the time of the First World War.

> 'There was one side of the building for us blind boys and the other side was for deaf boys. One of the worst punishments was to go and live on the deaf side for a couple of days. If we talked in the dining room or some such little misdemeanour they could hand out that punishment. That was the only time we ever went to the deaf side, when we were naughty. Now the thing was, of course, that the deaf couldn't hear and we couldn't lip-read. So it was a really pretty desperate situation there. Well, what you had to do was learn to spell on your fingers, to be able to make yourself understood with the deaf boys, I remember the manual alphabet even to this day. We used to take the deaf boy's hand and spell out the words on his hand. Without that we would have been completely cut off from the world, in absolute silence.'

Bedwetting was also often a punishable offence. It was a common problem caused principally by the atmosphere of fear and anxiety that the children lived in. In addition dormitory regulations which often prevented the children from leaving their beds at night and difficulties resulting from the children's physical disabilities all made the problem worse. The reaction of some members of staff to constantly soiled sheets was extremely brutal. Marjorie Jacques:

> 'I used to wet the bed a lot when I was little. Now they wouldn't let you have potties, they didn't allow those. If I wanted to go in the night and I woke up I used to have to crawl out of bed, right down the hallway and drag myself up onto the toilet, see. But mainly I couldn't get myself out of bed because of my legs and I used to just wet the bed. In the mornings we used to have to strip our beds and the nurse would come around to inspect them. If it was wet you were in trouble. I used to dread that inspection because, of course, mine was quite often wet because it was so difficult for me to get myself out of bed. The punishment for wetting was one I really hated. They made me knit a pair of black stockings on four needles, with a seam right up the back. And if you made a mistake then you had to unpick it and start again. I knitted God knows how many pairs of stockings with me wetting the bed a few times a week. I think now that it was because I was so homesick. I was only three and a half when I was first sent there. Anyway, every night after school I would have to go to my dormitory to do these stockings. They would bring up my tea, one piece of bread and treacle. I had to sit all on my own trying to knit and feeling pretty lonely and miserable. Another punishment for

bedwetting was to take things away from us, I remember once my mum sent me a lovely birthday cake and they wouldn't let me have it 'cos I'd been naughty, I'd wet the bed or something probably. They put it in a store room and locked the door. But when they got it out two days later it was full of ants so it had to just be thrown away.'

Chapter 6

Another world: experiences of residential special schooling. Now

Paul Cooper

First published in P. Cooper, *Effective Schools for Disaffected Students: Integration and Segregation*, London, Routledge, 1993.

Special educational provision in the 1990s still includes residential schools. Among those who are referred to them are children and young people who are seen as having 'emotional and behavioural difficulties'. Paul Cooper has studied these schools from the perspective of the students themselves and he presents a complex view of residential school life that includes both damaging isolation and positive support. Following on from the previous chapter, the themes covered here are: first impressions, being away from home, sanctions, and education and achievement.

FIRST IMPRESSIONS

Many of the boys interviewed arrived at their respective schools with little or no knowledge of what to expect. For some, the first they knew of their placement in a residential school was their arrival. Alan describes his feelings on arriving at Farfield thus:

> 'Well, it did annoy me a bit, because they didn't ask me first. Or they didn't tell me where I was going. I didn't even know where I was going. All I knew was I was going in the country somewhere . . . One day, my old key worker at Spenser House [previous placement] turned up. I said "Right, where am I going?" She goes, "Oh, don't worry about that, just get your watch and clothes ready for tomorrow. Make sure nothing's broken. Get your clothes in a bag." I didn't know where I was going . . . I don't normally wear a watch when I go out normally, but she said put my watch on then. So since then I've always kept my watch on, except for night.'

Greg, another Farfield boy, tells a similar story:

'I didn't know I was coming to Farfield on the same day . . . It gave me a bit of a shock really. They goes, "It's quite a few miles out." I goes, "Where's that?" I didn't know where it was at first, when Joe [present key worker, i.e. residential social worker with special responsibility for Greg] brought me . . . I thought it would be one of those lock-up places.'

Colin's move to Farfield was equally abrupt and unexpected:

'One Monday I got up, and as I was lined up for school, Uncle Fred [a residential social worker at Colin's former school] came over – he was brilliant – he goes, "Er, Colin, come with me." I says, "OK. Am I going to the dentist or something?" He goes "No, I've got a surprise for you!" "A surprise!" I says. He gets in where the head's office is – it's outside, and it smells of beautiful brewed coffee. I can't figure it out like. Anyway, it goes on. I keep mouthing, "What's going on? Go on, tell us!" "Alright then. Your dad's coming down." "God! Is that all! My dad's coming down to see me!" "No it's a surprise." Anyway, my dad comes down with this lady in a Citroen. They goes, 'Come on, we're going out!" I goes, "Brill! Where?" "We're going to visit a new school." I goes, "Are you trying to be funny? I've been at this school for five years and you want to move me for my last year!"'

PC: Who was the person in the Citroen?
Colin: I don't know. Some social worker from [home town].
PC: Your social worker?
Colin: I don't know. Just the school social worker who moves people.

BEING AWAY FROM HOME

Homesickness is a common feature of many pupils' early recollections of their life at residential school. Jim describes his earliest feelings in terms of the conflict he felt between the attractions of Farfield and his feelings of fear and loneliness:

PC: What did you think of the place when you first saw it?
Jim: Big . . . there was a lot to do . . . I thought it was going to be a bad place. When he [Mr Talbot, the principal at Farfield] says, 'You go to Butlins and Spain' [annual school holidays] it made me think again . . . When it was the day for me to come here, I got a shock a bit . . . I was scared . . . I didn't know how I'd get on with kids I'd never met before.
PC: How did you feel about being away from home?
Jim: I cried a bit. I was upset.
PC: How long did it take to get over that?
Jim: Until I went home really. When I went home and came back and

went home. I was just getting less crying and that. I just get used to it now.

Lewis describes a whole complex of difficulties which he had to overcome in his early days at Farfield, all owing to the differences between his home life and the life in a residential establishment:

PC: Can you tell me how you felt when you first came here?

Lewis: Well, I suppose I felt like a lot of other kids. When you're first away from home, it's not exactly the best place to be . . . I hadn't been away from home before, so it made it hard for me. I felt caged in; as if if I did anything wrong I'd get done for it.

PC: Why was that do you think?

Lewis: I dunno. I just weren't used to a place with so many kids there. And sleeping with kids you don't know – that don't exactly feel right to me . . . I think you should really have a room of your own, until you get used to knowing the kids; what they are like and who they are, if you know what I mean. So that is one thing that I didn't like about it. But after a while I got used to it. I didn't like having to shower with kids that I'd never known, and that felt bad towards me . . . It was so far away from home an' all. The only way you could talk to someone was on the phone. And when I did that it made me feel worse anyway. I felt weird with the town and that.

PC: Why was that then?

Lewis: Just all different. And that I was the only coloured person in the town. And it made me feel the odd one out.

PC: Yes, the town's a lot different from where you come from. How did you feel about this?

Lewis: It was dead. I wondered where everyone was, because there was only a few people walking down the street.

Being away from home is by no means a negative aspect of residential schooling for all of these boys. A large proportion of pupils from both schools indicate that they value their residential experience for the respite it gives them from problems they experience in their home environments. As we saw in the previous chapter, family, local schooling and peer-group experiences are often described in negative terms by the boys, and these experiences are seen as contributing to their adjustment difficulties. For many of the boys at Farfield and Lakeside (another residential school) the residential experience provides them with much-needed respite from the destructive pressures of home life:

'Some kids love being at home; I can't stand it! . . . I'm always glad to get back to Lakeside.'

(Jock, Lakeside)

It's [his relationship with his single parent mother] got a lot better, but it's still bad . . . I think it's got better because we've spent longer times apart . . . I reckon it's the break.'

(Ryan, Farfield)

'The school's helped me change by helping my mum . . . By [my] coming here, she can have a rest.'

(John, Farfield)

'It's helped my mum out. Like when I've been here I've been sorting myself out.'

(Ian, Farfield)

SANCTIONS

The boys of both schools agree that while there are certain obvious rules which regulate their daily school lives, the enforcement of rules and sanctions for rule-breaking depend very much on individual circumstances and contextual matters. Lakeside boys sometimes dismiss the staff as 'soft' because they do not enforce rules rigidly. Arthur sheds a different light on this however:

[the staff at Lakeside] 'they're a lot better. They're more like people! When I was at Rushforth [day special school], they were more like robots really. You do something wrong; the first thing they do is grab 'em and stick 'em in a room, and just lock them up! Like here, they just talk to you; just tell you what you've done wrong, and have a good go at you. And you know you've done wrong, so you just have to take it . . . Sometimes, you don't want to listen; they just let you go and have a walk, and come back, and talk to you later.'

Under the former regime, there was a good deal of corporal punishment used by staff against rule-breakers, and it is the absence of this that some boys complain of. However, as Arthur suggests, the more reasonable approach of the new staff can have a deep impact. Thus, like the systems of rewards and privileges, the sanctions at Lakeside are geared to giving the boys a sense of their own responsibility for their own actions. This leads to some discomfort among the boys. They complain about the lack of discipline in the school, the softness of the staff, and long for the days of less freedom and draconian discipline. They complain because the current staff do not force them to comply with rules:

'Donald [current head] is too soft. When Ed was here, if everyone was talking in the dining room, as soon as Ed walked in, everyone would be quiet.'

(Frank)

'As soon as Donald walks in, everyone carries on – kick the chairs and everything.'

(Bill)

'Donald tries to act strict, but no one listens to him. They just give him mouth, and walk off! . . . He doesn't do nothing.'

(Arthur)

And yet:

'I think it should be more stricter. But if they get it more strict, I'm going to be the one that's breaking all the rules!'

(Larry)

EDUCATION AND ACHIEVEMENT

The boys have mixed opinions about the quality of the formal education provided at the two schools. While many pupils claim to have benefited from the educational programmes, there are many who complain at the lack of breadth in the school curriculum and the lack of opportunities to take public examinations.

The most vociferous complainant, on virtually all subjects, is Tom from Lakeside:

'I feel I'm getting thicker whilst I'm here . . . There's less chance to do the subjects everyone else is doing in a normal school . . . You're missing out on physics and chemistry. If I go back to my old school, I'll have a lot of catching up to do. 'Cos if I go back, I'll only have a year-and-a-quarter left . . . to get ready for my exams.'

Tom's assertion that the school is 'rubbish' is perhaps strongly coloured by his anxieties about his educational prospects. Tom is heavily preoccupied with his desire to return to a mainstream school, in order to complete his education. At the time of the interview Tom was awaiting a reply to a letter he had written to his former school, requesting the opportunity to return. This was clearly a testing time for Tom. His concerns about the quality of the schooling he was experiencing, however, are reflected in the views of other, less obviously troubled Lakeside boys:

'The education here is pathetic! I was doing exams before I came here . . . My reading age hasn't improved since I was nine.'

(Tim)

'It's [Lakeside] helped me in other ways, but not with my education. I was doing O-level maths, before I came here; now I can't even do fractions.'

(Frank)

However, not all the Lakeside boys share this view, by any means:

'Before I came to this school, I couldn't do maths or anything.'

(Tom)

These views are echoed by Jock and Stan, both of whom claim to have made much greater educational progress at Lakeside than in previous schools.

Larry offers a more complex picture. He links what he perceives as a lack of strictness in the school with the suggestion that he is underachieving:

'It's nowhere near as strict [at Lakeside, in comparison with a comprehensive school], and you don't do half as much work here. That's bad, that is, I can't stand work myself . . . it's boring. But when you were at senior school, and you were made to do it, you learned a lot more. I don't want to do it, but sometimes, I think you've got to do it, or you'll regret it when you get older. So I have a go!

(Larry)

Chapter 7

'. . . some kind of bampot.' Young people in care and their experience of the education system

Felicity Armstrong, Melissa Clarke and Selena Murphy

In this chapter two sisters, Melissa Clarke and Selena Murphy, describe their experiences of education and being in care, and Felicity Armstrong discusses educational issues for children in care from her own perspective as a foster parent.

INTRODUCTION

The first part of the title for our chapter is a salute to a nameless young person quoted in a report published in 1985 by the Scottish Council for Single Homeless called *Where Am I Going To Stay?* (Morgan-Klein 1985). She was commenting on the attitude of others when they find out you are in care:

> 'When you tell folk you're in care an' that . . . they think you are some kind of bampot.'

This chapter is about the experience of school and being in care. It is an attempt to relate our personal experiences to some of the wider issues which confront young people in care as they make their way through the education system. Many young people in care experience good times at school and come across teachers and social workers who support and encourage them. School may be a lifeline at a time when it is the only stable element in a young person's life. But some young people may encounter crushing prejudice, low expectations, discriminatory and bullying behaviour from adults and other pupils, and a lack of commitment on the part of schools and social services to ensure that young people in care have the same opportunities as other students.

In addition to writing about our own experiences we also draw on more voices from the Scottish report cited above, and from a more recent report *Not Just A Name* (Fletcher 1993). After the introduction and a section on discrimination we have each written a short piece about education and being in care from our personal perspectives. This is followed by some extracts from a discussion we had about further issues we felt were important.

DISCRIMINATION

Approximately 65–70,000 children and young people in England, Wales and Scotland may be in care at any particular moment, or 'being looked after' to use the euphemism adopted by the 1989 Children Act. One danger in talking about whole groups of people under one label is that the members of that group lose their individuality and become stereotyped. In fact, like any other 'group' of 70,000 people, children and young people in care are a very diverse group. One popular stereotype of young people in care is the 'villains' and 'victims' paradigm with a smaller number of 'volunteers' (Fletcher-Campbell and Hall 1990). Young people in care, this version goes, have either done something wrong or have 'something wrong' with them, or there is 'something wrong' with their families. This pathological view is deeply stigmatizing to young people in care and one which they are acutely conscious of. This is well documented in the Scottish report *Where Am I Going To Stay?* (Morgan-Klein 1985) and *Not Just A Name* (Fletcher 1993).

There is a section in *Where Am I Going To Stay?* called 'The stigma of residential care', which testifies to public and private ignorance and prejudice through the comments of young people in care. One girl who lived in a residential home said:

'. . . folk get a different impression outside. Like folk who have never seen the place and think it's an old place – something out of *Oliver Twist*.'

Most of the young people interviewed (approximately fifty took part in the main study for this report) had experienced the effects of discrimination and prejudice at school:

'An' [the teacher] turns round and says "People who are in children's homes are only in there for one reason for things they have done" and all this. She really insulted me and B. I felt like getting up and punching her in the face and everybody turned round and looked at me and B.'

'the kids were horrid. They used to like call you wee orphans and things like that when you were in the home and tell everybody in the school where you came frae – "X Children's Home. She come frae X." We used to never go to school the first year we came in here – not one of us would go to school because of it.'

'Well the first reaction an' one that I really hated when I said I was in a hostel was "Are you in care?", "Aye", "Oh what a shame." An' I just felt anger right away an' I said "I'm a'right – I'm just as well as you." You ken it's really the thought o' people feelin' pity or sorry for you that you're somebody that you should feel sorry for, I mean, I'm *strong* I don't need anybody's pity.'

Commenting on these views, the authors of the report write:

> In addition to these more general comments one or two young people mentioned feeling ambivalent about media coverage of life in residential care. One girl felt that well-meaning critiques of the treatment children and young people received while in care increased the stigma attached to being in care while achieving nothing. It seems that, paradoxically, young people feel ignored by this sort of coverage. Perhaps it is because *their* views are rarely genuinely sought.
>
> (Morgan-Klein 1985: 13)

Attempts by teachers to approach students who are in care with special sympathy can be experienced by them as patronizing and discriminatory.

> 'If people know, I am teased and called a "charity scrounger", also if a teacher knows they treat me different, sympathizing, asking how I am.'
>
> (15-year-old)

> 'All they do is ask me how things are getting on at home.'
>
> (12-year-old)

There is also evidence of low expectations on the part of some teachers towards students who are in care. For example:

> 'I feel that the actual education is no different, but people generally tend to put you in a certain group and because of being in care people don't expect a lot of you. It's like people in care are classed as thick, but there are many who have proved them wrong.'
>
> (17-year-old)

> 'Before I went into care I was in top sets and everything. They put me in bottom sets as soon as I moved into care and moved schools.'
>
> (16-year-old)

> 'Teachers were much more lenient, no work was expected of me. Being a grammar school this kind of treatment was in a way suggesting that I was no longer good enough. Why should the grades change – after all I'd achieved A grades while being abused.'
>
> (20-year-old who had been in care)

EXPERIENCES OF SCHOOL

In the following sections we describe personal experiences which have arisen in contexts relating to school or college. Melissa and Selena write from their

Figure 7.1 Melissa and Selina
Source: Darren Murphy

perspectives as students and Felicity writes from her point of view as a foster parent.

Melissa's experience

I am 19 and hoping to go to college next year to train as a social worker.

I never really liked school except the first school I can ever really remember which was Pegasus School. I enjoyed it. There was a teacher at that school who used to love me. Her name was Miss Fryer. She knitted me a jumper and used to write to me when I was in Long House children's home. I never had any trouble at school when I was living at home. When I was 9 I was fostered a long way from my home town and I went to another school. I was one of the only black children in the school apart from my brother Darren and my sister Selena and one other boy. I was really naughty at school and I was always made to sit outside the classroom or go to the headteacher's office. I couldn't read or write properly so I was naughty to get out of doing the work. When we had spelling tests I used to put the book under my desk to copy it or I'd copy my foster sister's answers. (There were seven of us fostered with one couple.) I didn't know my alphabet or know how to spell my last name which was 'Murphy' at that time. The teacher never gave me any special help which I think I really needed.

My foster mum took me out of school because I was so behind and I was going to go to secondary school. She taught me at home and I worked from

9 am until 4 pm and did two hours' homework in the evenings. I had extra lessons in maths and French. I worked very hard like this for about eighteen months and I didn't really have much choice because I used to be scared of my foster mum. Whenever I got something wrong she would hit me. I didn't have any friends because I wasn't going to school.

At my secondary school there was only one other black person apart from me. I experienced a lot of racism. I used to get bullied nearly every day and nothing was ever done about it. I used to tell my foster parents and they used to say: 'Just ignore it.' I didn't want to go to school. In the end my foster mum talked to the teachers but I think that made it worse by doing that. As I got into the third year I started to stick up for myself and I didn't get bullied so much. I used to hate my French and Spanish lessons so much especially when we had to speak out loud because I could never pronounce it properly. I had difficulty pronouncing English (which is my mother tongue), let alone French or Spanish. I was always good at sports, cookery and RE which were the subjects I liked most. Some of the teachers were really horrible to me. When I left that school which was an all-girls' school I came back to Oxford where I was born and I went to Cheney School which I liked. It was mixed and it had a lot of mixed-race kids too. I found the work very different from the previous school.

Selena's experience

I am 15 and taking my GCSEs this year. There are three of us and out of the three I think I've had it the easiest. I've only really been in one foster placement before this one and at school I think I lead a so-called 'normal life'. I always had questions asked about why I am in care and why I am black and my so-called 'family' was white. At the time this didn't really affect me.

I remember an incident at my old junior school when everybody was asked to bring in photos of themselves. I got myself all worked up as I didn't have any. I felt left out of the project and all the kids picked on me because of it. As I got older I came to terms with being bullied. I think I was bullied partly for being in care and partly because of the colour of my skin.

Some months ago I left the foster family where I had been for nine and a half years. I was beginning to feel unhappy and I felt unwanted. This was making me feel unsettled in the home and at school and many of the teachers told me that it was affecting my school work and my behaviour was affecting others around me. I would be loud in lessons and I was always wanting attention.

I'm now with a new family and I had to start a new school. I missed five weeks of valuable school time in my GCSE year because it took so long to fix up. I was dreading going to my new school because again I would have to go through the making friends process. In fact, this wasn't as bad as I thought it would be because I think in a way being in care has made me a stronger character and it has made me more independent and mature.

I haven't had it as bad as some kids in care have (in terms of my education). I guess I've just been lucky. But to keep having to pick up your belongings and making new friends gets to be a nightmare and you never feel properly settled. You never feel you are in a proper, real family. When you are in care you have hassles at school like 'normal' kids but you also have to deal with the fact that you are in the care of social services, and that isn't a very secure feeling.

Felicity's experience

I have been a foster parent to Melissa and Selena's brother Darren for six years. Darren came to live with us just after his 11th birthday. We became a 'foster family' by accident. We heard about Darren when he was living in a children's home for adolescents in a village in Oxfordshire. Darren was much younger than the other young people there. He was very keen on watching television, sport, eating chocolate and going to art galleries. Because of the interests of the different members of our existing family, it sounded as if we might get on well together. I also thought he would enjoy living in the city in an area where he would be able to have regular contact with his own extended family.

I think we have been lucky in general with schools. We live in an area where there are all kinds of people living in all kinds of family arrangements. The ethos of a school is important for all students whatever their personal history. Darren attends Peers School in Oxford which values each student and does not categorize students by putting them into different sets. There is an acceptance of difference and diversity and the variety of family arrangements shared by the school population are regarded as ordinary rather than extraordinary. Of course, there are occasions when this does not always work out in practice, but in general I think it is a comfortable place to be.

Darren made only two brief visits to our home before coming to live with us. On that occasion he asked me if he had to call me 'mum'. We agreed this would be uncomfortable because he has a 'mum' already. In an earlier foster family he had been encouraged to call his foster parents 'mum and dad' and to refer to his real mother by her first name. He was just 7 at the time. We also needed to sort out the question of surnames. In the last foster family Darren's own surname had been changed to that of the foster parents. When he left that family it had reverted to his original surname. He wanted to stick to it this time. At school teachers often refer to us as 'your mum and dad' although they know we are not and this feels uncomfortable. Some children in care want this, but to others it is false and may be experienced as a gross disloyalty to their own family.

Another cause of mutual unease has been on occasions when a teacher has made a remark such as 'He's a very lucky young man' or 'You're doing a great job'. Children who have been taken into care for whatever reason cannot be described as 'lucky'. If they were 'lucky' they would be living with their own families with all the problems which lead up to them being taken into care being sorted out. Children in general want to live with their own families like other people.

Congratulatory remarks such as 'You're doing a good job' devalue children in care. The assumption seems to be that a child or young person in care is going to be more difficult than other children and only some kind of saint would be willing to look after them.

Children and young people in care have no power and no real voice. They are often present at meetings which are run by adults for adults, although they are meant to be concerned with the young person's views and needs. Often I have sat in meetings and Darren has said virtually nothing. I think this is because the agenda is set by the professionals concerned who have their own ideas about what needs to be discussed. This has been particularly true of meetings organized by social services but has also been true of meetings held at school to discuss Darren's 'progress', punctuality etc. Often – in both contexts – I have felt a decision has been made at a meeting at which Darren was reluctantly present but in which he took no part. A major part of the problem is that the things the young person really wants are not on offer. In addition, unlike other children and young people, they have to ask for things which should be theirs by right, like regular contact with their own family, the right to privacy and the right to say no to living arrangements which are unacceptable to them. All these issues spill over into school life, of course.

I think the issue of privacy is important. It's difficult to know what to pass on to schools in terms of information about your children. It is important to listen to *them* and to let them give you some indication of what they want other people to know about them. This can mean teachers feeling they haven't been given enough information about a pupil.

For me, the most difficult thing about being a 'foster' parent is the hardening realization that in spite of the Children Act (1989) children and young people who are taken into care do not have the same basic rights as other people.

DISCUSSION

'I used to think I had to be as good as the others . . . the normal kids'

After reading each other's contributions it was clear there were some issues raised which needed more discussion. This is an extract from the discussion which followed.

Felicity: What was your experience of living independently, Melissa?

Melissa: I *thought* it would be good. Social services wanted to put me in a hostel for young people because I had no one looking after me but I took one look at it and I knew I couldn't live there. It was dirty and there was no privacy. So I moved into my own place – independently – at 16.

Felicity: What happened about school?

Melissa: I stopped going really. We had a lot of friends round and I stayed up late. Then I enrolled at the College of Further Education but I soon stopped going because I wasn't getting enough sleep. People came round all the time and you can't tell people to go away because it's other people's home too. I couldn't live on what I had so I had to get a job in the evenings. I was always tired. At that time I got £32.60 a week to live on and out of that I had to buy food, books for college, clothes and 'girls' stuff' – which girls need and is very expensive. Then I had to pay the electricity, gas, telephone and washing machine. The electricity cost me £5 a week and the gas £17.50 a month. The telephone bill was a lot. I did get a free bus pass and free dinners when I went into college, but I couldn't live on the money I had. When I asked Social Services for money for sport they said no because I had chosen to go into lodgings and live independently.

Felicity: So you had about £20 a week for food, clothes and books and other essentials. I don't know how you managed.

Melissa: I didn't.

Felicity: Both of you have mentioned racism. Do you think there are any particular issues about being black and being in care?

Selena: I think it depends where you live. When I was fostered down in Sussex away from my home town there were hardly any black people there and there was a lot of racism. But in Oxford it's a lot better.

Felicity: What has been the hardest in terms of your education about being in care?

Selena: The whole thing. Having to change schools. I had to change in the middle of my GCSE year. And all the questions.

Melissa: I find it hard when people ask . . . I find it hard to say what happened and why I was fostered. I just say: 'I was adopted when I was little.'

Selena: When you are fostered, the other children in the family have to know everything about you.

Felicity: Why?

Selena: I don't know, but they do. I found out one of them was telling people at school about me.

Melissa: I've always found that. Everybody knew my business and asked questions.
        [pause]
Melissa: The other thing that has been really hard is not having anybody to talk to about how I was feeling.
Felicity: I know Darren feels pressurized because he thinks we have high expectations of him in terms of exams and going to college. Although we say we don't have these expectations and only 'want what he wants' perhaps he's right and underneath we *have* got expectations which don't correspond to the things *he* wants to do. Have you felt any pressure on you to do well in exams and so on?
Selena: I used to. I used to think I had to be as good as the others – the normal kids – the so-called 'normal' kids. I know I'm one myself now! But I used to feel I had to do better just so I could prove I was a normal kid. It was a pressure all the time, but it was good to know I was as capable as the others.
Felicity: Have you felt you were treated differently from other pupils by teachers at school?
Melissa: If anything, I think I've often been treated *better*. But I don't like it when people feel sorry for you.
Selena: When I left my previous foster parents and stayed with friends, all the teachers were really nice. One said I could come and live with them. They were all really nice.
Felicity: What could be done to make things easier for children and young people when they are taken into care?
Melissa: People should stay at the same school. Definitely.
        [long silence]
Melissa: I remember the day we were taken away. The social worker came to the house. We were all screaming. We got away and ran across a field and the social worker was running after us.
Selena: It was really horrible. They caught us. We didn't see our mum for a very long time.
Felicity: And you never went back to your school?
Melissa: No.

REFERENCES

Department of Health (1993) *Children in Care of Local Authorities, Year Ending 31 March 1991, England*, Crown Copyright, London: HMSO.
Donnellan, Craig (1993) *Children in Care*, Issues for the Nineties, Vol. 21, Cambridge: Independence Educational Publishers.
Fletcher, B. (1993) *Not Just A Name: The Views of Young People in Foster and Residential Care*, London: Who Cares? Trust/National Consumer Council.
Fletcher-Campbell, F. (1992) 'Stressing education: children in care', in T. Booth,

W. Swann, M Masterton and P. Potts (eds) *Learning For All 1, Curricula for Diversity in Education*, London: Routledge.

Fletcher-Campbell, F. and Hall, C. (1990) *Changing Schools? Changing People? The Education of Children In Care*, Slough: NFER.

Jackson, S. (1987) *The Education of Children In Care*, The Bristol Papers in Applied Social Studies, No.1, University of Bristol School of Applied Social Studies.

Morgan-Klein, B. (1985) *Where Am I Going to Stay?: A Report On Young People Leaving Care in Scotland*, Edinburgh: The Scottish Council for Single Homeless.

USEFUL ADDRESSES

Black and in Care
William Morris Community Centre, Green Leaf Road, London E1.

ChildLine
Freepost 1111, London N1 0BR. Freephone Helpline 0800 1111

Children's Legal Centre
20 Compton Terrace, London N1 2UN.
  Advice Line 2pm–5pm Monday to Friday. Tel. 071–359 6251

The Children's Society
Edward Rudolf House, 69–85 Margery Street, London WC1X 0JL.
  Tel. 071–837 4299

National Association of Young People in Care (NAYPIC)
20 Compton Terrace, London N1 2UN. Tel. 071–226 7102

National Children's Bureau
8 Wakely Street, London EC1V 7QE. Tel. 071–278 9441

National Consumer Council
26 Grosvenor Gardens, London SW1W ODH.

National Foster Care Association (NFCA)

England:
Leonard House, 5–7 Marshalsea Road, London SE1 1EP. Tel. 071–828 6266

Scotland:
1 Melrose Street, off Queen's Crescent, Glasgow G4 9BJ.
  Tel. 041–332 6655

National Foster Care Association Advice and Mediation Service, Wales
Valerie Capewell, Tralbuy, Brecon, Powys LD3 8HP, South Wales.

Robert Murphy, Bryn Glas, High Street, Llanfyllin, Powys SY22 5JB, North Wales.

Who Cares? Trust
Claybridge House, 235–245 Goswell Road, London EC1V 7JD.

Who Cares?
Magazine Advice and Information Service, 9 Wakely Street, London EC1V 7QE.
  Tel. 071–278 9441.

Part II

Developing inclusive curricula

Chapter 8

History for pupils who experience severe difficulties in learning

Judy Sebba

The writing of the National History Curriculum has been fired with heated debates. For example, should the content of an appropriate curriculum for British school students reflect a strictly British heritage or should it reflect the diversity of students' cultural backgrounds? In this chapter, Judy Sebba focuses on another debate, which is concerned with the value of teaching a subject called 'history' to children and young people for whom the concepts of place, space and time are difficult. She argues that the introduction of history into curricula for these students has been positive and she gives a range of practical examples.

INTRODUCTION

This chapter is aimed at those who may doubt the value of teaching history to pupils experiencing severe difficulties and at teachers who are searching for further ideas for their practice. I have made no assumptions about your knowledge of history.

It needs to be recognized that not all pupils will develop skills of communication and literacy, whatever opportunities are afforded, and that tokenism, for example claiming that pupils with profound and multiple difficulties are learning history through museum visits or historical recreations, should be avoided.

The context is set by considering some of the controversies surrounding the development of the programmes of study and attainment targets in history. The implications of the document for pupils experiencing special educational needs are considered. Most of the issues are in no sense specific to any particular category of pupil and, as has been suggested often elsewhere, it is assumed that good quality teaching will benefit all pupils, not just those whose difficulties have been identified. A range of examples from practice with pupils experiencing severe learning difficulties in special and mainstream schools will be used to illustrate the issues.

The publications available on teaching history have multiplied since the introduction of the National Curriculum. These have been predominantly in the primary field (e.g. Andreetti 1993, Bage 1993, Cooper 1992, Knight 1993), in which there was a previous dearth of appropriate information. Many publishers have produced schemes for primary history, sometimes closely tied to the current programmes of study and attainment targets which are unlikely to withstand the test of time given that revisions in the curriculum are inevitable. Teaching history to pupils with special educational needs has been addressed by only a few authors in recent publications. These include the identification of issues by Wilson (1992), the examples of practice for pupils with moderate and severe learning difficulties (e.g. Banes and Sebba 1991, Morris 1992, Sebba and Clarke 1991, Ware and Peacey 1993) and more extensive ideas for activities and teaching material produced by teachers or local authority advisory services (e.g. East Sussex 1991, Humberside 1992, Suffolk 1991–3, Warwickshire 1993). Examples from some of these are given below.

THE CONTEXT FOR NATIONAL CURRICULUM HISTORY

The programmes of study and attainment targets emerged amidst a raging debate about the definitions of history and implications for teaching. Simplified, the controversy was between 'facts and dates' and 'process', characterized by interpretation of evidence. The 'traditional' view demanded knowledge about facts while more recent trends in teaching were considered to be biased towards the historical skills. The fact that history is about human beings and human experience (Purkis 1987) was not in dispute, despite my own experience of being shown work on dinosaurs in primary and special schools that is claimed to contribute to the history curriculum.

The current National Curriculum document, as Bage (1993) points out, contains both facts and skills, while leaving enough flexibility for teachers to make some decisions about what to teach. The structure is similar to the current English, technology and modern foreign languages documents in which the content is specified in the programmes of study and the skills in the attainment targets. This is helpful to those committed to providing curricula for diversity as it enables pupils working at different levels to be tackling the same content which is virtually impossible in subjects which have level-related content (e.g. currently, geography, science, maths). Beyond Key Stage 1, the programmes of study comprise facts while the attainment targets address the central historical skills of accounting for change and continuity, interpretation and use of sources. Key Stage 1 focuses predominantly on historical skills with a close match between the programme of study and the attainment targets. The specific content of the programmes of study and attainment targets have been detailed in numerous publications (Cooper 1992, Sebba and Clarke 1991, Wilson 1992).

NATIONAL CURRICULUM HISTORY IN PRACTICE

Reports of the monitoring of the introduction of the National Curriculum have been provided by the Office for Standards in Education (OFSTED) and the National Curriculum Council (NCC). In the OFSTED report on history (OFSTED 1993a), which covers mainstream primary and secondary schools, it was noted that history is more evident as a discrete subject than it has been in the past but that most primary schools still deliver history through topic work. A separate OFSTED report on special needs and the National Curriculum (OFSTED 1993b) reported that half the pupils in special schools were not receiving a sufficiently broad and balanced curriculum. It was suggested that this partly reflected poorly planned and uncoordinated topic work which failed to cover history, geography and science adequately. This was the only reference to history in the report, making it difficult to get a national overview on history in special schools.

In NCC's (1993) report on special needs and the National Curriculum teachers identified a need for guidance on differentiating teaching in history. This matches the OFSTED (1993a: 3) finding that in both secondary and primary schools, 'the matching of work to pupils of different abilities is handled uncertainly'. Specific concerns were expressed in the NCC review by teachers of pupils with visual impairments who were experiencing difficulties in the use of historical sources.

It is clear that the volume of history teaching has increased in primary and special schools and that many pupils who experience severe learning difficulties may be encountering history for the first time in their school careers. However, as Bage (1993) points out, more history does not necessarily mean better history. A balance should be established between knowledge and skills and between the different types of skills (e.g. historical enquiry, communication, use of evidence, etc.).

IMPLICATIONS OF NATIONAL CURRICULUM HISTORY FOR PUPILS WHO EXPERIENCE SEVERE DIFFICULTIES IN LEARNING

Many of the aspects of history which have important implications for teaching are broadly similar for pupils in primary and special schools. They arise because these schools rarely offered history as a discrete subject prior to the National Curriculum and only a small proportion of these schools have subject specialists with any background training or experience on which to base their current responsibilities. Staff in smaller schools are required to coordinate several subject areas making it difficult to acquire the knowledge or skills in any one subject. The sheer volume of content makes it difficult for non-subject specialists to decide how much depth to teach in each content area or how to tackle the vast range of material. The OFSTED report (1993a) suggests this has led some teachers to teach every detail in the programme of study, leading to content overload. Hence, the planning strategies become crucial to whether teachers sink or swim.

Those teaching pupils with special educational needs may find the literacy and language demands of history daunting. However, as Morris (1992), Peter (1994), Purkis (1987) and Woodall *et al.* (1987) have illustrated, there are ways of tackling the same content and skills through oral work and drama which partly overcome these difficulties. Nevertheless, it is clear that the use of written sources and communicating historical understanding through writing is likely to be limited for pupils who experience severe learning difficulties.

The requirements relating to interpretation (currently, Attainment Target 2) have challenged primary and special schools alike. Pupils who experience severe learning difficulties may be able to describe a previous event within their own experience such as last year's school trip but are less likely to be aware that another pupil's description differs from their own. Moreover, the further into the past the event occurred which the pupil is attempting to recall, the more difficulties they may experience. Hence, Wilson's (1992) suggestion that history teaching begins with the most recent past and works backwards in time.

The major disadvantages for pupils experiencing learning difficulties of a curriculum structured in hierarchical levels are comprehensively considered by Swann (1992). He points out that the levels are particularly problematic as those who have to implement them assume they are in the correct order. Yet we know from recent revisions of some subjects, that this is not the case. Furthermore, Bage (1993) has argued that the statements of attainment in history are not necessarily either sequential in difficulty or representative of stages in the development of historical skills. He suggests that there is insufficient research with young children to be confident about the order in which historical skills are acquired.

This implies that difficulties are likely to emerge with assessment in history at the earlier levels for all pupils. Assessment of pupils experiencing severe learning difficulties in history may therefore remain problematic throughout their school life. In addition to any confusion about levels, there will need to be due regard for ensuring it is history that is being assessed rather than communication, literacy or other skills. Teachers will require further guidance on assessment and recording of achievements in history for pupils experiencing special educational needs.

EXAMPLES OF HISTORY TEACHING WITH PUPILS WHO EXPERIENCE SEVERE LEARNING DIFFICULTIES

The examples described mostly relate to the history study unit in Key Stage 1. This is inevitable since they are mainly from schools in which neither the teachers nor the pupils have prior experience of history. While the structure of the document theoretically enables all the history study units to be accessed at any level, the reality of attempting to start with the study of a past non-European society (e.g. the Maya) or medieval realms with pupils whose skills in other areas are akin to those of a 5-year-old or less, is somewhat daunting. Hence, most history teaching with these pupils begins with the earliest study unit in order to build up the confidence of both teacher and pupils and to establish history within the curriculum. A few examples of work relating to later key stages is included as this may provoke some interesting debate and provide further ideas.

Activities relating to personal history

Materials predominantly designed for primary schools such as the *Time and Place* resources (Harrison and Harrison 1990), the Tressell integrated infant pack *Ourselves* (Simkin 1990) and *A Sense of History* (Purkis 1991) all include useful material on personal history, addressing family trees, 'Our School', 'My Home', 'Our Gran' and 'About Ourselves'. These materials have been adapted and used effectively by teachers working with pupils experiencing severe learning difficulties.

Activities addressing personal history cover many of the requirements of the National Curriculum including chronology, for example placing photographs of family members into sequence by age; cause and consequence, for example recognising that one reason for a new school building was that there were more children; and similarity and difference, for example discovering that Grandma used to play the same skipping game that we do now. A wide range of historical sources can be utilized including photographs, simple documents, buildings, objects and music. In addition, some pupils may be able to 'interview' family members about the past, using tape recorders to reduce demands for writing. With all pupils it is important to remain sensitive to differences in family structure, backgrounds and stability and not to allow stereotypes to result in discomfort or embarrassment for particular pupils.

An activity we have explored with some pupils experiencing severe learning difficulties is the use of personal videos to encourage an awareness of change over time. This work is described in detail elsewhere (Banes and Sebba 1991). Sequences of video made for illustration purposes for annual review meetings were edited backwards (most recent first) and shown to the pupil. Questions were used to encourage the pupil to consider changes in clothes, hairstyles, activities, skills, toys, school staff and friends. Pupils with limited non-verbal means of communication (e.g. gestures, signs) were found to respond by indicating that they recognized some aspect which had changed (e.g. one pupil signed 'baby' when, on a sequence of video from a year ago, a member of staff appeared who had left school to have a baby).

Figure 8.1 Timeline of Personal History

Source: Banes and Sebba (1991)

Timelines were constructed using events, people or objects that had been significant to the pupil, as shown in the example in Figure 8.1.

A major advantage of personal history work is that it is relevant and meaningful to the pupil and is therefore more likely to encourage learning in areas such as communication skills as well as history. A discussion about a past event in the pupil's experience within school such as a school play, outing or party, may provide the earliest opportunity to explore different interpretations of history by drawing out how pupils' accounts of the event differ. This is one of the least accessible areas in history but may provide a teaching context in which awareness and sensitivity towards peers can be further enhanced.

Activities recording changes over time

Many schools for pupils with severe learning activities keep weather charts, calendars and charts of the seasons. These are often tackled in inspiring ways to increase access such as using symbols, drawings and photographs. Use of real objects such as the clothing associated with particular seasons can be most effective in developing pupils' understanding of the differences that occur between seasons and in establishing the sequence.

Similarly, timetables of the activities that occur in school over a week, made accessible to pupils using symbols or pictures, can be beneficial in helping pupils develop an understanding of sequence. History-focused projects in this area include farming cycles, building sites and creating gardens. An integrated scheme of work on creating and developing a garden in a school for pupils with severe learning difficulties is described in detail by Byers (1992) and included keeping a garden diary using words, pictures, charts and video.

Activities based around the idea of time capsules can be an effective means of considering change over time. Pupils select some objects including a few likely to decompose over a relatively short period (e.g. bread, cheese, etc.) and place them in a weatherproof container. They are then buried and after an appropriate period (which will depend on the pupils involved) they are dug up and examined for changes. Pupils are encouraged to predict the changes that might have occurred prior to opening the container.

These activities are popular with teachers and pupils, generate good discussion on change and often result in better communication skills than occur in lessons supposedly addressing language. This version of the activity covers part of the science curriculum. In terms of history, it would need to be seen as leading on to activities in which pupils begin to address what information objects that are discovered might provide about the people to whom they belonged.

Use of artefacts

The use of Museum objects to depict life from another period may be effective if an attempt is made to compare the objects with their equivalents from the present. Teachers working with pupils who experience severe learning difficulties have undertaken a range of activities including 'feely boxes', matching the objects to photographs of people using them in the past, pairing them with their present-day equivalents and trying to use them. The questioning by the teacher may be crucial in facilitating the development of historical skills. Examples of appropriate questions to address are provided in the Humberside County Council (1992) material on history for pupils with special educational needs. Pupils are encouraged to consider in relation to each object characteristics such as colour, weight, material, size, shape, smell, function, who might have used it, etc. Figure 8.2 is an example from the materials produced by the East Sussex Severe Learning Difficulties schools (1991) as a resource for staff. It demonstrates the range of possibilities for comparing similarities and differences in a project on 'Now and Then'.

NOW AND THEN

HERE AND THERE

Time
When were, or are the different pieces of equipment used?
Which method takes the longer time?
How have things changed through time?

Place
As a variation on the theme — which building materials could you use in different countries?
Which plants are suitable for different environments?

Society
Does everyone have access to these modcons?
Who has made the changes and why?

Concepts
Modern objects may be more convenient.
Lifestyles change as time passes.
Old objects have some advantages.

Skills
Interpreting data, and recording it.
Observation and comparison.
practical involvement.

Values and Attitudes
Is today's life-style better?
Do mod.cons. make our life easier?

Cross Curricular Opportunities

Maths — timing the various activities
recording data using graphs
surveys of preferred equipment.
comparative cost.

Science — study of heat.
electricity.

Language — use of comparisons — quicker, slower, better, worse etc.

Possible Activities

Cook sausages over a fire, and on a cooker.
use a flat-iron, and a steam iron.

Illuminate the room with a candle, and electric light

Write with a quill pen, and a word-processor

Ride on a horse, and in a bus

Clean with a dustpan and brush, and hoover

Sew by hand, and with a machine

Whisk an egg with a fork, and a mixer
and you could even.......

Cut down a tree with an axe, and a chain-saw !!

N.B. Certain children (and staff) may need to be supervised !!

Figure 8.2 Now and Then
Source: East Sussex County Council (1991:19)

Oral history

Pupils for whom written sources are difficult to access may benefit from more use of oral history. Common activities include getting older people to visit and describe some aspect of life when they were young, listening to stories that have historical content and re-telling them or acting them out and interviewing people in the family or community about the past. Both Purkis (1987) and Morris (1992) describe oral history work designed to increase access for pupils who find reading and writing difficult. Pupils with severe learning difficulties will need to work in pairs or groups to enable a pupil with some speech to conduct the interview while another operates the tape recorder.

Use of later key stage content

Use has been made of material from history study units in Key Stages 2 and 3 in some work with pupils experiencing severe learning difficulties. Warwickshire County Council (1993) have developed useful materials about the Battle of Hastings presented using a range of sizes of print, pictures and symbols. An example is given in Figure 8.3. Pupils are encouraged to sequence the pictures, re-tell the story in their own 'words', using signing or symbols as appropriate, pick out the pictures of the people who are kings, etc. For pupils who can read, flash cards of the story are provided without the pictures. Other material is currently under development.

Information technology provides an important means of increasing access to history for pupils with limited literacy skills. The example in Figure 8.4 from Humberside County Council materials illustrates how use of the concept keyboard can increase access to medieval realms. This simple introductory database can be used to search, group and print out information.

CONCLUSION

This chapter has briefly described the controversies surrounding the development of National Curriculum history and some of the implications of the current requirements for pupils experiencing severe learning difficulties. A few examples have been described of activities and materials which have increased access for these pupils. These examples share some common features. They seek relevance by focusing on aspects of interest to pupils and within their experience such as clothes, food, music, etc. They use a variety of sources such as video, photographs, real objects and other people and, in particular, avoid dependence on written sources. Access is increased through the use of signs, symbols and IT. Opportunities are taken to address individual priorities within historical activities. In some of the activities, history starts with the present and moves backwards. These strategies are

Figure 8.3 The Battle of Hastings

Source: Elspeth Brown, Warwickshire County Council (1993)

Breakfast		
Dinner		
Supper	Peasants	Nobles
FINISH		

Figure 8.4 Medieval realms: how do people live?

Source: Humberside County Council (1992:178)

likely to benefit all pupils, but without them, pupils with severe learning difficulties will be denied access to history and their opportunities to learn will be seriously curtailed.

REFERENCES

Andreetti, K. (1993) *Teaching History from Primary Evidence*, London: Fulton.

Bage, G. (1993) 'History at KS1 and KS2: questions of teaching, planning, assessment and progression', *The Curriculum Journal* 4: 269–82.

Banes, D. and Sebba, J. (1991) 'I was little then', *British Journal of Special Education* 18: 121–4.

Byers, R. (1992) 'Topics: from myths to objectives', in K. Bovair, B. Carpenter and G. Upton (eds) *Special Curricula Needs*, London: Fulton.

Cooper, H. (1992) *The Teaching of History*, London: Fulton.

East Sussex County Council (1991) *Don't Panic! A Hitchhiker's Guide to Humanities*, Lewes: East Sussex County Council.

Harrison, P. and Harrison, S. (1990) *Time and Place: History and Geography for Key Stage 1*, Hemel Hempstead: Simon and Schuster.

Humberside County Council (1992) *Access to History: History for Children with Special Educational Needs*, Hull: Humberside Curriculum and Professional Development Unit.

Knight, P. (1993) *Primary Geography Primary History*, London: Fulton.

Morris, C. (1992) 'Opening doors: learning history through talk', in T. Booth, W. Swann, M. Masterton and P. Potts (eds) *Learning for All 1: Curricula for Diversity in Education*, London: Routledge.

NCC (1993) *Special Needs and the National Curriculum: Opportunity and Challenge*, York: NCC.

OFSTED (1993a) *History: Key stages 1, 2 and 3*, London: HMSO.

OFSTED (1993b) *Special Needs and the National Curriculum*, London: HMSO.

Peter, M. J. (1994) *Drama For All*, London: Routledge.

Purkis, S. (1987) 'Personalizing the past: oral history in schools', in: T. Booth, P. Potts and W. Swann (eds) *Preventing Difficulties in Learning: Curricula for All*, Oxford: Blackwell.

Purkis, S. (1991) *A Sense of History*, Key Stage 1 materials. Harlow: Longman.

Sebba, J. and Clarke, J. (1991) 'Meeting the needs of pupils within history and geography', in R. Ashdown, B. Carpenter and K. Bovair (eds) *The Curriculum Challenge: Access to the National Curriculum for Pupils with Learning Difficulties*, London: Falmer.

Simkin, D. (1990) *Ourselves: An Infant Topic Pack for Integrated Humanities*, Brighton: Tressell.

Suffolk Humanities Advisory Team (1991–3) *Guidance Booklets on National Curriculum History*, Ipswich: Suffolk County Council.

Swann, W. (1992) 'Hardening the hierarchies: the National Curriculum as a system of classification', in T. Booth, W. Swann, M. Masterton and P. Potts (eds) *Learning for All 1: Curricula for Diversity in Education*, London: Routledge.

Ware, J. and Peacey, N. (1993) '"We're doing history" – What does it mean?' *British Journal of Special Education* 20: 65–9.

Warwickshire County Council (1993) Materials for teaching history to pupils with severe learning difficulties. Leamington Spa: Warwickshire County Council.

Wilson, J. (personal communication) Material from John Smeaton Community High School, Leeds.

Wilson, M (1992) 'History: issues to resolve', in K. Bovair, B. Carpenter and G. Upton (eds) *Special Curricula Needs*, London: Fulton.

Woodall, J., Carey, T. and Dodgson, E. (1987) 'Teaching history through drama', in T. Booth, P. Potts and W. Swann (eds) *Preventing Difficulties in Learning: Curricula for All*, Oxford: Blackwell.

Chapter 9

Group work in physics

Towards an inclusive curriculum

Christine Howe

Christine reminds us of the stereotypical view of physics as a subject inaccessible to nearly everyone and she notes that it is often taught to students who are working individually. From her study of Piaget's theories of cognitive development, however, Christine expected that a different pedagogical approach could enable many more children to make progress with physics. In a series of collaborative studies with colleagues in the Psychology Department at Strathclyde University, Christine investigated the value for children of working together in mixed-ability groups. Her results show that the children's disagreements over predictions and explanations were creative catalysts in the development of their understanding. And those children in the groups who were seen to be the least able, made the most progress.

INTRODUCTION

If we had to identify the discipline which best epitomizes a non-inclusive curriculum, we might very well turn to physics. There is evidence that only a small minority of pupils continue with physics beyond the minimum level. Thus, Sears (1992) shows that just 17 per cent of recent A-level candidates in England and Wales were registered for physics. Moreover, even when pupils do persevere, the conceptual content of the discipline frequently passes them by. Research reviewed by McDermott (1984) documents widespread misunderstanding at university level. For example, substantial numbers of physics undergraduates deny one of the central tenets of Newton's Laws, that objects can move in the absence of forces. Findings such as these are bad enough, but the situation proves even worse when we probe more deeply. Then, it becomes clear that access to physics is not simply limited but also the prerogative of well-defined groups. Gender is, for example, relevant, with only 4 per cent of Sears' A-level candidates being girls. Moreover, although the absolute proportions studying physics are greater for Scottish Highers, research reported by Croxford *et al.* (1992) shows that boys still outnumber girls by a ratio of 2:1. It is also possible that girls find the conceptual content of physics relatively challenging. Certainly, a large-scale survey of 8 to 14-year-olds (Scottish Office Education Department 1992) shows boys consistently outstripping girls in the knowledge displayed on written tests.

The non-inclusiveness of physics has long been recognized, and in that sense the figures quoted above simply confirm that the problem continues. Not surprisingly then, there has been extensive discussion as to why it occurs, with a range of answers offered. One favourite is poor teaching. It is sometimes argued (usually without evidence) that when physicists are rare and therefore valuable, the good ones are unlikely to be attracted to a low-paid profession like teaching. Another approach is to call on the nature of physics. It is said to be too mathematical or, with phrases like a 'massless rope' and a 'frictionless pulley', too abstract. Recently however, a third line has been followed. It is argued that when students come to physics they are not blank slates with respect to the phenomena they will be studying. Rather, they are holders of pre-tuitional conceptions which differ from the received wisdom of science and exert a subversive influence on it. Evidence for this is presented in a number of sources. McDermott (1984), for instance, shows that when students deny motion in the absence of forces, they correspondingly assert forces which operate (sometimes exclusively) in the direction of motion. Thus, pendular forces are erroneously attributed to playground swings and circular forces to roundabouts. When the forces being considered are tantamount to gravity, they are often expected to increase as the earth's surface is approached and/or be influenced by air pressure, both views far removed from conventional science.

There is little doubt, then, that pre-tuitional conceptions exist for physics. Equally, there is little doubt that these conceptions undermine teaching. Research by Champagne et al. (1980) shows that although conceptions are not the only significant variable, they certainly exert an influence on under-graduate attainment. Faced with such evidence, challenging conceptions has now been recognized as a high priority, and there have been several pro-posals as to how this should be done. One popular approach is to equate the conceptions with theories, and to argue that pupils should be taken through the procedures by which professional scientists evaluate theories (e.g. Screen 1988, Wellington 1988). Emphasis is placed on tasks where pupils make predictions on the basis of their conceptions, subject the predictions to empirical test, and construct explanations for what transpires. The approach is appealing, yet it is frequently restricted to the processes of science and excludes the context. Science, as practised professionally, is a collaborative activity involving teams of researchers and multi-participant conferences. Yet the teaching packages to date have been targeted at individuals. It could be argued that full mimicry of scientific procedures would emphasize the collaborative context, perhaps by organizing pupils to work in groups.

Theoretical support for a group-based approach can be found in the work of Piaget. According to Piaget (e.g. Piaget 1985), conceptual development depends on 'equilibration', equilibration being the reconciliation of conflict between existing and newly experienced conceptions. The implication is that children should be provided with ideas which conflict with their existing ones but which, by virtue of not being too advanced, are assimilable to them. As Piaget recognized (Piaget 1932), one context in which this might be achieved is group work between children who hold differing conceptions. So long as children are given tasks which tease the differences out and motivate their resolution, the synthesizing of new and existing ideas should be a real possibility. If this is correct, it would have major advantages for the teaching of physics. Research into children's conceptions has documented considerable variability within each age band, implying that groups with differing ideas could be easily achieved. Indeed, the emphasis on difference would make a virtue of the possible gender variation alluded to earlier. Equally, the requirement under the recent National Curriculum (Department of Education and Science 1989) to involve children with 'special needs' would become a strength. More generally, the implication would be a striking endorsement of mixed-ability teaching.

Accepting Piaget's argument as correct would then have major advantages. However, to do this, we need relevant empirical evidence, and until recently little was available. Piaget never observed group work directly, and sorties into this field by his associates (e.g. Doise and Mugny 1984) have emphasized logical, mathematical and spatial reasoning, and not the physical world. During the 1980s, studies appeared which did focus on physics, for instance Nussbaum and Novick (1981), Forman and Cazden (1985), Forman and Kraker (1985), Osborne and Freyberg (1985) and Gilbert and Pope (1986). However, with these studies, it is frequently impossible to differentiate the effects of group work from the effects of adult intervention. Moreover, although the studies all claim to address conceptual conflict, the guarantees that the children's conceptions differed were often far from convincing. Even when these difficulties were avoided, the studies rarely had comparison groups with similar conceptions to differentiate the benefits drawn from group composition from those drawn from task materials. In addition, they seldom considered whether the positive effects survived over time. Recognizing these problems, a group of us at Strathclyde University have embarked on a further programme of research. The remainder of the chapter will be devoted to summarizing the research, and documenting its relevance to inclusiveness in physics.

GROUP WORK IN PRIMARY SCHOOL PHYSICS

The research consists of two series of investigations, the first comprising three studies all conducted with primary school children (see Howe *et al.*

1990, Howe, Tolmie and Rodgers 1992). The studies addressed children's conceptions of why some objects float in tapwater while others sink (hereafter Study I); why some objects float in tapwater but sink in other liquids (Study II); and why some objects roll a distance off inclined planes while others do not (Study III). They all began with individual interviews (or 'pretests' as we called them) to around 120 Glasgow children aged 8 to 12. The aim of the pre-tests was to obtain information about the children's initial conceptions. For the Study I and II pre-tests, we presented small objects, for example a metal key, an ebony cylinder and a plastic ring, and asked the children to predict whether (and to explain why) these objects would float or sink in tanks of water. In Study I, we used one tank, half full with tapwater. In Study II, we used a series of tanks with the water varying in density (relevant to floating and sinking and achieved via salt) and depth or roughness (irrelevant but often thought by children to be important). We also outlined real-world instances, icebergs floating in the sea and anchors sinking, ice cubes floating in tapwater but sinking in whisky, and asked the children to explain them. Real-world instances also featured in the Study III pre-tests, for example skateboarders speeding down hills. However, the focus was apparatus which supported slopes of varying angle, friction and length. The children's task was to predict which of three squares toy vehicles would reach if rolled down the slopes, and to explain their predictions.

We noted what the children said in response to each pre-test item, for example 'I think it'll float because *it's got air inside*' and 'I don't think it'll go very far because *the slope isn't very steep*'. Subsequently, we extracted the explanations (italicized here) from the responses as a whole, reasoning that they were a relatively direct index of initial conceptions. Using the explanations, we attempted to group the children such that their conceptions were either different or similar. The children's conceptions differed in varying ways both within and between the studies, and the composition of the groups reflected this. Full details of group composition can be obtained from Howe *et al.* (1990) and Howe, Tolmie and Rodgers (1992), but Figure 9.1 presents a summary. One point to note is that, as signified by the DD label, half of the differing groups in Studies I and II and all of the differing groups in Study III contained children at different *levels* of understanding, equivalent to mixed ability in this context. Group membership was restricted to classmates, and the groups were always foursomes. The use of foursomes was motivated by pilot work and by Her Majesty's Inspectors (1978) who reveal that smaller groups are rare in primary classrooms. Gender was not systematically varied, but there were no differences between the different and similar groups in the total numbers of boys and girls nor in the gender distribution within each group.

Between four and six weeks after the pre-tests, the groups were taken one by one to work on tasks that we had prepared. These tasks had the predict–test–explain format which, as mentioned earlier, is widely believed

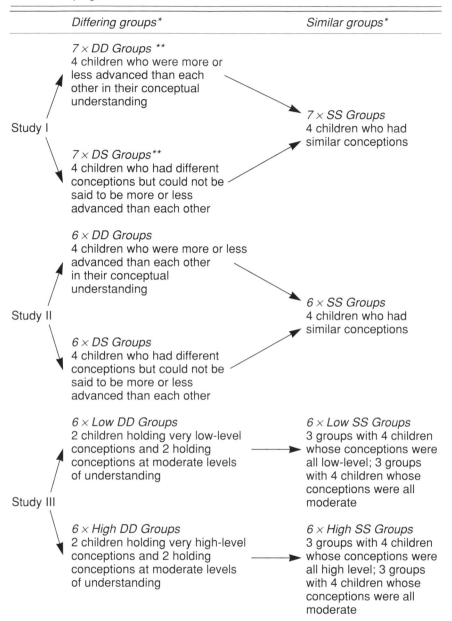

Figure 9.1 Composition of the groups in Studies I, II and III

* Children assigned to differing groups were required to have given different responses from all other group members to at least two-thirds of the pre-test items. Children in similar groups were required to have given the same response as all other group members to at least two-thirds of the items.
** DD means that the children differed by virtue of being at different levels of understanding. DS means that they differed despite being at the same level of understanding.

to be helpful. At the start, each child in the group was given a set of cards. Materials similar to the pre-tests were displayed and the children asked to make private predictions by ticking the correct answers from choices on their cards, for instance 'The key will float . . . /sink . . . in the water'. Once the children had done this, they moved to the group phase proper. They were given workbooks (see Appendix I) which invited them to compare their predictions and come to an agreement where these differed. Pilot work had revealed that comparing predictions after being committed in writing is an excellent incentive to lively discussion. The workbooks specified that once the predictions had been agreed, they were to be tested using the materials, and explanations of the outcomes were to be agreed. In addition to items relating to the predictions, the workbooks also contained descriptions of real-world instances for which the children were asked to agree explanations. We took the children through the first two items of the workbooks, avoiding comment on the decisions but checking that the procedure had been properly grasped. Thereafter we withdrew, with the children being videotaped as they worked through the remaining items.

Subsequent to the group tasks, we appraised the children's conceptions once more via individual interviews, referred to this time as 'post-tests'. In Study III only, there were post-tests to a 25 per cent sample within one day of the task. Data from these post-tests will not be reported here (see Howe, Tolmie and Rodgers 1992 for details). In all three studies, the major post-tests involving all group participants were after an interval, four to five weeks in Studies I and III and two weeks in Study II. These post-tests contained items equivalent to the pre-tests, and were administered in an identical fashion. Also identical were the procedures for identifying conceptions in each child's responses. Once conceptions had been identified for every pre- and post-test item, they were scored for approximation to the received wisdom of science. For Studies I and II, scoring was on a scale from 0 to 4, with conceptions receiving a score of 0 if they omitted physical factors (for example, 'things float when they want to' or 'ice sinks in whisky because whisky's bad') and a score of 4 if they included relative density (for example, 'things float when they're lighter than the same volume of water'). For Study III, scoring was on a scale from 1 to 4, with conceptions receiving a score of 1 if they showed confusion over angle, friction etc. (for example, 'steep slopes slow things down') and a score of 4 if they coordinated the factors adequately (for example, 'the higher things start, the further they go'). By averaging scores across items, we computed mean pre-test scores and mean post-test scores for each group participant.

Our approach to estimating conceptual growth was to look at pre- to post-test change (that is, post-test means less pre-test). We preferred this to performance within the groups because group performance was generally inferior to post-test suggesting, as is implied by 'equilibration', that the benefits took time to show. We focused on comparisons of the pre- to post-

Table 9.1 Mean conceptual change in Studies I, II and III

		Differing groups	Similar groups	
		Change from pre- to post-test		Change from pre- to post-test
Study I	DD (N=28)	+0.31**	SS (N=28)	+0.07
	DS (N=28)	+0.27*		
Study II	DD (N=24)	+0.42**	SS (N=24)	+0.05
	DS (N=24)	+0.32*		
Study III	Low DD (N=24)	+0.56**	Low SS (N=24)	+0.33
	High DD (N=24)	+0.19	High SS (N=24)	+0.22

Note: When the mean change of a differing group is marked with one or more asterisks, it was significantly higher than the mean change of the corresponding similar group using conventional statistical tests (*p < 0.05; ** p < 0.01).

test change in the children from differing and similar groups. As Table 9.1 shows, the change in the children from the DD and DS groups of Study I, the DD and DS groups of Study II and the Low DD groups of Study III was both progressive and substantially greater than the change in the children from the corresponding similar groups. This amounts to considerable evidence for group work where initial conceptions differ having beneficial effects. However there was one exception: the children from the High DD groups of Study III failed to differ from their similar counterparts. This is interpretable in several ways. First, ceiling effects may have been operating. The High DD children started from a relatively high level, and possibly group work is less powerful in these circumstances. Second, task design may have been exerting a dampening effect. Since the group tasks focused on agreed predictions, differences over predictions were a major context for making conceptions explicit. This can be seen from the following:

Barnaby: I think it's the same square.
Imran: I think it's the same square, the same square.
Emily: But Moien did the further square. I did the same square.
Barnaby: I think it's because *it's not on a steep slope*.
Moien: *But it's heavy on it.*

Although the High DD children differed in their underlying conceptions, they did not vary much in the predictions they made. Thus, their chance of recognizing their conceptual differences was limited. If this is what was undermining their performance, minor changes to the task ought to eliminate the problem. Thus, one motive for the second series of investigations was to see whether such changes would be warranted.

GROUP WORK WITH COMPUTER-PRESENTED TASKS

The second series involved two studies, Study IV whose topic was object fall and Study V whose topic was relative speed (see Howe *et al.* in press, Howe, Tolmie, Anderson and Mackenzie 1992). Besides clarifying the inconsistent result in Study III, Studies IV and V explored whether the superiority of differing groups generalizes to other contexts. As before, the studies began with individual pre-tests to over 100 participants, 12 to 15-year-olds in Study IV and undergraduates in Study V. The Study IV pre-tests were presented in written form. They started with 'prediction' problems relating to objects which moved in horizontal, pendular or circular directions and then began to fall. Examples include a golf ball rolling over a cliff, a conker falling from a string and sparks flying off a catherine wheel. Participants were asked to draw the paths that the objects would follow from starting to fall until hitting the ground. Next came 'explanation' problems, which utilized four prediction scenarios but asked participants to indicate the forces that would be operating. The Study V pre-tests involved a series of computer-presented problems (see Appendix II). For these, participants watched two trains move across a screen, one at constant speed and one at variable, and predicted at which of three points speeds would be the same. The distance/time information that was crucial for correct decisions could be obtained from a 'Help' facility but, whether this was accessed or not, participants were quizzed as to how they decided.

Pre-test responses were then scored. With Study IV, responses to the prediction problems were awarded 'prediction scores' from 0 to 5, the correct response (a parabolic path in the direction of the pre-fall motion) scoring 5. Responses to the explanation problems were awarded 'conception scores' from 0 to 6 according to the number of relevant forces (for example, gravity and wind resistance) specified and used appropriately. With Study V, prediction scores were obtained from decisions about where the speed was the same. Since the decisions were either right or wrong, prediction scores for each problem were either 1 or 0. Conception scores were obtained from the justifications participants offered for making their decisions. Conception scores ranged from 0 to 5, with high scores depending on reference to distance travelled per unit time. To resolve the prediction–conception issue raised by Study III, grouping considered both prediction scores and conception, producing four types of group as detailed in Table 9.2. As far as possible, grouping procedures followed the earlier work. Thus in Study IV, where school pupils were used, members of the groups always came from the same class. There were however two major departures from Studies I to III. First, the groups were pairs rather than foursomes. This reflects what

Table 9.2 Composition of the groups in Studies IV and V

Study IV	Study V
14 × SP/SC Groups 2 pupils with similar predictions and similar conceptions	*12 × SP/SC Groups* 2 students with similar predictions and similar conceptions
14 × SP/DC Groups 2 pupils with similar predictions and different conceptions	*12 × SP/DC Groups* 2 students with similar predictions and different conceptions
9 × DP/SC Groups 2 pupils with different predictions and similar conceptions	*12 × DP/SC Groups* 2 students with different predictions and similar conceptions
4 × DP/DC Groups 2 pupils with different predictions and different conceptions	*12 × DP/DC Groups* 2 students with different predictions and different conceptions

Note: DP and DC both signify different levels of understanding. Thus, the groups are equivalent to the DD Groups in Studies I to III.

McAteer and Demissie (1991) have established to be normal practice for computer-based work. Second, gender composition was carefully controlled, rather than allowed to fluctuate randomly.

The pairs were taken to work on group tasks between five and eight weeks after the pre-tests. As with Studies I to III, the tasks had a predict–test–explain format. However, this time they were computer presented. This was motivated by the ephemeral nature of real-world motion: by virtue of a computer, test outcomes could be preserved on screen for further discussion rather than lost in an instant. The tasks began by asking the pairs to compare their pre-test predictions. This involved returning pre-test answer booklets in Study IV and preparing printouts of pre-test decisions in Study V. After comparing, the pairs were requested to input joint predictions by clicking onscreen. They were then given feedback as to accuracy, a trace of the correct path for Study IV (see Appendix III) and 'Well done, that's the correct answer' or 'Sorry that's the wrong answer' for Study V. Finally, they were asked to discuss why things turned out the way they did. As with the earlier work, we introduced the group tasks, monitored the first few items but then left the participants on their own, interaction being videotaped.

All group participants were given individual post-tests, these taking place one to two weeks after the tasks in Study IV and about three weeks after in Study V. The materials used for the post-tests and the procedures followed were identical to the pre-tests. Post-test responses were also scored according to pre-test principles. The main interest was once more pre- to post-test change as a function of difference and similarity. Thus, as before, mean scores per pre- and post-test item were computed for each group participant,

Table 9.3 Mean conceptual change in Studies IV to V

	Study IV	Study IV
SP/SC	$+0.45_a$	$+0.61_{ab}$
SP/DC	$+0.02_a$	$+0.23_a$
DP/SC	$+0.28_a$	$+0.38_a$
DP/DC	$+1.83_b$	$+0.91_b$

Note: When subscripts differ within a *column*, means are significantly different ($p < 0.05$) using conventional statistical tests.

with pre-test means being subtracted from post-test. Using the means, change was examined as a function of difference and similarity in predictions and conceptions. The results, which are presented in Table 9.3, are straightforward: in both studies, the greatest gain was in the DP/DC participants. Thus, to gain maximal benefits, it was necessary to differ in both predictions and conceptions. From this, two conclusions can be drawn. First, the superiority of groups with differing conceptions has been demonstrated in studies which differ from the previous ones in participant age, group size, topic area and task presentation, implying considerable generalizability. Second, insofar as differing predictions did appear to be necessary, the rogue result in Study III was most likely a reflection of task design.

GROUP WORK AND AN INCLUSIVE CURRICULUM

As intimated already, the variability of pre-tuitional conceptions means that differing groups would be easy to organize in classroom contexts. Even random assignment would do the trick. It would also be straightforward to organize task materials so that differing conceptions mean differing predictions. Thus, although our research was experimental in nature, it could readily be applied to educational practice. Should this happen? The answer might seem self-evidently 'Yes', yet there is room for doubt. Although the differing groups generated the greatest *mean* progress, they may not have generated progress in every participant. It is possible that only some individuals learned. Suppose that this was the case. Suppose also that these individuals were physics highfliers, given confidence by the discovery of their relative superiority. In these circumstances, we would be justifiably unhappy about educational application. The scenario is, of course, hypothetical, but it suggests that we ought to relate progress to initial level. Taking this to imply considering change as a function of pre-test score, the picture from the five studies is encouraging. In Studies I to III, there was no association between pre-test score and pre- to post-test change. In Studies IV to V, there was a moderate association, but it was the participants with relatively low pre-test scores who learned the most. Moreover, participants with high pre-test scores showed some benefits even if not as much.

Perhaps looking at change relative to pre-test score is insufficient. It is possible that even though progress was unrelated to initial level, definable subgroups were differentially affected. The data preclude a general commentary on this issue, although it is worth pointing out that the participants were fully representative in demographic terms of the City of Glasgow. Social background varied from middle class to highly deprived; ethnic minorities participated, 38 per cent of the sample in Study III; and children with special needs were included. However, while we cannot go beyond this by way of generalities, something further can be said about the specific case of gender. The background literature (e.g Swann 1992) gives few grounds for anticipating gender differences with the primary school age group of Studies I to III, and this is essentially what was found. Unpublished data indicate that as the number of boys in the groups increased from zero to four, so did the time devoted to interpreting test outcomes. As the number of girls increased, so did the time devoted to making predictions. However, neither the form of the interaction nor the magnitude of progress was related to gender. The background literature does on the other hand hint at gender differences with older individuals, particularly when computers are involved, and this was strongly endorsed by the results of Study IV.

It is not that there were gender differences over individual progress in Study IV. On the contrary, as documented by Tolmie and Howe (1993), the pre- to post-test change of the boys and girls was indistinguishable, regardless of whether they participated in same- or mixed-gender groups. This was true even when allowance was made for the lower pre-test scores of the girls (and as pointed out already, the slight association between low pre-test scores and greater progress). Where the gender differences occurred was in the forms of interaction associated with change, particularly in the same-gender groups. In general, the boys progressed most when differences over predictions led to an increased focus on the current problem and exchange of views about the factors at work, and when careful input of predictions was followed by the discussion of test outcomes and the subsequent refinement of conceptions to take outcomes into account. In other words, the boys had to coordinate testing activity with underlying conceptions, a tendency well documented in the following:

Alan: Well, we got that one completely wrong.
Barry: I was thinking of the speed it was travelling at, it would have had more arc and travelled up, you're saying that the weight would have pulled it straight down.

For the girls, progress depended on differences over predictions leading to awareness of differences in conceptions. The differences did not have to be resolved ontask, and indeed resolution seldom occurred. However, they did have to be linked with earlier problems. Thus, for the girls it was the coordination of conceptions across problems that was crucial, as illustrated in the following:

Jane: I think it'll fall straight down; it's heavy.
Beth: But the crate was heavy and it didn't fall straight down.

There were no gender differences with the undergraduate sample of Study V. However, the helpful strategy for all pairs in Study V regardless of gender was to coordinate conceptions with both testing activity *and* previous problems. Thus, to succeed at the undergraduate level the forms of interaction helpful to boys in the 12 to 15 age group had to be united with the forms of interaction helpful to girls. This might be taken to suggest a powerful role for mixed groups at 12 to 15 to precipitate union, but the Study IV results counsel against. As intimated already, helpful forms of interaction were hard to identify with the mixed groups. This was in part because the acute unease many pupils felt in the mixed context led to dramatic reductions in the quantity of dialogue. In view of this, a preferable solution would be to allow pupils to work in the groups of their choice, almost always same gender at this age level, and via some method of external support foster coordination across both the crucial dimensions. Our current research (see Tolmie *et al*. 1993) is trying to achieve this via computer-based prompts. Should we succeed, the hope is not simply to encourage the forms of interaction that undergraduates find helpful, but also to increase the intelligibility of physics for school-aged pupils. This might prove a small step towards an inclusive curriculum.

ACKNOWLEDGEMENTS

Studies I, II and III were made possible by ESRC Research Grant C00232426 to the author; Studies IV to V by ESRC Research Grant R000231287 to the author, Tony Anderson and Terry Mayes. Thanks are due to the ESRC for their support. Thanks are also due to Stewart Fleming, Karen Greer, Philip McEachern, Mhairi Mackenzie, Cathy Rodgers and Andy Tolmie for their work on these studies. Finally, a great debt of gratitude is owed to the children who participated in the studies and the teachers/headteachers who allowed the studies to happen.

REFERENCES

Champagne, A., Klopfer, L. E. and Anderson, J. (1980) 'Factors influencing the learning of classical mechanics', *American Journal of Physics* 48: 1074–8.
Croxford, L., Gooday, M. and Taylor, J. (1992) 'A common curriculum: to what extent do Scottish boys and girls follow a common curriculum?'. Paper presented at Gender and Education in Scotland: Creating a Research Network, University of Dundee.

Department of Education and Science (1989) *Science in the National Curriculum*, London: HMSO.

Doise, W. and Mugny, G. (1984) *The Social Development of the Intellect*, Oxford: Pergamon.

Forman, E. A. and Cazden, C. B. (1985) 'Exploring Vygotskyan perspectives in education: the cognitive value of peer interaction', in J. V. Wertsch (ed.) *Culture Communication and Cognition: Vygotskyan Perspectives*, Cambridge: Cambridge University Press.

Forman, E. A. and Kraker, M. J. (1985) 'The social origin of logic: the contribution of Piaget and Vygotsky', in M. W. Berkowitz (ed.) *Peer Conflict and Psychological Growth*, San Francisco, CA: Jossey-Bass.

Gilbert, J. K. and Pope, M. L. (1986) 'Small group discussions about conceptions in science: a case study', *Research in Science and Technological Education* 4: 61–76.

Her Majesty's Inspectors (1978) *Primary Education in England*, London: HMSO.

Howe, C. J., Rodgers, C. and Tolmie, A. (1990) 'Physics in the primary school: peer interaction and the understanding of floating and sinking', *European Journal of Psychology of Education* V: 459–75.

Howe, C. J., Tolmie, A., Anderson, A. and Mackenzie, M. (1992) 'Conceptual knowledge in physics: the role of group interaction in computer-supported teaching,' *Learning and Instruction* 2: 161–83.

Howe, C. J., Tolmie, A. and Mackenzie, M. (in press) 'Computer support for the collaborative learning of physics concepts', in C. O'Malley (ed.) *Computer-Supported Collaborative Learning*, Berlin: Springer-Verlag.

Howe, C. J., Tolmie, A. and Rodgers, C. (1992) 'The acquisition of conceptual knowledge in science by primary school children: group interaction and the understanding of motion down an incline', *British Journal of Developmental Psychology* 10: 113–30.

McAteer, E. and Demissie, A. (1991) *Writing Competence Across the Curriculum*. Report to Scottish Office Education Department.

McDermott, L. C. (1984) 'Research on conceptual understanding in mechanics', *Physics Today* 37: 24–32.

Nussbaum, J. and Novick, S. (1981) 'Brainstorming in the classroom to invent a model: a case study', *School Science Review* 62: 771–8.

Osborne, R. and Freyberg, P. (1985) *Learning in Science*, Auckland: Heinemann.

Piaget, J. (1932) *The Moral Judgment of the Child*, London: Routledge and Kegan Paul.

Piaget, J. (1985) *The Equilibration of Cognitive Structures*, Chicago: The University of Chicago Press.

Scottish Office Education Department (1992) *Science 1990: Assessment of Achievement Programme*, Edinburgh: HMSO.

Screen, P. (1988) 'A case for a process approach: the Warwick experience', *Physics Education* 23: 146–9.

Sears, J. (1992) 'Uptake of science A levels: an ICI and BP sponsored project for ASE', *Education in Science* 149: 30–1.

Swann, J. (1992) *Girls, Boys and Language*, Oxford: Basil Blackwell.

Tolmie, A. and Howe, C. J. (1993) 'Gender and dialogue in secondary school physics', *Gender and Education* 5: 191–209.

Tolmie, A., Howe, C. J. and Sofroniou, N. (1993) 'Computer-supported hypothesis testing in primary and secondary school science'. Paper presented at CAL-93, University of York.

Wellington, J. J. (1988) 'The place of process in physics education', *Physics Education* 23: 150–5.

APPENDIX I:
EXTRACT FROM GROUP TASK WORKBOOK (STUDY I)

[The extract relates to the first object about which predictions were made. The text is successively abbreviated to avoid labouring points that are well understood. Thus, by the last object, it is roughly half the length. In the book, text relating to the objects is illustrated by photographs and text relating to the real-world instances by coloured pictures.]

Key

To start, each of you must find your card headed *Key*. Do this before reading on.

Have you done this? If you have, look at what each of you has ticked. Did you all think the *Key* would sink? If so, go on to Page 3. If not, read on.

Did you all think the *Key* would float? If so, go on to Page 3. If not, read on.

Did some of you think the *Key* would sink and some of you think it would float? If so, look at the *Key* and talk about what it will do until you all think the same way. Then go on to Page 3. Do not go on to Page 3 until you all think the same way.

[Text from Page 2]

Now you are going to find out if you are right. Take the *Key* and put it into the tank of water. Do this before reading on.

What has happened? Are you surprised? Talk very carefully about what has happened. Try to work out *why* things turned out the way they did. Make sure everybody in the group says what they think. Then talk about the different ideas until you all think the same way. Take your time and do not go on until you all think the same way.

Did you all think the same way? If so, take the *Key* out of the tank. If it floated, put it on the *Floaters* tray. If it sank, put it on the *Sinkers*. Then turn to the next page.

[Text from Page 3]

APPENDIX II:
EXTRACT FROM COMPUTER-BASED PRE-TEST (STUDY V)

1 Initial problem display

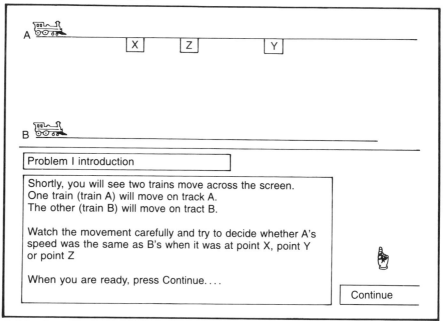

Problem I introduction

Shortly, you will see two trains move across the screen.
One train (train A) will move on track A.
The other (train B) will move on tract B.

Watch the movement carefully and try to decide whether A's
speed was the same as B's when it was at point X, point Y
or point Z

When you are ready, press Continue. . . .

Continue

2 Display of help options

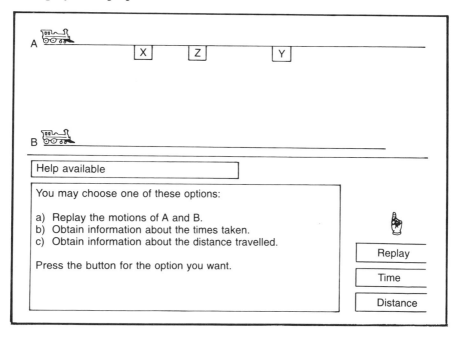

Help available

You may choose one of these options:

a) Replay the motions of A and B.
b) Obtain information about the times taken.
c) Obtain information about the distance travelled.

Press the button for the option you want.

Replay

Time

Distance

3 Choice of distance information

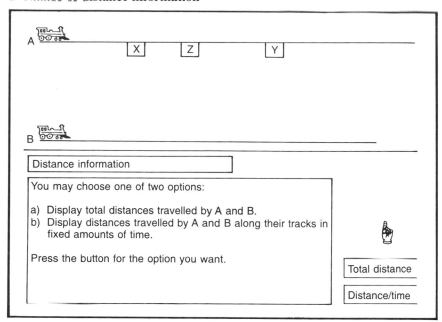

Distance information

You may choose one of two options:

a) Display total distances travelled by A and B.
b) Display distances travelled by A and B along their tracks in fixed amounts of time.

Press the button for the option you want.

Total distance

Distance/time

4 Display of distance/time information

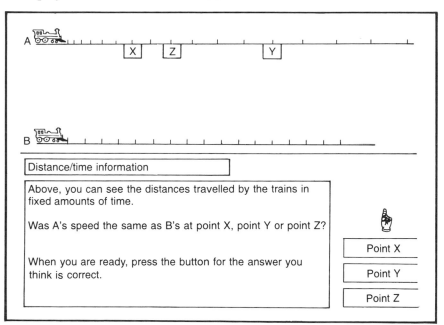

Distance/time information

Above, you can see the distances travelled by the trains in fixed amounts of time.

Was A's speed the same as B's at point X, point Y or point Z?

When you are ready, press the button for the answer you think is correct.

Point X

Point Y

Point Z

APPENDIX III:
EXTRACTS FROM PRE-TEST AND COMPUTER-BASED
GROUP TASK (STUDY IV)

1 Example of paper-and-pencil prediction problem plus typical response

When there is an emergency and people are desperately short of food, aeroplanes bringing relief do not always land. Instead, they fly low without losing speed and drop the food in heavy crates. Suppose the plane pictured below was travelling in the direction shown and dropped a crate from its hatch. Indicate where the crate would be when it hit the ground, and show the path it would follow as it fell through the air. Use X to show where the crate would end up and remember to show the path from the hatch to the ground.

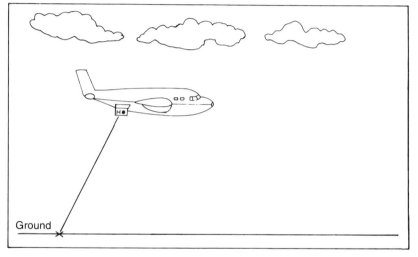

Ground

2 Computer-based group task: request to formulate joint prediction

Talk very carefully about where the CRATE will fall until you both think the same way.

If you both think the same way and are ready to show me the path then press the "Continue" button.

Continue

If you wish to see the PLANE flying again, just before the CRATE is dropped, then press the "Show Again" button.

Show Again

3 Computer-based group task: input of joint prediction

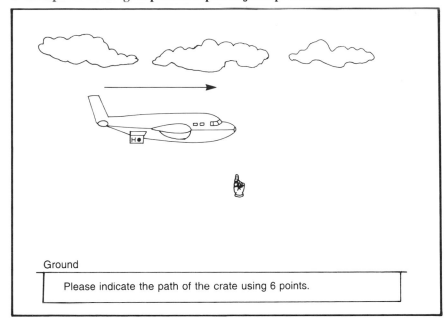

Ground

Please indicate the path of the crate using 6 points.

4 Computer-based group task: comparison of joint prediction and correct solution

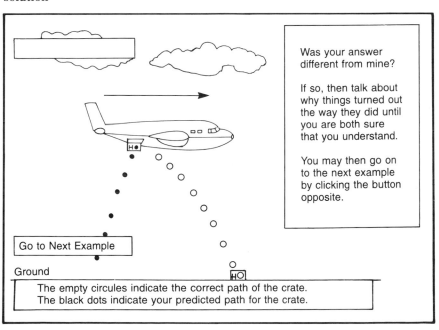

Was your answer different from mine?

If so, then talk about why things turned out the way they did until you are both sure that you understand.

You may then go on to the next example by clicking the button opposite.

Go to Next Example

Ground

The empty circles indicate the correct path of the crate.
The black dots indicate your predicted path for the crate.

Chapter 10

Drama for all in a primary school

Caroline Haycock

Caroline is the Special Needs Coordinator in a large primary school. She works with small groups of children who experience difficulties and is actively involved with the after-school drama club, open to all children in Years 3 to 6. This chapter is based on the curriculum development project Caroline completed for the Open University Advanced Diploma in Special Needs in Education. Her aim was to see how the use of drama in the classroom could help children to overcome their difficulties in learning by boosting their self-esteem, autonomy and enjoyment.

INTRODUCTION

For this project I have chosen to explore and investigate the use of drama in the curriculum. My philosophy is that all children learn more effectively when they are motivated and interested and can find meaning and relevance in what they are asked to learn. Any child coming into school brings with him or her a rich variety of experiences and interests. If these can be employed, then, I believe, the learning experience of all involved is the richer.

Drama has great potential to facilitate this, allowing children, teachers and parents to explore the world around them. It draws on personal experiences and interests, can be open-ended or problem-solving and encourages empathy with other people and their situations. As I will go on to show, it can be exciting and fun, and a great motivator for children who would otherwise experience learning difficulties. It makes the children 'active learners', with ownership of their ideas and thoughts, and can improve their self-esteem and personal worth.

I am the Special Needs Coordinator in a large urban primary school, which is situated in a socially disadvantaged area in a West Midlands borough. There are 624 pupils on roll, and these range from Nursery to Year 6, i.e. 3 to 11 years of age. During this year I am acting in a support role in the Upper Phase (9 to 11-year-olds), and do not have a class. I am responsible for teaching a small group of about twenty children, who are experiencing difficulties with a wide range of literacy skills. I have attempted to give each group of about three and four children two 40 minute sessions during the week in a withdrawal situation. In these sessions I do a variety of activities, one of which is to use a recently introduced reading scheme called 'Wellington Square', based on the local community and its familiar characters.

The school has teams of teachers who work together to develop areas of the curriculum. The Creative Arts team has recently introduced an after-school drama club, which is open to all children from years 3 to 6. This has proved to be very popular and they now have, on average, about thirty children who attend regularly and voluntarily. Staff and pupils are presently engaged in developing a small original production based on the theme of 'Giants'. I shall be using some of the children's comments further on in this report.

As an extension to this, the team decided to invite the LEA's adviser for Drama into the school to provide an hour's in-service training for staff on the use of drama in the classroom. This was to be followed up with nine lessons of drama being taught by the adviser in Years 1, 3 and 6. Staff were to be involved and to participate and follow it up. I shall comment briefly during the report on the impact of this training.

THE AIMS OF THE PROJECT

- To analyse the extent of drama being used in my school
- To analyse the teachers' perceptions of the value of drama in the classroom
- To briefly analyse the impact of the drama club
- To develop some drama with a group of children with learning difficulties, focusing on increased lesson participation, and based on reading material that is linked to the children's interests and experiences
- To analyse the drama lessons that I have developed
- To make recommendations for the value of drama and its practice linked to classroom learning in the light of my project development

BACKGROUND TO THE PROJECT

Most of the children I teach, and who are in my learning support groups, live on one of the borough's council estates. The children's backgrounds are varied and their reading experiences often lack breadth. The children who are the focus of my project are experiencing difficulties in learning literacy skills. Their vocabulary is quite limited and so to motivate these children the reading material must have some credence and relevance for them. Many of the children's experiences are gained 'playing out', often in the street among their friends and the community, which is close-knit. Again, many of them have cousins in the same school and class, with their extended families living on the same estate. Often the children will have been no further than the estate itself or just beyond. The children therefore bring to school a variety of mixed experiences from the home, the street and the community in which they live.

I decided to use drama as an extension to the reading scheme and draw out their experiences, encouraging empathy with some of the characters, and helping develop a greater understanding of the stories. I felt it would help them to use language, communicate ideas and thoughts, collaborate and share, whilst participating and motivating their learning, and having 'fun' at the same time.

ANALYSIS OF DRAMA IN THE CURRICULUM IN MY SCHOOL

In order to find out the teacher's views on drama in the classroom and the extent of the drama being used in the school, I compiled a questionnaire. This I have been able to analyse and will comment on it in a later section. I also devised a simple questionnaire for the children who attend the drama club.

The extent of drama being used in my school

I chose to use a questionnaire because I could obtain a wide response. I designed it to gain some answers to the following questions:

- Have teachers used drama in the classroom in the last year?
- If so, how has it been used?
- If not, why?
- What areas of the curriculum do they use it for?
- Do they see it as a valuable experience for all children?
- What value is it to those experiencing difficulties, especially in language?
- Has the recent INSET had any impact on their views?

I found the response to the questionnaire very positive. I received fifteen back from a possible twenty-two which I felt gave a reasonable sample of opinions. Questionnaires are a good way to extract information, but they rely on the 'good will' of people to return them and their time to fill them in.

I was surprised how much drama had been done in school during this year. Nine staff answered that they had used drama in a mixture of curriculum subjects – religious studies, including assembly, environmental studies (endangered species) and history, especially for projects on journeys and explorers. Other areas mentioned were Christmas, science and maths counting. I would have liked to know what topics they specifically used their drama for, but I didn't ask that.

The drama tended to be in the nature of role-play which comes in the National Curriculum English document (but three said they had had the children making up their own plays). The following extract is from Programmes of Study for Key Stages 2 to 4:

8 The range of activities should include:

- the preparation of presentations, *eg. to the class, the school assembly or to parents*;
- planning and problem-solving activities across the curriculum;
- assignments where specific outcomes are required;
- talking about stories, poems, playscripts and other texts;
- taking part in shared writing activities;
- role-play, simulations and group drama.

(National Curriculum for English, p. 25)

The teacher's perceptions of the value of drama

All agreed that drama is a valuable part of the curriculum and gave a variety of reasons. Here are some of the responses:

'children learn through play . . . drama focuses on their feelings . . . it gives enjoyment . . . they can act out their fantasies . . . it is good for social development . . . it gives them real situations . . . helps with language development . . . gives them insight and empathy, . . . experience ideas . . . helps them to work with others'

Again, the responses that I received agreed that children of all abilities could participate, especially children with learning difficulties. Answers ranged from 'children being able to take part because they didn't need to read' to 'facilitating oral participation and observation.' One response was 'drama makes a valuable contribution regardless of ability as it has no constraint in language'.

Only four replies stated that they felt they hadn't done drama because of the lack of time, or because they lacked confidence to tackle it. (I thought I would receive more responses of this nature, and was pleasantly surprised.) This did not undermine the value of drama.

All who replied felt the in-service training was of benefit. Several felt that it gave good non-threatening ideas for use of drama in the classroom, and two thought that it reinforced the value of drama. Most of all, it was felt that the training gave good ideas for classroom practice, and starting points for further development.

The impact of the drama club in school

To find out what the children themselves felt about drama, I devised a simple questionnaire that they could fill in. The children enjoyed the opportunity to share their thoughts and, again, they were positive. I asked them what they liked best about drama club, and why they joined. Did they think it was a good idea to do drama, and if they wanted their friends to share the experience. I noticed that several of the children, whom I know have difficulties with classroom learning, attended. This made me feel really happy . . . and they were so positive about what they were achieving!

Here are some of the children's comments:

'We have fun . . . everyone takes part . . . we work in groups . . . we listen to others . . . we act things out . . . listen to stories . . . play games and do "spots" '

Why did they join?

'it looked fun . . . it sounded exciting . . . my friend budged me . . . the idea of drama got me thinking . . . it was a chance to learn how to act'

What do they like best about drama?

'the acting out . . . watching people doing their play . . . the teachers . . . being at school late . . . working in groups and meeting friends . . . plays . . . talking . . . sharing parts'

The impact that the club has had on the children is such that when I asked the children would they like to do drama in the classroom, seventeen said yes, and only four said no. This was because they thought there would be too many people, and some children would be 'naughty' (interesting comments!). Three children said that they had joined because their friends had said it 'was such fun', and one said that they had liked it when the drama club had shown the rest of the school some of their work on 'the circus'. This 'showing' to the school had obviously had an impact since the numbers who wanted to attend went up the following week, and there is now a waiting list to join. All the more reason to have classroom drama, as it would allow a wider range of pupils to participate.

These are the children's views. So, what do the teachers think about the club? What impact has it had on them? I briefly asked the teachers who had been taking the club to comment on the impact the club has had on them.

'The drama club gives you a sense of achievement. It is so satisfying to watch an end result in a performance for other children and parents.'

'It heightens your awareness of the way that drama can be used in the classroom. It helps you mix with children other than in your own age group, and it fosters mutual respect.'

'The club gives them ownership of the material as it's voluntary. They attend because they enjoy it and you can see it on their faces.'

From these comments it is clear that the teachers have positive opinions about the worth of the club, and its value to the children.

The club has therefore been good for the school, and children of all abilities have found it 'fun' to learn, and rewarding to attend and try.

The drama that I would develop would include elements of empathy, language, participation and collaboration, but linked to the children's own experiences and reading material that they had enjoyed.

A SMALL-SCALE CURRICULUM DEVELOPMENT BASED ON THE ANALYSIS OF DRAMA IN MY SCHOOL

My development was able to use the heightened awareness of drama in the school, the positive approach that the children were able to bring to it, my own interest in the 'Wellington Square' scheme and a belief that the children learn best when motivated. In my development I particularly wanted to bring out the richness of the children's experiences, whilst keeping the following in mind:

Does drama particularly increase involvement in the language curriculum?
Does it help to base it on reading material?
Does it help to link it to children's interests and experiences?
Is drama a vehicle to improve learning?
Can it be supportive of classroom learning?

The children chose a book from the 'Wellington Square' scheme that they found particularly interesting.

The Yellow Canary

Three lessons focused on this book. It is about Jamila, whose father owns a corner store in Wellington Square. She finds a yellow bird, a canary, in the park, and takes it back to the shop. Her father is not keen for her to keep it. In a previous book Mr Patel, Jamila's father, had objected to dogs in the shop, so the children were able to relate to this part of the story.

Mr Keeping, who is the local animal man, and who 'knows all about animals', comes into the shop, and Jamila asks him about the bird. He says that he will take the bird, and look after it. Some days later, he returns with the bird, but it is no longer a canary. The bird has become a sparrow.

Mr Keeping says that there must be someone who is painting birds in the square, and selling them as canaries which are valuable as pets. Jamila decides to let the sparrow go, and it flies onto the statue of the Duke of Wellington, and sits looking down at them.

From this story I decided that I would get the sixteen children aged 9 to 11, to empathize with Jamila, her dad, and Mr Keeping. I would allow them a chance to mime out actions, as well as speak words that the characters might have spoken in the story. Most of all I wanted to get them to use their experiences as much as possible, and try to relate them to me and the group.

The first lesson (8 June 1993)

To warm up, the children were asked to work in pairs on a game called 'Word Tennis'. I gave them a topic – school – and they had to take turns to say words relating to this. (This encouraged them to use vocabulary, take turns, and to think.)

In the main part of the lesson they then had to work in pairs and mime a box (any size) and show what was inside the box by using facial expressions, or mime. Partners had to guess what it was. Each pair had a turn. Pairs were then asked if they would like to show them to the class. (Some excellent ideas came out – a computer, a motorbike, a football.) The children had to watch, and guess.

I'd introduced 'mime' to them, so I decided I would use teacher-in-role, and be Jamila who finds the bird. As I aimed, each child in turn had to say what I was thinking. All the children joined in – at no time did I force them to join in. They had to feel comfortable sharing. This activity was excellent for observation, and for getting them to think what I would be thinking as Jamila herself. It also taught them the difference between direct and indirect speech, which they picked up quite quickly. This was most noticeable when I introduced the idea of using a hat to represent the character – as the child put on the hat they had to speak as that person. It noticeably changed from 'He says . . .' to 'I . . .'

Next I got the children together and told them that they (as Jamila) had now got to 'sneak' the bird past their dad into their bedroom. I decided to try this, as I felt that 'to sneak' something past someone, parent, teacher, etc. was in most children's experience.

The children talked in groups of three, and thought of ways they could get away with it. They could then act it out, using words.

They then had to discuss how they would show the group the most important 30 seconds of the story. They could show the group if they felt comfortable.

This proved most illuminating. They had obviously had experience of 'sneaking', and some ways of getting the bird into their bedroom were very imaginative. (Waiting for Dad to be serving in the shop . . . at night putting the bird in a box and raising it to the bedroom on a rope! . . . putting the box up their clothes . . . telling lies about what was in the box!)

All the children wanted to show their ideas, and willingly answered questions about their ideas.

As a final activity to this session, I got the children to choose the part where Dad actually caught Jamila with the bird. They had to 'freeze' the picture, and hold it still for 30 seconds, as if it were a photograph. This encouraged discussion, mime and being able to hold a facial expression for a length of time. I encouraged the children to think who certain people were in the 'picture', and get them to communicate what they were thinking.

Again, this was in their experience. They had obviously been caught doing something, and were able to relate this story to those situations.

One group said that Jamila had been naughty, and had told lies. We started to discuss what was 'bad' about lies, and the discussion turned to the topic of being 'grounded' (being kept in by their parents, and not being allowed to play 'out' with friends). The whole group were most open about reasons for being 'grounded', and their opinions of it. Some actually liked it, and one boy said that he had been 'grounded' for swearing at a teacher! Others said that they had got into the local 'zoo', under the fence (they asked if I would like to know where it was!), and played on the roundabouts. They were grounded for that.

This was totally unplanned, and quite sudden. The children sat and listened to each other in a way I had not experienced before. I was able to question openly, and get their feelings about doing wrong and being punished quite freely without any threat. It was an opportunity to share in a non-threatening situation things that had happened to them. I felt privileged to know I had that degree of trust!

Activities from the lessons (9 and 10 June)

I decided to introduce the idea of persuasion. Jamila, in the story, had got to persuade Dad to allow her to keep the bird. Dad didn't want Jamila to keep it.

The children chose who they would like to be . . . Jamila or Dad, and they had to get together some really good reasons to persuade each other.

Some of the reasons were imaginative, and resourceful. The children being Jamila said that she needed a pet, she'd look after it, etc. Those children being Dad said she couldn't keep it because of the 'bird mess' and that it was a shop.

They all listened to each other and discussed in a very animated way. They were totally engrossed in the suggestions, and criticized their suggestions openly and without argument.

After discussion, the children acted out the part of the persuasion. Some felt threatened by this, and did not join in, others openly acted it out. It was interesting to see that part of the persuasion included one child (being Dad) actually hitting the other (being Jamila) to make her do as she was told.

Had time allowed I would have liked to discuss this further. Did they feel this was an effective way of getting someone to do something? This was obviously within their experience, and had its origins in reality for them.

The lessons were a great success. The children enjoyed them, and so did I. I had no problems with behaviour . . . the children were engrossed . . . I had full cooperation, and the children and I felt comfortable with each other, enough to share personal thoughts and experiences.

ANALYSIS OF MY DRAMA WORK AS A CURRICULUM DEVELOPMENT

Was I successful? In my opinion, the development was a resounding success.

The children thoroughly enjoyed the lessons as was evident from their follow-up interviews afterwards. On being asked if they had enjoyed all three lessons, their replies were positive. Some did not want to show any of their work to others, but ten said positively that they were keen to show some of the activities to their peers, and in some cases to the children in the earlier years. All wanted to do it again, and were keen to come the following week for this. On being asked what they liked best, all the children said that they had enjoyed it all, and were unable to think of any area that they had enjoyed the most. As I have been asked I shall do another three lessons for them in the next week, but choose another book that the group had shortlisted.

During the period of the development, I asked our Deputy Head to observe one lesson to stated criteria, which were the following:

- offering ideas and sharing them with others
- listening to each other and responding to comments
- use of their own experiences to relate to the subject
- empathy with the characters in the story
- improved use of language

Her comments on the observation were very positive. She states in her report that she found the children highly 'motivated', and using a 'high level of collaboration'. They readily 'drew upon their own experiences in a lively and imaginative way', and 'negotiated turn taking' successfully. Their sentences were 'fairly structured' and often relevant to the character they were portraying, thus reflecting thoughtful understanding.

Further to this, I feel that this development was certainly helped because I based it on a book that the children had chosen themselves. There was no argument about it being the 'teacher's choice': they chose one they, themselves, had shown interest in. I hasten to add here that it was not a book that I would have chosen, so it proved challenging for me to think of interesting, motivating activities for them to do. Following a story gave some structure to the drama, and the children knew where we were 'going', as we had read the book first. It also helped me in the planning.

As one of the aims was to improve, and provide opportunities for language, I felt I successfully achieved this. This development proves that drama can be a valuable vehicle for increased language participation, as well as offering the chance for children of all abilities to express themselves and their opinions, and to practise the skill of listening to others.

I felt that there were few weaknesses in my study. I did have to keep the pace of the lessons going, which someone with little experience might find difficult and daunting. I also found that I had to be really well prepared and confident in my own ability. A teacher not confident in this subject could lose the children quite quickly. As one teacher pointed out to me 'I can see the value of drama, but I don't like the children out of their places.' Children need to know the 'ground rules' for these activities and I started my first lesson by telling them some of the rules that they had to follow. Some teachers are afraid that the children will become undisciplined. It depends on the class, and the relationship the teacher has with the children. I have a good trusting relationship with these children, so I felt confident tackling drama work.

A CONCLUSION – WHERE COULD I GO FROM HERE?

As I was limited to a small group of children, I would like the opportunity to share the lovely stories of 'Wellington Square' with other children in a full class situation. How lovely for the children who have reading difficulties to be able to offer 'their stories' to a wider audience. What a boost to their morale! Hopefully, this chance may arise as I have already had one member of staff ask if I would like to do some drama with her class. She had been passing the classroom and noticed the activities, and the involvement of the children, and thought her class would benefit from such experiences.

I shall definitely be doing some more drama with this group on another book in the scheme . . . they have asked me to! So how can I refuse them?

Here could be the chance to allow those who want to, the opportunity to show their work to others – to the younger children and to parents.

It is also a chance to share the 'drama experience' with other classes. The group were quite willing to 'show their work' to their classmates. One boy came to me and said that his friend had said, 'I wish I could do Wellington Square then I could do drama as well!' What a lovely comment.

I also intend to involve the LEA adviser in our next work. She was keen to come and take part in this development but time did not allow. She is very enthusiastic for drama to have a valuable place in the work with children experiencing learning difficulties and has taken an interest in this development.

As I have used drama in the past to stimulate creative free writing, and because these children were really motivated, I am sure that it would be possible for them to write a short story or poem from their work, as they would have had 'first-hand experience'. This I would be keen to try also.

Some of the stories in the 'Wellington Square' scheme have strong community issues. These books could be used to develop a stronger community awareness, and how enjoyable it would be to use drama to encourage this awareness, especially as my school is endeavouring to become a 'community school'.

Does drama have value when linked to classroom learning?

- It has value in that it makes a substantial contribution to the development of children's language. It gives them the freedom to speak without the constraints of workbook/worksheet language which can lead to confusion.
- It certainly has great value when linked to a child's immediate experience, and helps them to explore their environment at their level of understanding.
- Drama has value when used cross-curricular – in history, humanities, certainly in RE, and in the creative arts.
- It is another method to use to raise children's awareness of the world around them, and gain some understanding of it.
- And finally, because it forces children to work in groups. It encourages collaboration, and develops social skills, which are important parts of classroom learning.

Having observed the value of drama in the curriculum for children of all abilities, especially those who are language impaired, it is a great shame that more weighting isn't given to it in the National Curriculum. Mention is made of it as 'role-play', and in 'listening and speaking', but it has so much more to offer, in the broader curriculum, across the subjects and especially for children who experience difficulties with classroom learning.

Chapter 11

Personal, social and sex education in the mainstream

Conversations with disabled and able-bodied teenagers

Inge Hempstead

Disabled students in the outer London borough of Hounslow have been supported within the mainstream since the local special school closed in the summer of 1990. Discussions between teenagers as part of their personal, social and sex education curriculum are therefore enriched by the diversity of experience in the resulting mixed groups. Inge Hempstead is in charge of the borough's support services and she knows all the disabled students well. She recorded and transcribed for us two conversations in which students at Feltham School discuss the following issues: self-esteem and self-confidence, stereotyping in relation to sex or disability, sex education, relationships, teenage pregnancies, abortion and homosexuality. There is a strong feeling among the young disabled people at the school that able-bodied people need much more information about the feelings, needs and aspirations of disabled people.

INTRODUCTION

Feltham Community School is one of the largest secondary schools in Hounslow with about 1,200 pupils, aged 11 to 18. It has a thriving sixth form. The school moved to a new campus eight years ago and has excellent facilities, including a drama and music block and a very well equipped sports hall. It has a lift which is used constantly by the fourteen disabled pupils on roll at the moment. As the closure of Martindale Special School was not under discussion ten years ago, the plans for Feltham School did not include any facilities for disabled pupils.

Martindale School closed in July 1990. For two years prior to this closure Feltham School had integrated some of the more academically able pupils from Martindale School and gained valuable experience of the needs of disabled pupils. Headteacher and staff at Feltham School therefore agreed to become the receiving school for all pupils aged between 11 and 16 when Martindale School closed. In September 1990 eight pupils joined Feltham School.

During the summer the school underwent major adaptations and changes. A special resource room was created for back-up lessons, particularly for pupils dependent on computers and switches. A physiotherapy room was equipped. A small office was provided for the teacher in charge of integration. Ramps were built wherever it was deemed necessary. Several toilets, suitable for disabled people were installed.

Specialist staff from Martindale School were transferred to Feltham School: initially one teacher and two classroom assistants.

The education authority also created a service to oversee the borough-wide integration of disabled pupils. This service initially consisted of one head of service, an IT teacher and a music therapist. Two additional teachers have been appointed since then.

Staff at the school had a series of training days to discuss the changes that were going to take place and the needs of all the pupils, parents and staff involved in such an important innovation. Since then there have been regular reviews and evaluations of integration and regular INSET days on a variety of topics.

Three years later the presence of disabled pupils in lessons is no longer seen as an innovation but as a positive aspect of normal school life at Feltham School. All the disabled pupils who joined the school in 1990 have made a success of their move from a special school. The oldest pupil left in July 1990 after gaining five GCSEs and is following an-A level course at a neighbouring college. Each year the new intake includes disabled pupils, mostly from the primary school which has specialist facilities for disabled pupils.

Hounslow no longer has a special school for physically disabled pupils. Wherever possible, these pupils attend their local school. If their disability is severe and requires substantial support in the classroom, Feltham School is best able to meet their needs. There are now two specialist teachers and five classroom assistants. The service for disabled pupils also supports. Several of the pupils are severely disabled, mostly by cerebral palsy. This does not prevent them from taking part in all curricular and extra-curricular activities. Laptop computers, switches, speech synthesizers, page turners, etc. are used to enable the highest level of independence and empowerment possible. Dependence on other people is kept to a minimum. Support is provided in classroom situations, withdrawal is kept to a minimum. Physiotherapists and speech therapists support this and ensure their work relates to school life and school work.

It has been a pleasure to watch the disabled pupils grow in confidence and competence over the last years. The commitment of the staff and the enthusiasm of the pupils have created an inclusive education model at Feltham School which is quite close to perfection.

Table 11.1 Sex education programme content

Science	
Year 7	Basic factual information on puberty, the menstrual cycle, human reproductive system, pregnancy and birth.
Year 8	Reinforcement of factual information from Year 7.
Year 9	Detailed information to include films on aspects covered. Begin work on sexually transmitted diseases to include AIDS, use of video to heighten awareness of the issues.
Year 10	In-detail factual information on reproduction, sex determination, population control, parental care; all work is now based on examination syllabuses.
Year 11	Continuation of Year 10.
PSE	
Year 7	Personal hygiene, developing relationships, self-awareness, self-esteem, looking at how others perceive you.
Year 8	Self-awareness, moral judgements through case studies and role-play, understanding oneself in relation to others, sexual maturity, your rights – your body is your own and no one can invade.
Year 9	Emotional and bodily changes that occur during puberty; stereotyping, contraception and choice.
Year 10	Appropriate and inappropriate behaviour, relationships, accepting other people and contraception.
Year 11	Parenting.
Year 12	Focus on problem-solving situations to include pregnancy, legal aspects of sex, moral and social implications relating to AIDS.
RE (compulsory module)	
Year 10	Attitudes to sex both religious and non-religious. Questions of life and death (abortion, euthanasia). Factual and moral issues relating to contraception.

Source: Feltham School curriculum document

THE TEACHING OF SEX EDUCATION

The teaching of sex education is embedded firmly within the whole-school curriculum. The aim of the school is to build up each child's sense of worth and self-esteem, at the same time as valuing others and breaking down stereotypes, so that they are able to make informed decisions about their lives. It is our belief that pupils should recognize the importance of personal choice in managing relationships so that they do not present risks to health and personal safety, with the understanding that organisms, including HIV/ AIDS, can be transmitted in many ways. It is for this reason that we envisage sex education taking part in many curriculum areas.

The sex education programme is one based on the continuity and progression of each pupil throughout the school continuum. It reflects the need for each child to explore and discuss similar issues at different levels in their school career, considering the different conceptual levels of each pupil at each stage. The programme accommodates the experiences that each child brings into the classroom.

It is considered that sexuality is a lifelong process from birth to death, with the school programme playing a part in the experience, to aid and enhance experiences in later life. It is important to include in the teaching some reference to sexually transmitted diseases and more particularly HIV/ AIDS education.

A CONVERSATION AT FELTHAM SCHOOL IN JULY 1993

Participants: Kerry, disabled
                Matthew, disabled
                David, disabled
                Amanda, disabled (no speech)
                Zoe, ablebodied
                Amanda, ablebodied
Moderator: Inge Hempstead

Inge: We are at a large comprehensive school in Hounslow which has been integrating pupils with physical disabilities for three years now and we have come together today to have a chat about this. Tell me, what has been good about going to a large comprehensive school, Kerry?

Kerry: We get more education and the work is a lot more . . . you get a lot more work and instead of lazing around all the time which we did at our other school, you don't. You have to really concentrate, you get a lot of homework, it is really hard but you learn to cope in the end.

Matthew: Coming to this school you get to make a lot more friends, you learn about more interesting subjects and you got a more wide variety of subjects and as Kerry said you get a lot of hangups but you can cope in the end.

Inge: David, how do you feel about things?

David: Ah . . . well . . . ah . . . the lessons are great, the teachers are great, people . . . they get on my nerves, most of the disabled people's nerves, even in lessons, they take the mickey.

Inge: So, there have been some difficulties, you feel?

David: Yes.

Inge: Can you tell us a little bit more about them?

David: Well, they take(?) names, out of all the swear words, they take the mickey out of our disabilities, he can't walk well, he is dumb, or something like that and that really gets up my nose.

Inge: Kerry, has that been your experience as well?

Kerry: Yeh, when I was in about the first year, I did have a girl that used to be with me but first of all I used to go home and I used to be really upset and I could not take it because I was not used to it, now we are the best of friends, now. It was all over and done with by the time we got into the fourth year.

Matthew: Yeah, they do take the mickey out of you and they do think you don't get disciplined and say, 'Oh, you never get any detention but we are always getting told off by a teacher and you should get told off as well.' But if they do take the mickey out of you, you just brush it off and you go 'Yeah, alright' because they are being stupid, you are not the one who is stupid, you can't help it.

Inge: Matthew, I remember when you first came to the school, you were having some problems with your class. Do you remember what you did about it?

Matthew: Yeah, I got up in front of the class and I told them all about my disability and it educated them, so I could get on with my own life and have my own education, they still sometimes, they take the mickey out of me but I can cope with it now.

Inge: So you feel that was a good way of dealing with it?

Matthew: Hm, because that educated them as well as allowing me to get on with my own life and have an education in this school and just learn, which is what I am here to do anyway. Now they get on with me much better and I get on with them much better now. So, I found it a good way to cope with it.

Inge: Thank you. Amanda and Zoe, you do not have a disability but you have friends in your class who have disabilities. How do you feel about it?

Amanda: I think it's good that they have come to this school so that people can learn about the disabilities and so that they can have a proper education.

Zoe: I think it educates people that haven't got a disability where if they go into the outside world to understand that people that are disabled are still the same as them.

Inge: So do you feel that other schools should do the same as this school is doing?

Zoe: Yeah, it causes problems sometimes, I think, but in the end it is worthwhile.

Inge: Kerry, has it been easy to make friends?

Kerry: In one respect yes it has but on the other hand, it's like, when they are bullying you you find it hard and you think, why do I bother, but then . . . but then you get used to it all and then you think, oh, it was all worthwhile, and it's all going well, and when things are going well you feel pleased with yourself, and it's all going well and I'm OK, I'm alright.

Inge: Have you been on any holidays with your school?

Matthew: I have. I went on the French trip last year and I found it interesting because I learned more about France, actually being in France, and a couple of people in my class went and I got to know them better outside school because they were on the trip.

Inge: Do you have a chance to see any of your schoolfriends after school hours?

David: No, well, no well, where I used to live, where I used to live I had friends, right but now, but now when I moved down to Shakespeare [Road] I haven't got many friends there now because I don't know them all. And I haven't got many friends because they can't come and see me, they can't play . . . or if they come and see me, it's a long way and it's knackering.

Inge: What can we do about that, David?

David: Well, there's . . . not . . . you can do really.

Inge: I understand there is talk of a sports club at school for able-bodied and disabled pupils. Would that be one way of making friends?

David: Yes, that would be an excellent way of making friends, because if you don't know a lot of people you can make friends there.

Inge: Now, Zoe and Amanda tell me, do you feel that the disabled pupils are getting away with murder at times, or do you feel that most teachers treat them the same way as you?

Amanda: Some teachers treat them the same way as us, but some teachers because they are in a wheelchair, they think they shouldn't have detention because it's not their fault. But they [the disabled pupils] do the same things as we do, they do . . .

Inge: You mean 'naughty things'?

Amanda: Yes, they do naughty things.

Inge: Like what?

Amanda: Ahem . . . they are cheeky to the teachers, don't hand in homework . . .

Inge: I see, what do you think Zoe?

Zoe: Sometimes the teachers let them get away with it. A lot of teachers like let them get away with it but I think that the welfares sort of catch them up on it, so they don't get away with it in the end.

Inge: So the welfare assistants are stricter? . . . yes . . . Do you complain to the teachers if they are too soft on the disabled pupils?

Zoe: No.

Inge: Well, what do you think about it then, those of you who are in wheelchairs, do you think you should be treated the same? Matthew?

Matthew: Sometimes we do not get disciplined and we do get away with a bit more than we should but I don't think that's right because we have not been in the school as long as people without disabilities and we come in to learn about education and I think we should be treated the same as them.

Inge: Is there anything . . . remembering your special school . . . you feel you are missing out on now you are in a school which integrates? Kerry, can you answer that?

Kerry: I enjoy coming to this school but the only thing I miss was we went out a lot more at my old school and we do a lot more work, as I said, but I wanted to come to this school and I wasn't that bothered once I got here, so it doesn't really bother me. I was one of the people that was really enthusiastic about it.

Inge: I know Amanda is really keen to say something to you, would you like Zoe to speak for you, Amanda? . . . Yes. OK.

Zoe: She feels that the trips that they used to go on quite a lot, like afternoon trips down, to say, shopping or something, and being here she hasn't got time to go out and they can't plan to go out as much and she misses out on that. But also the welfare assistants, she agrees that they are quite strict here, sometimes over-strict, aren't they? You keep relaying . . .

Inge: Do you feel it is a disadvantage having a classroom assistant with you a lot? Do you feel you get more supervision in a way and don't get away with things quite as much as the other pupils? What do you think, David?

David: Well . . .

Inge: Sorry, I didn't hear that . . . Do you have support in class sometimes from a welfare assistant or a classroom assistant?

David: After school?

Inge: No, no, during lessons.

David: Well, I do . . . well I do have some but that is only in science . . . when anything can go wrong, and in science, see teachers can . . . in case I cut off my hands. In other lessons, ah . . . ah . . . like PE like PE just in case I fall . . . I fall . . . football, football.

Inge: Well, my question was, I don't know whether somebody wants to volunteer to answer. If you have a classroom assistant in class, if you are with another teacher, if your base room teacher comes with you or one of the service teachers, do you feel sometimes you, you have to behave better and work harder and somebody who doesn't have that extra pair of eyes trained on them, has an easier time in class? Kerry?

Kerry: Well, I think, they do involve themselves too much at times, because I think we do get too much from them, too much help and I think they sometimes they tell us what we should be doing and what we shouldn't be doing, and that really gets up my nose. Because I think we should, I think we should just lead our own lives without people pushing us and telling us what to do.

Matthew: In some ways it's good we have the support because if we do not have time to listen to the teachers or if we have got to do things and can't listen to the teachers we get told what to do. And I start writing so I get help on that level but otherwise it is a bit more hard to get away with things because they are more used to what you are doing.

Kerry: If they see you doing something which is wrong, they sort of give you a dirty look or something or say: 'Kerry, should you be doing this? Shouldn't you be getting on with your work?' and things like that. It really gets up my nose. You are only trying to fit in with all the people.

Inge: Do you feel able to direct the help you need? I mean, do you feel you have been here long enough now to ask for the help you want, the type of help you want, and the amount of help you want? Do you have the chance to do that or is it just handed out to you willynilly?

Matthew: We don't have much chance to say: 'Oh, I think I need more help in this lesson than I'm getting', because there is also other children that need help and you just take the help when you can get it, but I think I might need some more help in other lessons than I am getting now.

Inge: You seemed to be saying just now that you were getting too much and not the right kind. So I'm saying can you discuss that with your classroom assistant or your teachers, your specialist teachers?

Kerry: We do need help, I'm not saying that we don't need help. In some classes, like Matthew said, we need more help than in others. We don't get that. We ask, like we come to the head, that is in charge of us here, and we ask, and she tries to sort it out but it takes quite a long time so you just got to try and cope with it, you know.

Inge: Are some of your able-bodied friends too helpful?

David: No, not really, because I am . . . because we have to do everything for ourselves . . . only when we have a wounded shoulder or a wounded neck then somebody has to go and get the stuff . . .

Kerry: I disagree with that. I think in some ways they are more helpful than the welfare. They understand you in a different way. I think it is because they're the same age as you, so they understand you in the same way you understand them. You can relate to them a lot more.

David: Yeah, I know, Kerry, but most of the kids in my form, in my year, are nowhere near below me, but some kids are in my same age group keep on . . . what's the word . . . keep on . . . pestering me, yeah.

Matthew: But, there are some people like Amanda or Shazia that need more help from their friends and do deserve it and do get it. We have friends but we don't need as much help as them, so we don't get as much help from friends as they do which we don't mind because we don't need it as much as they do.

Inge: Amanda, I am looking at you now. Are you getting as much help as you want or are you getting too much? You are getting too much from your friends? What are you telling me, yes or no? Hmm? . . . You get enough. Do you want to be more independent? You would like to be more independent. Do you feel you have all learned to be more confident and independent since you have been here? Are you more confident about meeting people? About speaking up for yourself now? Kerry?

Kerry: Yeah, because when I first came here I was really quiet, believe it or not. Yeah. And . . . now, as you can hear, I can, I rabbit on all the time, so I think it really has brought my confidence up. And the teachers and the welfares have really been praising me for my work and that and saying I am doing really well so I feel really happy and that.

Matthew: Yeah, well, I am more confident but that must happen, that must come naturally, because you wouldn't stay unconfident if you come into this school. You can't because otherwise you just sink. It's a game of sink or survive. Gee . . . and I am swimming.

Inge: How do you feel about your relationship with the opposite sex? Anything good happening there, are you making friends with, are you acquiring boyfriends or girlfriends? How do you feel other pupils in the school see you, of the opposite sex? [Lots of giggling]

Matthew: Well, that's difficult one to answer because at the moment I can't answer because I am confused and I don't know what to say diplomatically. So, for once . . . .. [giggles] No, David can have that question.

David: Well, ahh . . . well . . . all the girls that I have gone out with keep on taking it as a joke and all that, so really . . . I have no hope until later.

Matthew: You do have some difficulties some time, because girls will come up to you and say: 'Do you want to go out with me?' but that is their way of having a joke, taking the mickey out of you, so you've got to try and decide who is serious and who you like and you think likes you to the ones mucking around.

Kerry: A lot of the boys are more helpful than the girls. Because the girls can be quite bitchy at times. But the boys . . . they just take it in their stride, and, like . . . I like a lot of the boys in the school, but . . . like they said . . . they take it . . . they think it is one big joke and they think because you are in a wheelchair that you are going to be different from anyone else. And they can't . . . and they . . . and sometimes they are ashamed to go out with you because you are in a wheelchair.

David: Yeah, and they also . . . they do take it as a joke but they also don't mean . . . they also don't feel what's going on in your heart, because we are sensitive, we take it for real, but they take it for a joke and then go along with this joke. . . .

Inge: Do you feel you would go out with somebody who has a disability, now you have been at school with people for three years?

Zoe: I don't know, it's hard to answer . . . I don't know.

Inge: What would it depend on?

Zoe: I mean, yeah, I maybe would . . . because it is not the wheel-chair, it is the person, I mean, if you found the right person, the wheelchair wouldn't matter.

Inge: Yes, I think sometimes people have to become more mature to take that attitude but when we are young we still very much go by looks and sometimes people have to get used to the idea that somebody is in a wheelchair, because you suddenly see the way other people look at you who haven't gone through the same experiences. It is a very difficult question, possibly it was a bit unfair asking it.

SIOBHAN (SHIV) GIVES HER VIEWS: OCTOBER 1993

In answer to the question 'might able-bodied young people treat disabled young people differently when it comes to dating?' Shiv says:

Some older men might get a kick from going out with a disabled young girl. You got to be careful because some men do get a kick out of it. When

I went out with somebody I also got a kick out of it and then I realized I had to be careful or I might get seduced by an older man.

On abortion, she says:

Well, if you are talking about abortion it is always the woman's right to decide it's her body and she has the right do to what she wants and I think if . . . if a young girl gets pregnant and she can't cope I think it is better she accepts this and considers adoption or even abortion. If she cannot cope and look after the baby and love it, she should talk to the doctor and get an abortion.

Inge: What about aborting disabled babies? Should they be allowed then to abort that pregnancy?

Shiv: Yes, I think they should because as I said it is up to the woman to say whether she can cope because it isn't fair on the kid to be brought up in a world where nobody loves it.

Inge: What about the situation where a woman can cope but it is the fact that it is a disabled child that makes her mind up to have an abortion?

Shiv: Well, personally I would think very hard before I would even consider it, but I still think it is up to the woman.

Inge: Shiv, can I ask you whether you have thought about the area of homosexuality at all, whether it has been discussed and whether you have any views about it?

Shiv: I think people should be able to do . . . I think people should be able to be themselves and be with whoever they want to be. I know a little bit about homosexuality because my mum and dad have a lot of friends and I have a lot of friends and some are homosexual and I like them, I think they are great.

Inge: When I talk about homosexuality do you mean men and women?

Shiv: Yeah, I mean men and women. I think they are quite exciting and . . . [not intelligible] . . . they are just like everybody else, people are prejudiced against them because they think they are different, but they are not.

Inge: We are coming back to stereotypes in a way, aren't we, that some people find it hard to accept that somebody isn't all man or all woman.

Shiv: Yeah, I think there is a lot of . . . about homosexuals I think they are very kind. My mum's got a friend, he is very nice, very kind. He isn't at all like what people expect of homosexuals. . . .

Inge: It is a bit like . . . once you met somebody who is out of the ordinary and you realize what they are like as a person, you forget about any prejudice you might have had. It's like disability, isn't it, a minority in society, yes.

At this point the tape had to be turned over. The next question got lost. Inge had asked Shiv whether she knew any girls who had got pregnant while still teenagers. Shiv replied that she knew two girls.

Shiv: One of them has had the baby and the other one is about to have it.

Inge: And how are they coping?

Shiv: They are coping very well. I saw her the other day with her baby and she is lovely.

Inge: Are you a bit envious?

Shiv: [laughs] Yes. When I see them I get all broody about it. I picked it up and I want one. I get all broody about having a baby!

Inge: So, you would rather have a baby than do your A-levels?

Shiv: Well, I don't want any kids until I am prepared for it properly. So I need to stay on at my school, right, and wait until I am a little bit older.

Inge: So, do you feel . . . I mean you are an intelligent girl anyway . . . you have had enough advice in school about contraception and AIDS and generally about relationships, you know, the emotional and the sexual side?

Shiv: Well, before I did it at school my mother told me all about it. She told me about contraception and AIDS and pregnancy and my period. When we did it at school I already had enough information. . . . I think I know everything there is to know.

Inge: So you feel comfortable about that. And do you feel comfortable with your own body?

Shiv: Sometimes, I think my . . . I am too fat, that my hips are too fat.

Inge: Look at mine, goodness me, I wish I had your hips.

Shiv: [laughs] Mostly I am alright with my body. I can fit into size ten. I think I have quite a nice figure but I also get like other girls sometimes, when I am depressed I pig out and then I think I am getting fat.

Inge: Ah well, we all need some treats at times. Do you feel you would want a chance to talk about getting married, or not getting married, having a relationship and having babies, related to your cerebral palsy or do you feel alright?

Shiv: I think that I am alright because I feel comfortable with myself now. The fact that I have cerebral palsy is not a big part of my life, I am a big part of my life and what I am actually doing is the big part of my life, but cerebral palsy is not a big part of my life. My education is.

Inge: Thank you.

Chapter 12

Personal development and young people with communication difficulties

A lesson in sex and love

Karen Muskett

Many children and young people with disab'lities and learning difficulties are denied knowledge and access to information about relationships and sexuality because it is not a part of the curriculum in their school or because issues are not explained and explored in a way they can understand. In this chapter Karen Muskett describes how she developed a sex education programme over a number of years for young people with speech and language difficulties in the special school where she worked. Many of the young people used signing to communicate. The programme developed and grew in response to the real-life experiences and interests of the young people themselves, although she discovered that she had to question many of her own assumptions and overcome the prejudice and suspicion of others on the way.

I was born in Liverpool in 1954 and was educated at one of the North West's first comprehensive schools. My own sex education consisted of how rabbits reproduce and a one-off lesson on VD. I was lucky enough to go on to university where I studied zoology, learning a great deal more about reproduction! During my postgraduate teacher training course sex or reproduction were never mentioned.

My first job was at a large comprehensive for girls in Stockport, where three weeks into my teaching career I found myself faced with giggling fifth-formers waiting to be 'sex educated'. I had specific instructions as to what to do and what to cover. I had one lesson a week for a half-term and then I would get the next lot of fifth-formers and so on until they had all been through my hands. Each group was more eager than the group before to watch the blushing 22-year-old fumble with her box of tricks! Six years (1981) later, a lot wiser and armed with more resources, I began a new job at a special school in a large city.

The school opened twenty-five years ago under the auspices of the local education authority. At the time the Department of Audiology and Speech Therapy at a neighbouring university was coming across children who were deaf and not using or understanding language. These children were not responding to teaching or speech therapy. As these children matured they became increasingly confused and frustrated and some needed psychiatric help. Little was known about speech and language impairments. The school was set up as a residential school to serve the whole of the region. Other authorities paid to send children there. One of the primary aims of the school was to prevent students from needing psychiatric treatment. Over the twenty-six years it has become an internationally renowned school and a centre of excellence for children with speech and language impairments. It is an all-age school 5 to 16 years and has fifty-eight pupils. The staff to pupil ratio is 1:6. Each child receives an individual education programme with individual speech therapy and language development. A child with a severe speech and language difficulty is a child for whom language is not functioning well enough for him or her to communicate with other people. Although there are around sixty children and young people in the school and each one is unique, they can be split into three groups.

1 Expressive language difficulty
   This group could range from the child having no spoken language at all to a child having severe word-finding problems, or an inappropriate use of language. The majority of the children also have a very limited functional vocabulary.
2 Receptive language difficulty
   Children with receptive problems experience difficulty in making sense of the language around them. Again, this could be very severe and spoken language could have no meaning at all or, more usually, a child has difficulty in understanding certain aspects of language.
3 A combination of both expressive and receptive difficulties.

As language is the essence of learning, anything which affects language may have a profound effect on a child's ability to learn. From my teaching point of view this meant that the teenagers I taught often had 'normal' age-appropriate interests but a language level of very much younger children. It can be likened to an intelligent person going to a foreign country with no knowledge of the spoken or written language.

At the time, the nearest I had ever got to talking about sexuality with my pupils was leading discussions with those fifth-formers on issues such as abortion or sex before marriage, something that had been quite definitely frowned upon. I had also had long conversations with some of my A-level students about issues such as lesbianism, pleasure, abuse, and so on. These conversations would very definitely have landed me in serious trouble but I trusted the girls and they trusted me. In all these conversations I answered questions honestly and let the girls take the lead.

In planning the 'sex education' programme in my new post at the special school, I wanted it to be an integral part of health education, not just a six-week special. I wanted it to be an ongoing thing that didn't cause a stir. I needed the support of the head and the parents to implement this. When I coolly talked to the headteacher about my ideas he blinked, gulped a few times and told me that previously the school nurse came into school to give the girls a talk about periods. My heart sank. However, after further discussion he gave me his full support. We agreed not to push the sex within marriage aspect but to promote the idea that sex should be a part of a deep, loving, long-term relationship. All I was intending to do was to give these teenagers the simple basic facts about human reproduction, growing up, conception, pregnancy, birth, contraception and sexually transmitted diseases. The parents were happy to give their consent. It should be quite simple. I would take my time and do the job thoroughly. All I had to do was to find the right words and draw some good clear diagrams. My main concern was that this would be taught to groups with both sexes and I was worried about teaching the boys! I need not have worried on that score. None of the pupils were embarrassed or silly and it didn't bother them being in mixed groups (in the twelve years at the school this was never a problem).

Simple it was not. The first problem was that none of these pupils appeared to have any idea about sex. Sexuality was apparently something that had never occurred to them. Most, though not all, had some idea about girls/boys, men/women looking different. These young people were 12 or 13 years old and I felt it was important they find out correct information.

I soon ran into tremendous communication problems myself. I discovered that at that time there were no Paget Gorman signs for words such as sex, sperm, ova, vagina, penis. Half of the pupils were totally reliant on Paget signs. I felt frustrated there were no signs for important bodily functions and parts especially as you could find signs for port and claret. I suspect this reflected the life style of Pierre Gorman the genius who along with Paget developed the system (of which I am a great advocate).

I wrote to the society and requested signs. They replied immediately and said they would produce some as soon as possible. Now, ten years later, I believe they are in the new manual and in use elsewhere. The society were very appreciative that the omission had been pointed out and worked hard to produce new signs. However, our need was immediate, so taking a lead from one of the more streetwise and able pupils I set about inventing some signs. Here are some of them (see also Figure 12.1):

Sexy   Hold each hand up like a person, bring them together and make them 'embrace'

Sex   As for 'sexy', but then lie them down flat

Vagina   Sign 'woman' (person with the left hand touch cheek with right hand) then make a small 'o' shape with the right hand in front of the 'person' hand in the correct anatomical position

"person"
(this sign is a constituent part of the other three)

"vagina"
(the first part of the sign means "woman")

"penis"
(the first part of the sign means "man")

"intercourse"

Figure 12.1 Signs created by students

Penis   Sign 'man' (person with right hand touch chin with left hand) then
          using the small finger of the left hand place it in the correct
          anatomical position in front of the 'person' hand
Period   Sign 'woman' then 'month' and 'blood'

Later we invented:

Homosexual   Sign 'man' loves 'man'
Lesbian   'Woman' loves 'woman'

The signs shown in Figure 12.1 are not those of British Sign Language, but were developed from the Paget-Gorman system, which was the system used in the school. Signs are not static symbols, but consist of several elements, moving in three-dimensional space. Hence the need for more than one photograph to represent one sign.

Some of the older more able pupils were very happy to invent some signs which were all very graphic and still in use today. If you just think about the word sperm how do you describe it to pupils with severe language difficulties? 'It is like a minute tadpole. No, no it doesn't turn into a frog. No, you can't see it because it's so small you need a microscope. Well it's, you know, one of those machines that make things bigger, yes, yes it comes out of the penis. It isn't wee, I don't think it's a good idea to look at your sperm now, how does it get out? Well you have to, you know, masturbate. Well that is when you . . .' Clearly I had a lot to learn and none of the mainstream materials were going to be of use. Often I thought I had done a good job only to find to my dismay I hadn't. One of the advantages of being in a special school was that I didn't have to worry about exams and tight schedules, so I was able to return to areas of confusion and try again. Very slowly I began to understand what was needed and I began to develop resources specifically for each group, differentiated to meet each pupils needs. My ability to communicate with these pupils grew and our trust in each other developed.

One or two of the pupils had a great deal of difficulty in understanding their own emotions and desires. They just did not have the language to describe their feelings. They suffered a great deal of frustration and confusion. Some of the pupils did begin to express a need to talk about related issues such as pleasure, their own worries and their own sexuality. I encouraged them to do so but often asked them to do this out of lesson time so as not confuse further some of the other pupils. Another mistake.

I decided that I needed to extend the sex education policy further. It would have to include opportunities for the pupils to express their feelings; after all, these pupils needed more than ever the forum my A-level students had had. They were not likely to pick up on these issues from other pupils, parents and myself. I would approach the head about it when the time was right. I was due to go on maternity leave. My pregnancy had been much 'used' in the lessons.

1986

I returned to school with my head full of motherhood. I would really have to improve the way in which I had taught about childbirth. These girls would have to know much more than I had previously taught them if they were to stand any chance of making informed decisions and of understanding the experience of childbirth. The boys needed to realize they had a very important role to play too.

Not long after my return to school the headteacher asked me into his office and introduced me to a detective, investigating an incident involving one of our ex-pupils, who had been raped by two adult men. They claimed he had consented. The detective wanted to know how much the pupil knew about homosexuality. Would he understand what he had consented to?

I had to answer that as far as I knew he had never asked about it nor had anyone else in his group so I had never talked about it. He had great difficulty in understanding language and concepts and it was my opinion that despite my efforts he was still probably confused about heterosexuality, he certainly would not have understood an invitation to go back to someone's flat let alone an invitation to have sex. I was horrified. Why, why hadn't I talked about homosexuality and why hadn't I told students about abuse, rape and ways of keeping yourself safe? This must never happen again.

This issue plus the dawning awareness of AIDS made the time right to go for a very much broader sex education policy as part of an all-embracing sexual health and well-being programme. The rape of this student promoted often heated discussions in the staff room but in the end the staff agreed that much more was needed.

It would be very important to put over the idea that ignorance could make our pupils even more vulnerable and that by introducing issues such as abuse and homosexuality into the curriculum our pupils would be better equipped to deal with life. These two issues produced the first ever complaint from a parent, a very articulate parent who spent a great deal of time and effort in trying to have me silenced or removed. I will remain grateful to the head and other staff for their support.

In 1987 I presented a half-hour talk to the governors asking them to approve a new sex education policy. I was extremely nervous but I needn't have been. After a lively debate I was given unanimous support. I was helped greatly by the fact that the local education authority were encouraging governors to promote very progressive sex education policies. It is also worth pointing out that in recent years a great deal of money and effort had been spent on training teachers to teach 'sex education'. Their courses were excellent. Seventeen years after beginning to teach I finally got some useful training!

The last six years have seen great changes in the way things are taught at the school. The initial information about growing up, etc. is taught at an earlier age, 11 (I would like it to be taught much earlier). The pupils are encouraged to express their own feelings and concerns right from the beginning and therefore topics such as masturbation are talked about quite openly. It is interesting that the majority of the pupils are not embarrassed to do this and take it in their stride. The one or two who have been more embarrassed are those who are more 'streetwise'. One of the problems with being this open is that you then have to teach them when it is appropriate to be open and when there is a need for privacy. Earlier this year one of the older boys proudly announced that he had tried on a condom and it fitted! He was really pleased with himself but the visiting potential parent nearly fell off her chair with shock.

Expressing our feelings is something which is very difficult for many of us and it is even more difficult if you experience speech and language difficulties. It is an area where a lot more work is needed. I have found role-play very useful. However, this too has its drawbacks. I was reminded by Mary, one of the house parents, about the following incident which clearly shows that sometimes young adults with language difficulties don't have any idea when they haven't understood. The group of six pupils, Mary and myself had been working on the idea of a teenager getting pregnant and going to tell her parents. They had decided that the father would be so cross that he would kick the girl out. The whole afternoon was spent working on the role-play. The teenage girl, the boyfriend, the doctor, the mother all played brilliantly, but Brian the father just stood looking bewildered. I realized he hadn't understood and carefully explained the whole thing to him. I even took the role myself to give him more of an idea, 'Come on Brian you are her dad and you're really mad at her, be angry.' He carefully walked up to her, put his hand on her shoulder and in the calmest voice said 'Be Angry.'

It was as a result of role-play that I learned that one of the pupils was being abused. On another occasion I also realized that a whole group of girls had missed out a really important bit of information. The girls, all school leavers, had had extensive sex education. We had been over the basics time and time again. We had discussed their feelings and their sexuality. They had visited the family planning clinic and they understood about 'safer sex', indeed one of them was enjoying a relationship and using contraception reliably. I had set up a role-play in which I was the GP and one of the girls was coming to me to tell me she thought she was pregnant. Everything was going very nicely until I asked why she thought she was pregnant. Thirty-five minutes later with every clue under the sun, not one of that group could tell me that the patient had missed a period. How can this type of thing happen? I knew I had taught them this many times and once I had reminded them they all nodded. This fact is fundamental and yet somehow had not been put over. It was a small consolation when we repeated the role-play the next week that they all remembered the vital clue. Role-play, time consuming as it is, can be extremely useful.

I asked a small group of parents and governors if they would like to work with me to produce a resource book for parents to use at whatever level they felt comfortable with. This turned out to be very interesting. The parents shared their fears, anxieties and aspirations and I shared my experiences of teaching their children. Two very important things emerged from this. Firstly, all the parents worried about their child's sexuality and were extremely anxious about their child's future regarding sexual relationships. They were very much afraid of their children being abused and hurt. Secondly, they nearly all underestimated how much their children knew and understood. They tended to see their children as much younger than they were. I learned a great deal from this group and wish that I had had the foresight to start eighteen years ago. We all benefited from it. The resource book was published by AFASIC. Figures 12.2a and b show extracts from the book (Muskett 1993).

In January of this year I attended a course on lesbian and homosexual issues in education. I arrived at the course feeling quite sure I was doing all the right things. This opinion was bolstered when during introductions it became obvious that many schools did nothing in this area. My smug satisfaction was short lived, when I realized that there were big gaps in my teaching. For example, when I first talked about adolescent boys having wet dreams I always talked about heterosexual feelings, never mentioning possible homosexual feelings or dreams. Very soon afterwards I had the opportunity to amend the situation. I was amazed to find that the young group I was talking to did not bat an eyelid when I added some boys may dream about other boys and having sex with them. It was a good start. Clearly talking about homosexuality was important but presenting positive images of gay and lesbian teenagers is even more important. I do know that some of the pupils I taught both at the special school and in mainstream were gay or lesbian and I hope that I gave enough of a positive image to them.

I could write another chapter on what these young adults talked about in terms of their own sexuality, desires and feelings. It is important that I note that not all the pupils were able to do so. Of the ones that did the vast majority were open and honest. They welcomed the opportunity to do so because problems with communication made it difficult for them to do this at home or indeed with peers outside the school environment. I am happy to say that the pupils who have enjoyed an enlightened curriculum appear to have been able to cope well with the huge changes that their bodies and minds go through. All of them expressed desires to find someone to share their lives with and to have children with and they expect to do this. They appear to understand the threat of AIDS and they know about using condoms. In some ways they may be better equipped than their mainstream peers who still think AIDS is something that won't happen to them. The

vagina

This is the opening or passage that joins the womb to the outside of the girl's or woman's body. It is found between her legs. Inside the vagina is made up of folds of skin. These folds can open out to allow the vagina to stretch. The vagina is the passage where a man puts his *penis* during sex and it is the passage through which the baby is born.

penis

Boys and men have a penis, this is the *male sex organ*. It has two jobs to do

1 lets wee out
2 puts *sperm* into the woman's body.

Most of the time you penis is small and floppy but when you are feeling sexy it goes *erect* (hard and sticking up). If the penis is rubbed gently then the sexy feelings get very great and the *sperm* come squirting out – this is called *ejaculation*. The very nice sexy feeling is called *orgasm*.

Mens' penises can look different sizes when they are limp but when erect they are more or less the same size. The size of the penis does not make any difference to the way it does its job.

Figure 12.2 (a) Definitions of 'vagina' and 'penis'. (The copy in the original is set larger than here.)

Source: Muskett (1993: 143; 91–2)

sexual intercourse

This is when a couple have *sex* or *make love*. When a man and woman make love the man puts his erect *penis* into the woman's *vagina (vaginal intercourse)*. If two men make love one man puts his penis into the other man's

anus (anal intercourse) . The couple then move gently up and down together until they have an orgasm.
Making love often feels very good and it is a way of showing how much you love someone. It is very special.
If a man and woman make love the *sperm* from the man may reach the woman's egg and make her *pregnant.*

Figure 12.2 (b) Definition of 'sexual intercourse'. (The copy in the original is set larger than here.)
Source: Muskett (1993: 124)

pupils I taught know that they must always use a condom to protect themselves and they probably will. They have also experienced buying them, getting them free from the FPC, they have seen their use demonstrated on cucumbers and bananas and they have had a chance to pull them apart and twang them, and some of them have tried them on in private.

I have throughout all my teaching emphasized love and long-term relationships. The vast majority of pupils see sex as an adult activity and they don't see themselves as adults. I hope that through this programme of health education they will go into adulthood and enjoy a healthy and safe sex life.

In 1992 some of the older pupils asked me to make a dictionary for them which they could keep and when they didn't know a word they could look it up and understand what it said. A year later, we were awaiting the publication of the A to Z, a simple guide to sex and love (Muskett 1993). A book which I toiled over for many months but it is specifically written for young adults who have a language problem. The pupils helped me by 'proof reading' it and by giving me ideas. Without them it wouldn't have been possible.

A great deal more work is needed, particularly in the area of feelings. It has to be acknowledged that there will always be a small number of young adults with severe language difficulties who will, despite the very best efforts, still find very great difficulty in understanding.

I feel very strongly that the achievement at this school would not have been made if these young adults had been integrated in mainstream. The work we did in this area of the curriculum took a great deal of time and that time is not available in mainstream schools.

REFERENCE

Muskett, K. (1993) *A Simple A to Z of Sex: A Guide for Young Adults with Speech and Language Impairments*, London: Association for All Speech Impaired Children.

Chapter 13

An inclusive curriculum within a nursery school

Marian Ellis

Burton Grange Nursery School flourishes in one of Barnsley's most de-prived areas (see also the chapter by Julian Wroe in Part I of Equality and Diversity in Education 2: National and International Contexts for Practice and Research*). Marian Ellis sets her discussion of the work of her school in the context of Barnsley LEA's entitlement curriculum and com-mitment to equality of educational opportunity. She details the pattern of support for children, which starts before they are admitted, then goes on to describe a 'typical' morning in the nursery. She introduces us to four children who are seen to have 'special educational needs' and whose diversity of interests and abilities are catered for within the nursery's well-planned and creative approach.*

INTRODUCTION

Burton Grange Nursery School is a small LEA school catering for forty children in the morning and forty in the afternoon; there are no full-time places. It is staffed by a headteacher, a teacher, two nursery nurses and a clerical worker.

Built in the 1940s, the school consists of a small kitchen and staff room, a tiny office/stock room and two teaching rooms joined by a corridor, the bane of our lives – what 3 or 4-year-old can resist the temptation to run as fast as possible down a long, narrow corridor?! Every inch of space in the tiny building is utilized.

The school is in north-east Barnsley, which includes some of the most deprived communities in the borough. There are few childcare services, with just one registered childminder in our immediate locality. Nevertheless, like so many coal-mining areas, the community is characterized by close family ties and a strong community spirit. It is the spirit which families bring to our school that enables us to provide an exciting and effective education.

PROVIDING A CURRICULUM FOR ALL CHILDREN

It has to begin with a commitment by staff and governors, that *all* children will be welcomed into school, and that *all* children will benefit from what is on offer. The ethos of the school must transmit a positive message, so that all members of the community believe that they have a right to education in their own local school, and that the education offered will be the most appropriate for their children.

Our starting point for each child has to be based on each child's life experiences as part of the family and the community. Whatever knowledge, skills and attitudes the child has already acquired from his/her early experiences will form the basis of our curriculum planning. The children enter the school having had an enormously varying set of experiences and at many different stages of development. Each child has an entitlement to the curriculum and our role is to design routes of access to their entitlement: see Figure 13.1.

SUPPORT RIGHT FROM THE START

The route must start from where the child is now, so communication with the people involved in the child's early life is crucial. This will inevitably involve discussions with parents and carers, but it may also include health workers, portage workers, social workers, etc. From this sharing of information we are able to establish an accurate picture of the child's knowledge, skills and achievements and the context in which they have been acquired. This information provides the base from which we can negotiate an appropriate curriculum for each child, whatever his or her particular needs may be.

A home visit

This gathering and collating of information usually begins on a home visit. Each member of staff has responsibility for a pastoral group of ten children per session, and this relationship starts on an initial home visit before the child enters school. The visit offers the opportunity for the family and the worker to establish a bond and to begin to work together to meet the child's needs. If there is involvement with other agencies, the worker will liaise with them and take responsibility for passing on information to the rest of the staff. Because of the close involvement between staff and parent or carer it is possible to both establish our starting point for the curriculum, and to ensure continuity through an ongoing dialogue and sharing of information.

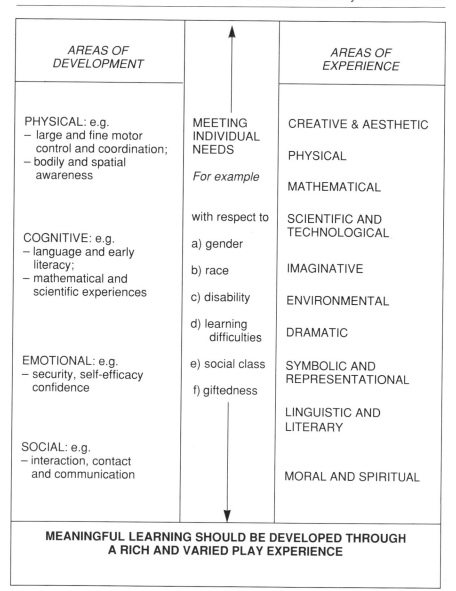

AREAS OF DEVELOPMENT		AREAS OF EXPERIENCE

PHYSICAL: e.g.
– large and fine motor
  control and coordination;
– bodily and spatial
  awareness
	MEETING INDIVIDUAL NEEDS
	
	For example
	
	with respect to
	
	a) gender
	
	b) race
	
	c) disability
	
	d) learning
	   difficulties
	
	e) social class
	
	f) giftedness
		CREATIVE & AESTHETIC
		
		PHYSICAL
		
		MATHEMATICAL
		
		SCIENTIFIC AND TECHNOLOGICAL
		
		IMAGINATIVE
		
		ENVIRONMENTAL
		
		DRAMATIC
		
		SYMBOLIC AND REPRESENTATIONAL
		
		LINGUISTIC AND LITERARY
		
		MORAL AND SPIRITUAL

COGNITIVE: e.g.
– language and early
  literacy;
– mathematical and
  scientific experiences		

EMOTIONAL: e.g. – security, self-efficacy confidence		
SOCIAL: e.g. – interaction, contact and communication		

MEANINGFUL LEARNING SHOULD BE DEVELOPED THROUGH A RICH AND VARIED PLAY EXPERIENCE

AN APPROPRIATE RECORD OF THE CHILDREN'S ACHIEVEMENTS

Figure 13.1 Content of the entitlement curriculum 3–5

Source: Barnsley LEA (1989: 2)

a) Teaching and learning within the Entitlement Curriculum will promote:

- feelings of personal worth (about self and others)
- values which reject racist views
- equality of opportunity with respect to gender
- positive attitudes towards disability
- values which celebrate diversity in culture, race and gender

Figure 13.2 Values and attitudes
Source: Barnsley LEA (1989: 8)

Children with a statement of special educational needs

If a child entering the school already has a statement of special educational needs there is a high chance that s/he will also have individual support in the form of a Curriculum Support Assistant (CSA). The CSA will work alongside staff in the school to support the child in his or her learning. The assistant will not generally work one to one with the child, but will structure group situations in order to meet specific learning objectives from which other children can also gain. Suggestions from therapists will also inform our curriculum by providing ideas for more structured group activities in which all of the children can join. Regular meetings with therapists, parents and carers and staff ensure their involvement in the planning sessions. If specific goals or targets are agreed, these will inform and influence the planned curriculum activities on which staff will focus throughout the nursery. Consequently, the nursery curriculum *includes* the particular needs of this child; they are not added on as an extra or afterthought.

Joint training sessions

In addition to the regular meetings, we as staff also attend joint training sessions. Most of the in-service training for early years workers takes place in twilight sessions, thus enabling staff and parents and carers to train together. Creche facilities are provided. It may be that therapists will join us, or they may be helping to run the courses. The consequence of the joint training is that all the people involved with a child seen to have special educational needs become familiar with useful teaching and therapeutic techniques. It also facilitates the pooling of information about the child's stage of development from different observers in different settings: home, school, clinic, thus enabling a full picture of the child's achievements to be drawn up.

DAILY LIFE IN THE NURSERY SCHOOL

Perhaps the easiest way to illustrate our work is to describe 'A Morning in the Life of Burton Grange'. It can't be described as a typical morning as I'm not sure we ever have such a thing.

A wet Wednesday

9.00 am The children are arriving at school. It's pouring with rain, so everyone comes in shaking coats and brollies – buggies pile up in the tiny entrance. Mrs B. is waiting to greet children and their parents or carers, paying particular attention to our newer pupils. Even the new children know us quite well as they've usually visited school several times and their 'special teacher' has already been to see them in their home. Parents and carers feel comfortable, too, as the home visit has given them the opportunity to discuss any queries or worries.

9.05 am Karen finds her own name and puts it up on our self-registration board, before heading straight for the reading area. She enjoys sitting on the settee with her mother and listening to at least three stories before she decides that it's time for 'mam' to go home.

David and his dad are already busy in the studio, mixing up paint for the first painting of the day. Dad says that the school must be doing something right: 'It doesn't matter how poorly he is, he still insists on coming!'

9.15 am The tiny building is filling up fast. Parents and grandparents, uncles and neighbours are busy settling children into activities, some speaking to staff, others chatting together; 'Who's staying behind today? Shall I put the kettle on?' A small group of women settle themselves in the kitchen, making tea and toast, before they get down to their task of the day – making new games for the nursery's toy library. They cost 10p a week to borrow and have been very popular, eliciting comments such as: 'They learn a lot about counting from this game, you know!' or 'It kept them quiet for ages!'

Back in the nursery, children have made their choices and are very busy with their play. Paul is engrossed with a selection of pipes and U-bends in the water tray, trying to predict where the water will flow from next, explaining to the NNEB student exactly how he fixed them together. Shrieks of laughter as the water gushes out unexpectedly, soaking the floor and their shoes!

Several children have selected their milk, and sit round the table chatting as they munch on their apples.

The CDT (Craft, Design, Technology) area is very popular this morning. Selena is choosing boxes, ribbons, bottle-tops and buttons from the self-service selection, ready to start her very carefully thought-out model. With the help of Miss O., she has already drawn a plan, and is now ready to translate it into three dimensions. She will persevere with this until she is satisfied – often up to 50 minutes.

At the same table, Mark is smearing glue over every surface of a cereal box. He resists any encouragement to add anything to the sticky surfaces, but checks to make sure that no 'unglued' areas remain. Mark has only been in the nursery a few weeks; Selena will move up to the infant school next term. In the wet sand, Robert is exploring the concepts of heavy and light with large weighing scales and buckets, whilst around the dry sand, children are discussing which is the biggest bottle, and predicting who will be the first to fill it to the top.

Other activities going on around this room include clay modelling, wood-work, large construction bricks and mark-making with many different media. Children move purposefully from one area to another, choosing the equipment and resources they require from the open shelving.

10.00 am The rain has stopped, so the doors can be opened, puddles swept leaving the children free to play indoors or out. Outdoor play is usually an extension of the indoor provision with the added attraction of large equip-ment to climb on, or jump over, or make dens with. . . . On into the quiet room – here children are busy in the office area. Katie is not very happy about the mess, so she makes a sign to pin on the notice board telling everyone to keep the office tidy. She loves to write and is supremely confident about her skills. When trying to explain something which I was having trouble understanding she said: 'Hang on, I'll write it down for you!'

10.30 am Everywhere children are busy with real and imagined activities: constructing train tracks, listening to stories, dressing up, feeding babies, cooking dinners, booking holidays at the travel agents, peering through magnifying glasses, organizing picnics.

And the adults are busy: staff, students, parents and a schoolgirl on work experience are listening, suggesting, discussing, comforting, intervening and observing.

When the children have gone home, the morning's observations will be discussed and noted for individual records and to inform future planning.

11.00 am Now the children are in small groups with their 'special teacher'. They've collected their pictures, reviewed the morning's work and struggled into coats and wellingtons.

The workers in the kitchen show off their newly completed batch of games, ready for the toy library tomorrow. Working together like this has given several of the women a boost of confidence and heightened self-esteem. Some (including one dad and one grandma) have joined adult education classes in maths and English, others have made friends and given a lot of support to each other, and all have become more actively involved in their child's learning within school.

As they leave, some people pick up leaflets and books from the parents' library, housed in the cramped entrance porch – the most popular tend to be the ones tackling issues such as temper-tantrums and bad language!

11.45 am The children have gone now, so all we have to do is tidy up, prepare for the afternoon session, write up notes, make phone calls, and hopefully have some lunch before the afternoon children arrive.

MARTIN, BARRY, CHRISTOPHER AND DEBBIE

Martin is 3 years old; he has a statement of special educational needs and a curriculum support assistant has been appointed to support his learning in the school. We know Martin well, as he visited many times with his mum and sometimes his portage worker. Nursery staff, parents and therapists have jointly drawn up long-term aims for Martin and these have been incorporated into our long-term curriculum planning.

Through our process of information gathering and discussion we know that we need to encourage Martin to use both hands together, to use a twisting wrist movement and to develop a signing system.

In our weekly curriculum planning session it is agreed that the construction kit with large nuts and bolts should be re-introduced to the construction area. We also plan to change the water play resources to 'tipping and pouring' – jugs, teapots, cups and beakers.

The construction kit provides the ideal medium for practising the wrist movements that Martin needs, whilst playing in the area with other children. He enjoys water play so much that he has devised his own sign indicating his desire to play there. The jugs and cups ensure that he needs to steady a cup with one hand while pouring water from a jug with the other, and at the same time supporting his body against the water tray.

The same equipment is being used by other children in different ways.

Barry has recently been fascinated by machinery and has spent a lot of time investigating how a cuckoo clock works by examining the workings inside. On a recent trip to a traditional flour mill, he was shown how the heavy sacks of flour were transported to the upper floor by a pulley system. Using the same construction kit as Martin, he is now attempting to construct a pulley system which he hopes to suspend over the beams in the nursery.

In the water play, Christopher is being encouraged to pour 'cups of tea' and offer them to other children. He has difficulty relating to his peers and his play is often aggressive and threatening.

Debbie is counting out how many little cups of water it takes to fill the big red teapot. When it is almost full she estimates how many more will be needed to fill it up to the top.

Each of these children is using the equipment in a different way, influenced by their stage of development and by the intended learning outcomes planned by the staff. Throughout the nursery, resources are organized this way into workshop areas where children can have free access to equipment.

But how can we ensure that all our children have access to all the areas of learning and experience which form the framework of our curriculum, and how can we provide evidence to support this?

Our attempt to answer this lies in our observations and record-keeping. Detailed records of experience are collated for each child based on daily observation notes. The observation notes are recorded by staff, students, parents, volunteers – anyone who has observed the child is encouraged to make notes which are then filed in wall pockets. The pastoral group worker is responsible for transferring these notes onto record sheets, analysing them, and then planning what further action may be needed. Alongside photographs and samples of work, this documentation provides the written evidence of each child's experiences within the nursery, and ensures that his/her progress continues to be planned and monitored. As it is a record of experiences and progress, not a checklist to be ticked off when the child has reached the required level, it is much more suited to the individual needs and development of each child.

A visitor entering the school would meet children who have reached different stages in their development:

- Martin, who is now walking with the aid of a trolley, and is still a little unsteady.
- Barry, who can describe what he has observed and found out in his exploration, and can ask questions which help him to identify needs and opportunities for design and technological activity.
- Christopher, who can now tolerate sitting in a small group situation for short periods of time, and loves outdoor play.
- Debbie, who can count, read and write numbers up to 10 and who makes predictions based on experience. She loves to write, and will sign her name anywhere and everywhere!

The common thread is that each child is involved in a curriculum based on their particular needs and their individual experiences at home and school, which aims to maximize the learning possibilities for each and every child. This is one nursery school's attempt to provide an inclusive curriculum which recognizes and values each child and the community to which they all belong.

ACKNOWLEDGEMENT

Some of the material included in this chapter is taken from: M. Ellis, 'Making a mark in early education', *Childcare Now*, 1993, vol. 13, no. 1, pp. 6–8.

REFERENCE

Barnsley Local Education Authority (1989) *Barnsley LEA Entitlement Curriculum. A document for discussion and consultation*, Barnsley: Barnsley LEA.

Chapter 14

Bilingual education in Wales

June Statham and Sian Wyn Siencyn

This article examines language policies in Wales and the extent to which they take into account the needs of children with disabilities and learning difficulties.

INTRODUCTION

In Wales, the notion of an inclusive curriculum needs to take into account an additional factor, the Welsh language. Children in schools in Wales are either taught through the medium of Welsh, in some or all subjects, or they are taught Welsh as a second language. The central government policy was stated in the document '*Welsh in Schools*' on which the decision to include Welsh as a core subject in the National Curriculum was based:

> In English-speaking areas all pupils should be given the opportunity of acquiring a sufficient command of Welsh to allow for communication in Welsh, while bilingual education should be available to pupils whose parents desire it for them.
>
> (Welsh Office 1981)

The eight local education authorities in Wales have developed their own language policies, which vary greatly in the extent to which they aim to promote a bilingual society by providing a Welsh-medium education for all children, or to respond to the wishes of particular parents.

What does this mean for children with disabilities and learning difficulties? Are they included in the language policies, or treated separately? Is there any evidence that bilingualism can hinder or help the education of children with special needs – and does this depend on the nature of their difficulty? What is the interaction between different factors, such as whether the child's first language is Welsh or English, whether they live in a Welsh-speaking or anglicized community, whether the school they attend has a policy of teaching through Welsh or teaching Welsh as a second language? We will not be providing many of the answers in this article. It became clear

Table 14.1 Place of education, % of children with statements

County	Special school	Special class	Mainstream class
Clwyd	44	14	42
Dyfed	22	13	63
Gwent	23	41	30
Gwynedd	34	19	47
Mid Glamorgan	17	77	4
Powys	25	13	57
South Glamorgan	39	57	3
West Glamorgan	8	17	74

Source: Calculated from figures in Welsh Office (1993)

as we tried to gather the necessary information that not only was the relationship between bilingualism in Wales and special educational needs a complex one, but that much of the information was not there to be found. There are few published statistics, no clear policies and little research relevant to the particular situation in Wales. Everyone we spoke to agreed that the situation was confused and needed attention. What we have tried to do in this article therefore is to bring together the data that are available, highlight where there is a need for further research, and raise some of the issues that need to be considered, through providing a number of case studies of children in different situations. We start off by looking at the background to special education in Wales and at Welsh language policies for all children, and then consider how the two interact.

SPECIAL EDUCATION IN WALES

In 1992, there were 61 special schools across Wales. An average of 3.1 per cent of children had statements of special educational needs, ranging from 1.1 per cent in the rural mid-Wales county of Powys to 4.2 per cent in the southern counties of West and Mid Glamorgan. Policies on where children with statements should receive their education clearly differed between authorities, as shown in Table 14.1. In West Glamorgan, nearly three-quarters were in mainstream classes; in Mid Glamorgan special classes were favoured, and in Clwyd nearly half of children with statements attended a special school.

Special education in Wales has been subject to the same legislative influences as in England. This includes the 1981 Education Act, with its emphasis on the integration of children with special needs into mainstream education, and the Education Reform Act 1988 and the Education Act 1993, which transferred power and resources from LEAs to individual schools and have affected the planning and support of services for children with special needs. The Children Act 1989 has also affected children with disabilities, including them for the first time as 'children in need' for whom local authorities have to provide services, and requiring all services to take account of the child's linguistic, cultural, religious and ethnic background.

A particular development in Wales is the All Wales Strategy for the Development of Services for People with a Mental Handicap, introduced by the Welsh Office in 1983, which provides additional resources to encourage agencies to work together and support people with learning difficulties in the community. The Strategy applies to both adults and children, and in a recent review of future directions after the first ten years the Secretary of State recommended that school-age education provision should be a key area for development, and that local education authorities should have a clearer role (Welsh Office 1992a). The Strategy funds the Special Needs Referral Scheme operated by the voluntary sector, which pays for helpers and equipment to enable children with learning difficulties to attend their local playgroup. Many of these places are in Welsh-language playgroups, thus providing integrated pre-school experience through the medium of Welsh for children with learning difficulties. However, children with other kinds of disability are not catered for by this scheme.

POLICIES ON THE WELSH LANGUAGE

At the beginning of the twentieth century, Welsh was spoken by nearly half of the population in Wales. In 1991 this had dropped to only one person in five, although wide variations exist between counties, with three-quarters of the population speaking Welsh in some districts of Gwynedd in the western heartland, compared to only 2 per cent in the border county of Gwent. From the mid-nineteenth century, the education system contributed to the decline of the language, blaming Welsh for the low standards achieved in many schools and introducing customs such as the 'Welsh not', whereby any child caught speaking Welsh at school had to wear a board around their neck and the child wearing this at the end of the day would be beaten. Towards the middle of the twentieth century however this position began to reverse, and schools are now one of the main agencies promoting the Welsh language.

In Wales today there is an established system of Welsh-medium public-funded education in both primary and secondary schools which is increasingly popular not only with Welsh-speaking families but also for children from monolingual English backgrounds. The first officially designated 'bi-lingual' secondary school was opened in 1958, and by 1990 there were 18 such schools. In addition many schools in traditional Welsh-speaking areas use Welsh as the medium of education. Welsh Office statistics for January 1992 showed that there were altogether 445 primary schools and 46 secondary schools which taught wholly or mainly through Welsh. These catered for 16 per cent of primary-aged pupils in Wales, and 12 per cent of secondary pupils. A widespread system of Welsh-medium pre-school education has also developed since the 1970s with the rapid growth of the Mudiad Ysgolion Meithrin, a Welsh-medium playgroup movement which by 1992 had nearly 1,000 groups across Wales, providing places for some 20 per cent of 2 to 4-year-olds.

The likelihood of a particular subject being taught through Welsh at secondary school varies greatly. Physical education and religious knowledge are learnt through Welsh by around one secondary pupil in ten, compared to only one pupil in 100 for subjects such as chemistry and physics. This is due partly to a lack of specialist teachers, and partly to a lack of specialist resources. When curriculum materials were developed in Welsh to support the teaching of secondary maths, for instance, there was a noticeable increase in numbers taking the subject through Welsh.

Those children in Wales who do not learn through the medium of Welsh, are taught Welsh as a second language. The Education Reform Act of 1988 gave Welsh the status of the need to prepare children for life in a bilingual society. Welsh therefore plays a role in the education of all children in Wales, but the particular emphasis depends on the language policy of the local education authority. At one end of the spectrum is Gwynedd, with a declared aim of making every child in the county thoroughly bilingual. Welsh is the main medium of instruction in all primary schools in the traditionally Welsh areas of Gwynedd and in the designated Welsh schools, although in the more anglicized areas English is used to teach academic subjects. At secondary schools all pupils study both Welsh and English to the end of the fifth year and some subjects are taught through Welsh. The policy applies equally to children who move into the area speaking only English. Such primary-aged newcomers receive concentrated Welsh tuition for three months at a specialized language centre, with back-up in the schools from peripatetic language teachers (*athrawon bro*). At the other end of the spectrum is Gwent, where the policy is to teach Welsh as a second language to the majority of children, and to provide a few bilingual schools or units for those who want a Welsh-medium education.

WELSH FOR CHILDREN WITH SPECIAL EDUCATIONAL NEEDS?

We saw above that there has been an increase in Welsh-medium education for children in general. This should result in more children with disabilities or learning difficulties learning through Welsh, unless this is either seen as inappropriate because it is in some way incompatible with other needs, or because resources and support facilities are not available for such children in Welsh. However there is no hard data that would show how far children with disabilities are able to receive their education through Welsh, or are taught Welsh as a second language. There is also no published information on how LEA policies on special needs interact with policies on the Welsh language, although this would be a fruitful area for research. Are children with learning difficulties, for instance, taught Welsh as an essential part of the National Curriculum? Do children with impaired hearing or sight have to receive their education in English, even if they come from a Welsh-speaking community? Does the LEA have a clear policy for such situations, or is the decision left to individual schools and teachers?

There certainly appears to be a lack of direction at a national level on this issue. A working party set up by the Schools Council Committee for Wales in the early 1970s to enquire into the feasibility of establishing bilingual schools in response to the Gittins report on primary education, contained a paragraph on 'slow learners' which stated that there was no consensus among teachers on the appropriateness of a bilingual approach for these pupils and that decisions should be made on an individual basis.

> Some teachers felt that language work should concentrate on great control of the mother tongue and that the addition of a second language would lead to frustration and excessive burden, others that a second language could be a potential source of interest and enthusiasm.
> (Schools Council Committee for Wales 1972)

A consultation document on special educational needs, *Access to the System* (Welsh Office 1992b) also has nothing to say on the subject of access to Welsh-medium special education.

RESEARCH ON BILINGUALISM AND EDUCATIONAL ACHIEVEMENT

One of the difficulties for policy-makers is the lack of research on which to base decisions about the appropriateness of bilingual education for children with disabilities and learning difficulties. This is particularly true of the situation where virtually all children speak the more commonly used language, English, as well. Most of the early studies on bilingualism and educational achievement were carried out in situations where a child speaking a minority ethnic language was introduced to education through English, with their first language receiving little reinforcement from the mainstream culture. Jim Cummins, a researcher who has studied bilingualism in Canada and Ireland, which like Wales offer immersion programmes in the less well-used language (French or Irish), draws a distinction between what is termed 'additive bilingualism' and the 'subtractive bilingualism' of many minority children.

> Additive bilingualism [is] generally achieved by children whose first language is dominant and in no danger of being replaced by the second

language. The bilingualism of these children is termed 'additive' since another socially relevant language is being added to the bilingual's reper tory of skills at no cost to proficiency in the first language.

(Cummins 1984)

In this situation, Cummins reports, most studies suggest that bilingualism helps rather than hinders children's learning, by reinforcing basic linguistic skills that underpin cognitive growth. But is this the case for all children? Again, we come up against a lack of knowledge. Cummins states that 'the question of whether . . . immersion programmes are suitable for all children is currently extremely problematic for Canadian policy makers, educators and parents because the two major research efforts concerned with the issue, involving almost a decade of research, have reached diametrically opposed conclusions'. One of the Canadian studies reported that learning-disabled or 'language-impaired' children in immersion programmes acquired basic academic skills at a comparable rate to similar children in English programmes, and in addition developed fluent interpersonal communicative skills in their second language, although at a slower rate than non-language impaired children. The other study, by a neurologist, claimed that some children were hampered educationally by learning in a second language, and should be identified early and switched to an English programme without delay.

RESOURCES TO SUPPORT WELSH-MEDIUM EDUCATION FOR CHILDREN WITH DISABILITIES

The availability of Welsh-speaking teachers and Welsh-language teaching resources are key requirements for successful Welsh-medium education. For children with disabilities or learning difficulties, particular resources are necessary:

- Assessment: staff who can carry out initial assessments in Welsh, including educational psychologists, health visitors and speech therapists. Children, especially pre-school children from Welsh-speaking homes, cannot be adequately assessed if they are tested in English.
- Support: staff who can provide support and specialist help in Welsh. This includes welfare assistants, speech therapists, physiotherapists, special needs teachers and specialist advisers.

Again, information on how far such resources exist is hard to come by without undertaking further research. The Welsh Office publishes figures on the number of educational psychologists in each local authority, but does not say how many of these are able to make assessments in Welsh. Training for speech therapists is available in only one college in Wales, in English but with an option of taking some of the course in Welsh, and anecdotal evidence suggests many Welsh-speaking children are not being assessed or given specialist help in their first language. Information on the availability of teaching resources in Welsh for children with special needs is similarly patchy. A resource centre for the production of Welsh-medium materials at the University College of Wales in Aberystwyth has produced a provisional list of the written materials that have been developed in each county, often by individual teachers, to support the education in Welsh of children with learning difficulties (Owen 1993). However the author notes that there is little coordination or sharing of this work, resulting in gaps and duplication of effort. The centre at Aberystwyth and the Dyslexia Unit at the University College of Wales in Bangor are collaborating in adapting into Welsh a teaching programme for dyslexic children, and a working group coordinated by the Pwyllgor Datblygy Addysg Gymraeg (the Welsh Education Development Committee) is currently standardizing Welsh Braille so that it can be used for standardized attainment tests and developing Welsh reading materials.

It may appear that such resources will only benefit very small numbers of children. It could be argued that there is little point in standardizing Welsh Braille, since all Welsh-speaking blind children will have learnt Braille in English as there are so few Braille books available in their own language. But which comes first, resources or the demand for resources? As we saw earlier, the production of curriculum materials to support maths teaching in Welsh created a demand. Also there will be an increasing demand for communication aids in Welsh because of the requirement that Welsh be taught to all children as part of the National Curriculum.

THE ISSUES

Given the lack of hard data to show how far children with disabilities are able to receive ther education in Welsh, or how effective this is likely to be, we will use the rest of this chapter to illustrate through case studies some of the issues which arise when thinking about what an integrated education should mean for a child with disabilities in Wales. The examples have been chosen to cover a variety of situations, including whether Welsh is the child's first or second language, the nature of the child's particular needs, and the language policy of the LEA. Some of the issues that need to be taken into account are represented in Figure 14.1, and it may be helpful to bear these in mind when considering the case studies.

CASE STUDY 1: GERAINT

Geraint is 3 years old and has Down's Syndrome. He lives in the predominantly English-speaking county of Gwent. Both his parents are monolingual, but are very keen that their children should be able to speak Welsh.

SiâP

Mae **siap** pendant ym mhob llun.
Dyma rai ohonyn nhw.

Defnyddiwch un ohonyn nhw fel siap ar gyfer eich llun.
Bydd arnoch angen:

Papur lliw A4   } Dewiswch ddau liw sy'n apelio
Papur lliw gludiog   } atoch.
Siswrn
Pensil

Pa siap ydych chi wedi'i ddewis?
Torrwch chwe siap o'r un maint (tua 4cm ar draws) a'u gosod ar y papur
lliw.

Symudwch y siapiau i wahanol leoedd ar y papur lliw.

Unwaith yr ydych chi'n hapus gyda'ch patrwm, gludiwch y darnau yn eu lle.

Gwnewch gyfres o batrymau gan ddefnyddio'r un siap a phapur lliw.
(Gellwch newid lliwiau'r papurau.)

Gellwch ddefnyddio siapiau wedi'u rhwygo neu wedi eu torri.

Er i'r cylch yma gael ei
rwygo, mae'r siap yn
dal yn amlwg ac yn
bwysig i'r llun.

Figure 14.1 'Shape' worksheet using paper, scissors, pencil etc

Source: This worksheet comes from a set of materials produced by a Welsh support team, which has now been disbanded due to cuts in resourcing

Geraint's mother feels deprived of her roots as her grandparents were Welsh speaking, and is learning Welsh at morning classes with her children. Geraint's father, a social worker, is also learning at evening classes twice a week, and they are beginning to use Welsh at home as far as they are able. Geraint's older brother Hum attends the Welsh unit at the local primary school, and his baby sister Angharad will start there when she is old enough.

Geraint's mother teaches part time, and while she is working he is looked after by a Welsh-speaking friend of the family. He also goes to the local *cylch meithrin* (Welsh-medium playgroup), where he receives individual support from an NNEB-trained helper funded through the Special Needs Referral Scheme. This is an acknowledged community initiative recognized by public funding through the All Wales Mental Handicap Strategy. Geraint is doing well there; he is friendly and confident and everyone knows him. Although he has little speech he responds well to spoken language addressed to him in both Welsh and English. He is in the process of being assessed for a statement, and has been visited in the *cylch meithrin* by an educational psychologist. Unfortunately none of the authority's psychologists are bilingual, so it has been difficult for an accurate assessment of his Welsh language skills to be made.

Geraint's parents have been thinking hard about his future schooling. One choice is the local English-medium school, which is new and has excellent facilities. It has integrated children with learning difficulties before and offers Welsh as a second language through the National Curriculum. The other is the Welsh unit at a nearby primary school, where his brother goes. However, the unit has no remedial or special needs expertise, and none of the teachers feel confident in dealing with children with perceived learning difficulties. Its facilities are also poor compared to those in the English-medium school. Geraint's parents feel very torn. They are very keen that he receives his education in Welsh and goes to school with his siblings, but are having to balance this against the better facilities and support at the English-medium primary school. Ideally, they would like to have both.

CASE STUDY 2: CARYL

Caryl is almost 6 years old and profoundly deaf. She lives on a farm in the heart of Welsh-speaking Dyfed with her parents and her 2-year-old sister Anna, who is also deaf. Caryl's *mamgu* (grandmother) and her Uncle John live in a bungalow on the farm, and her father and uncle work the farm together. Caryl's mother used to work in a bank, but has not worked outside the home since having her children.

Caryl was admitted to the local village primary school, a traditional Welsh-speaking school of twenty-eight children, two terms earlier than normal, at the suggestion of LEA officers. Her early school experience, like her home life, was all through Welsh. She was assisted at school by an unqualified but very keen teacher's aide, and also had weekly visits from the peripatetic teacher for the hearing impaired, who was bilingual. This specialist advised the class teacher and the teacher's aide on appropriate curriculum delivery and methodology.

However, the peripatetic teacher left to take up another post, and even though the authority advertised widely they were unable to appoint a properly qualified Welsh-speaking teacher for the hearing impaired. This meant Caryl would then have an English-speaking speech therapist, and an English-speaking expert teacher. The situation brought to a head discussions that had been going on for some time between the professionals involved with Caryl about her educational future. It was clear that there were no easy answers, and that decisions were having to be made on the basis of personal opinions rather than hard facts or official policies. Having discussed the whole issue of resources, the relationship between hearing community and adult services for the deaf and so on, Caryl's parents were advised to use only English at home with Caryl and her sister.

This obviously had an impact on the life of the extended family, since Uncle John and Mamgu were also required to speak English to the two girls. Mamgu found it particularly hard to adapt to using a less familiar language within the home. The village school, which taught entirely through Welsh, could have found it difficult to change its language to accommodate the perceived needs of Caryl, in which case she would have had to travel 18 miles to an English-medium school in the nearest big town. However, the school managed to cope by employing a bilingual NNEB assistant who can work in English with Caryl alongside the Welsh-speaking class teacher.

Physically, Caryl has been able to stay in her family and community and be educated alongside her peers. But using English at home and school has isolated her from her community and to some extent from her extended family. Within the resources it has available, the authority has offered Caryl the best solution that can be found, but it has been unable to take account of her needs as a particular individual within a particular community. As the experts discovered, there are no easy answers.

CASE STUDY 3: ALED, SIONED AND HELEN

In Gwynedd in north Wales, remedial help for children with specific learning difficulties is offered by a dyslexia unit, which is part of the University of Wales but supported financially by the LEA. A team of peripatetic teachers visit and support children in their schools.

Most of this remedial help is provided in English. This is partly because the majority of the peripatetic teachers are monolingual (since the unit is part of the university, the LEA's policy of requiring all primary school teachers to be bilingual does not apply), and partly because the assessment procedure results in fewer Welsh-speaking children being identified as having specific learning difficulties. One of the criteria used by educational psychologists is the difference between chronological age and 'spelling age'. Both reading and spelling tests are available in Welsh, but the spelling test is not standardized so assessment of literacy skills in Welsh-speaking children is largely based on reading tests. Because Welsh is a more phonetic language than English this may not identify the underlying problems, and Welsh-speaking children with specific learning difficulties are less likely to get on the priority waiting list for specialist support.

Aled comes from a Welsh-speaking background and was seen by the LEA's special needs team when he was 7 because both his teacher and his mother were worried that he was not progressing well at school. His reading age was only a little below average, but he misread small words, and had particular difficulty with concepts involving sequencing such as the days of the week, left and right, and telling the time. The specialist teacher who assessed him thought that Aled would benefit from attending the Dyslexia Unit and asked for an educational psychologist's report which would entitle him to receive this help. However because Aled's score on the Welsh reading test was relatively high, the educational psychologist turned him down. Aled's difficulties in school continued, and three years later his mother pressed for another assessment. This time he was seen by a different educational psychologist, who agreed that Aled had specific learning difficulties; but by then he was 10 and soon to leave the primary school, and it was merely recommended that his difficulties be noted and addressed by the secondary school.

For children from English-speaking backgrounds, such as Sioned and Helen, the issue is not so much assessment as which language should be used for remedial support. Both girls received statements entitling them to specialist help from the Dyslexia Unit, and are withdrawn from lessons at their schools to work with a peripatetic teacher from the unit. Both attend schools where their education is through the medium of Welsh. Sioned's remedial teacher is not Welsh speaking and her extra help is provided in English. One advantage of this is that her parents can help with paired reading work after school, but the disadvantage is that it conflicts with the language used during the rest of Sioned's school day, and does not reinforce her work in the classroom.

In Helen's case, the peripatetic teacher is bilingual and provides most of the remedial help in Welsh, using English only where there is a particular difficulty. This is more consistent with the rest of Helen's education, and reinforces her oral Welsh skills as providing help with specific difficulties. It is more difficult for her English-speaking parents to be involved, but the peripatetic teacher has spent time with Helen's mother helping her to learn the Welsh letter sounds, and the school has found a volunteer helper to work on a one-to-one basis with Helen on her reading.

CASE STUDY 4: LUKE

Luke is 8 years old. He has severe visual impairment and the prognosis is that what vision he has will deteriorate. He moved with his parents and older sister to a smallholding in Welsh-speaking Gwynedd almost two years ago. His father has recently returned to England to take up a new job, but as the family is happy in the country they have decided to stay there with the father coming back at weekends. Luke loves the smallholding. He knows his way around and takes his responsibilities of feeding chickens and collecting eggs very seriously.

When Luke arrived in Gwynedd at 6 he had no Welsh but his parents accepted the LEA offer of a place at the incomers' language centre where children are taught Welsh as a second language by a language specialist teacher (*athro bro*). It is the LEA's policy that children be taught mainly through the medium of Welsh up to 7 and their bilingual skills be developed up to age 11, with the aim that all children should be bilingual by the time they leave primary school.

Luke did very well at the centre and within six weeks was deemed fluent and confident enough in Welsh to start at the local village school, which teaches through Welsh. He has since settled happily there. His bilingual spoken skills are excellent and he is doing well academically and socially. He speaks Welsh with the other children in the classroom and playground, and is often called on to help them with computer work. Luke is particularly good with computers, and the school has software which allows the computers to respond in spoken Welsh so Luke is at no disadvantage because of his lack of sight. He uses the computer for producing his written work.

An advisory teacher for children with visual impairments visits the school once a week. She is teaching Luke Standard English Braille, using Welsh as the medium of instruction. Because Braille uses symbols to represent whole words and common endings as well as to represent individual letters, it needs to be adapted for different languages. Although a Welsh Braille has developed over the years it has been inconsistent with English Braille and therefore difficult to use in a bilingual context. A new standardized Welsh Braille has just been developed which can be integrated with English Braille, so that children will be able to read in both languages. Luke's mother is pleased that he will now have access to the written as well as the spoken word in Welsh. She likes to think that he will stay in the area as an adult, and wants him to be as well integrated as possible into his local community.

(a)   Child's best interests: in line with the spirit and letter of the Children Act 1989, the welfare of the child is paramount. All decisions made by every-one concerned with the child must be made on the basis of what is in her best interests. This then needs to take account of:
(b)   Community: does the child live in a Welsh-speaking community? Will English-medium education exclude her from village life? Where is she likely to live as an adult?
(c)   Siblings: what is the language of the family: What is the language between her brothers and sisters (which is not necessarily the same as the language between children and parents)? Where do the other children in the family go to school?
(d)   Parental choice: what do her parents want for her?
(e)   National Curriculum: every child has the same right to the National Curriculum, and if they are to be disapplied it must be stated and explained in the state ment of special educational needs.
(f)   Resources: are there Welsh-speaking educational psychologists and speech therapists who can assess the child in Welsh: Are there NNEBs trained to be teachers' aides for her: What about her needs in secondary school: Is there a sufficient and ongoing supply of teaching and testing materials in Welsh for her needs in integrated classes?
(g)   Legislation: what does the law say the child should have? What authorities have statutory responsibilities to supply and deliver? Have those responsibilities shifted?

Figure 14.2 Issues for integrated education

CONCLUSION

The case studies provide a basis for discussion rather than a set of answers. They illustrate the complexity and interdependence of the various factors which need to be taken into account when considering the concept of 'inclusive curricula' for a child with disabilities or learning difficulties in Wales. One important aspect of such a curriculum however must be the opportunity for Welsh-speaking children with special needs to receive their education through the medium of Welsh, in their local community. It is difficult to say how far this is happening. As a minority group within a minority group, the needs of Welsh-speaking children with disabilities appear to have received little attention. There is a need for clearer local authority policies on language and special needs, better collection of data to show how far the policies are working, research on the relationship between bilingualism and learning in children with various kinds of difficulties, and resources to support Welsh-medium special education. There is currently no clear evidence as to whether there is an inherent conflict between the cultural/linguistic needs and the educational needs of Welsh-speaking chil-dren with disabilities.

REFERENCES

Cummins, J. (1984) *Bilingualism and special education: issues in assessment and pedagogy*, Clevedon: Multilingual Matters Ltd.

Owen, E. (1993) *Deunyddiau angenion arbennig Canolfan Astudiaethau Addysg*, Aberystwyth: Coleg Aberystwyth, Prifysgol Cymru.

Schools Council Committee for Wales (1972) *Development of Bilingual Education in Wales*, London: Evans/Methuen Educational.

Welsh Office (1981) *Welsh in Schools*, Cardiff: Welsh Office.

Welsh Office (1992a) *All Wales Strategy Framework for Development from 1993*, Cardiff: Welsh Office.

Welsh Office (1992b) *Access to the System*, Cardiff: Welsh Office.

Welsh Office (1993) *Statistics of Education and Training in Wales*, no. 1, Cardiff: Welsh Office.

Chapter 15

Language through the curriculum
Equality of access

Felicity Armstrong

Most schools and colleges in England still take it for granted that all teaching and learning should take place in English. This assumption often leads to some students being excluded from areas of the curriculum and to their own language and culture being devalued and marginalized. Alperton High School, on the contrary, draws on the cultural and linguistic differences of the school community to enhance and create opportunities for inclusive learning for all students. This chapter describes some of the ways in which students gain access to the curriculum through collaborative learning and the threats to these practices from government legislation.

This chapter is about ways in which language can be developed both through the formal and informal planning and delivery of the curriculum, and through the ethos and organization of the school. I shall take a broad definition of language as meaning 'ways of communicating'. This definition can include written and spoken forms of language used by students from different cultural groups as well as verbal and non-verbal communication through the expressive arts. To illustrate the discussion I shall focus on Alperton High School in the London Borough of Brent.

TERMINOLOGY

'Language', categorization and segregation

'Language' is often seen as something separate from the rest of the curriculum but essential for gaining access to it. The assumption seems to be that without possessing some prior 'standard' in the skills of language, learning cannot take place. From this view of language (a discrete and separate skill) can arise a range of practices in schools which place an emphasis on separating the teaching of 'language' from the rest of the curriculum. This can take the form of students being excluded from some ordinary lessons so that they can receive extra help with their 'language' in small groups or individually. Another variation is the organization of students into different sets for learning, those whose language is judged to be inadequate being placed in the lower sets with other students who often carry the label 'special needs'. These students often remain in the 'low' sets years after they have been assessed as needing help with their English (Troyna and Siraj-Blatchford 1993).

'Curriculum'

The term 'curriculum' is another which is used in different and sometimes confusing ways in discussions about learning. It is frequently used to refer to what is taught in lessons. More broadly, the curriculum can be seen as the ethos and organization of the school and the values which these represent. Within this view of the curriculum, which is the one adopted in this chapter, are included all aspects of school life as well as what is taught and learnt in classrooms. This is not, of course, a new way of thinking about the curriculum but with the recent and current emphasis on curriculum as subject areas divided into key stages and levels of attainment, it is timely to re-emphasize an alternative view which sees what is taught explicitly as part of a larger cultural framework. One justification for holding this view is that much of what is taught in classrooms is a reflection of the values of the school and the interests of the community which it serves. This may come into conflict with other interests which are those of national governments, industry or other local and national pressure groups.

I shall argue that language is best learnt in an environment which is shared, relevant and collaborative and which values the cultural and linguistic background of all students. I shall also argue that there is clear evidence that this model is coming under threat from recent government legislation.

LEARNING TOGETHER AT ALPERTON HIGH SCHOOL

In 1993 I met Kay Campbell, who was working on a curriculum development programme in the Art and Design Faculty at Alperton High School as part of her work for the Open University course 'Curriculum, Learning and Assessment'. There are a number of Somali students in her school who have experienced sudden separation from their homes, their culture, their friends and families. Kay wanted to develop a curriculum which would specifically recognize this. During our discussions I became increasingly interested in the language diversity in the school as a whole.

Alperton is situated on two sites – the Lower School on the Ealing Road and the Upper School on Stanley Avenue. It has nearly 1,000 students, most of whom are bilingual and English is their second or third language. More than 10 per cent are Tamil speakers from Sri Lanka, nearly 8 per cent have recently arrived from Somalia, about 60 per cent of students speak Gujarati as their mother tongue and there are also smaller percentages who speak Urdu, Hindi or Arabic as their first language. There are nearly 10 per cent Afro-Caribbean students. There are also students from Cyprus, Turkey, Portugal, Iran and a number of different African countries. The number of white, indigenous English mother tongue speakers is below 10 per cent. The composition of the school population has changed considerably over the past few years and the arrival of Tamil speakers and Somali speakers is recent. A considerable number of these students are refugees.

Access to the curriculum

How do students whose mother tongue is not English and who have only lived in England for a short time gain access to the curriculum? How are these language needs reflected in the ways in which students are grouped for learning? It came as a surprise at first when I realized that English is not regarded as essential for gaining access to the curriculum, although all the class teaching takes place in English. This view means that a lack of English is not seen as a barrier to learning, so there is no question of routinely teaching students English first and then allowing them to follow the full curriculum with the other students. Although some who arrive with little or no English in the higher year groups may initially have an intensive period of English teaching, in general students in the lower age groups are full members of ordinary lessons from the outset. Access to the curriculum is not just a question of understanding. It is linked to the way in which the experiences, language and culture of different students are recognized, valued and included. During my visits I gradually understood how this principle, arising out of the importance given to equality of value and of opportunity in the broader ethos of the school, underpinned the planning and organization in different areas of the curriculum.

Technology

I visited a Year 7 technology lesson. Students were working in twos or threes on different projects which they were planning themselves. They consulted printed guidelines headed 'Technology Portfolio' which explain the requirements of the projects and suggest ways of going about meeting these. Chris Close, the technology teacher, showed me guidelines which are available in Gujarati, Arabic (Fig. 15.1), Somali (Fig. 15.2), and English (Fig. 15.3). He wants to get them translated into other languages. The students read the guidelines to each other, sometimes translating from the English version or into English from another language. They discuss the meaning and interpretation in terms of what they have to do. They exchange ideas for their projects, and talk about size, shape, purpose, materials. During my visit to the lesson Taneesha (12) and Heran (11) worked together to design a box. They are both from Ethiopia. Taneesha has been in England for two years and is able to translate the guidelines into Amharic for Heran who has only been in the UK for eight months. They discussed their ideas in Amharic, breaking off to explain what they were doing in English. A boy hurried past me to get an Arabic version of the 'Technology Portfolio'. 'There's a word we're not sure about,' he said as he returned to his group which included a Tamil student and an Afro-Caribbean student. They were drawing on three languages to develop their project as well as the subject-specific terminology of technology. The only language which they share is English which is the language they use to collaborate in their learning. This way of working which involves planning, negotiating, hypothesizing, and questioning in English differs radically from the more familiar model in which a support teacher or assistant acts as an intermediary – and gatekeeper – between the student and the curriculum.

Chris Close explained the approach:

'The problem is the same for all of them [the students] – it's a problem of access. They need to understand what they have to do, what the objectives are – then they can get on with it. All pupils are different . . . but it does come down to a question of understanding the work. It is not just a question of understanding the language, is it? It's about understanding what is going on. Some just translate everything into their language, but it doesn't mean they understand it . . . We don't have support in the classroom for technology because it is basically a practical subject and pupils work collaboratively. Those who don't know enough English work with someone else who speaks their language, so they can translate where possible. They can copy from the others and gradually they learn. The important thing is that they can gain access to technology.'

In a Year 10 technology class students were working on their GCSE projects. A group of girls worked together using Gujarati as the main language of communication but drawing on the English technical terms. One of them explained: 'We are making a toy car. We are researching the use of different plastics for it and using different techniques and equipment such as injection moulding and vacuum foaming.'

Although students work collaboratively in groups in the GCSE technology class as they do in Year 7, Chris Close explained that there is an important difference: because of pressure to get projects finished on time for assessment purposes, there is not time for everything to be explained carefully in mother tongue languages to those who are not experienced users of English. This means that students who have only recently arrived in this country may struggle in lessons. Some students who were clearly potentially excellent technologists had to be immersed in the English of technology not only so that they could understand the lessons but also because the GCSE

تعليمات

الملاحظات التالية لمساعدتكم ايجاد الوسيله المناسبه لإعداد التقرير الذي لدكمال المشروع . يُطلب منكم تقديم اشارات عن عملكم لغرض الحصول على نتائج جيده في الامتحان الوزاري. ان الاستاذ المشرف والاساتذه الاخرين مستعدين لتقديم المساعدات اللازمه في عملكم .

مكونات البحث

١ ـ غلاف التقرير

٢ ـ صفحه المحتويات (فهرست) . سوف لا تتمكنون من اكمال هذه الصفحه الا بعد انتهاء المشروع .

٣ ـ البحث : يجب ان تحتوي على المعلومات والتفاصيل التي استطعت جمعها

٣ ـ ماذا اكتشفت (تحتوي هذه الفقره على المهارات واكراسات والصور التي استطعت جمعها)

ب ـ من اين حصلت على هذه المعلومات (بما في ذلك اسماء وعناوين الامكان التي زرتها واسماء الاشخاص الذين تحدثت معهم .

٤ ـ ملخص : هذه الفقره يجب ان تحتوي على وصف وتحليل للمشكله التي سنقوم بعلاجها في المشروع (والرجاء التفكير في اختيار الموضوع بعنايه وذلك انه تم بالد عتبار قابلياتك والمواد والاجهزه المتوفره في المدرسه) .

٣ ـ اشرح المشكله التي اخترتها .

ب ـ اشرح توقعاتك لحل المشكله .

Figure 15.1 'Technology portfolio' guidelines, Arabic

امثله :-

- يجب ان تكون لها بعد الدهريين لتفهم شيء ما
- يجب ان تكون جديه
- يجب ان تكون جنديه وملفته للنظر.
- يجب ان تمنو شئ ما من الحدوث.

٥ ـ افكار اوليه : استخدم المخططات والملاحظات لشرح امكانك لحل المشكله (يفضل تقديم اكثر من فكره)

قرر اوا خيار الفكره التي ستستخدم شا واشرح السبب (من ثانيه ـ يجب التفكير بقدراتك والادهزه المتونره في المدرسه.. عكن المناقشه مع الاستذه).

٦ ـ حل المشكله : يجب ان تحتوي علت تفاصيل كامله لحل المشكله ,ما هيي المشكله ومقدار حاجمها (يجب الرسم برقته. وليس من الضروري ان تعمل نموذج في هذه المرحله).

٧ ـ التخطيط : اكتب الخطوات التي ستتبعها لحل المشكله.

٨ ـ نفذ الخطط.

٩ ـ تقيم.. انظر بدقه (للمرحله ٤) واشرح كيف كان حلك للمشكله يطابق معه (قد تحتاج لتطويره). اكتب من التغيرات التي عكن اجراؤها لتطوير التصميم.

ـ ٦ ـ

Figure 15.1 Continued

Saabka Tiknoolaziga

Waxyaalaha soo socdaa, waxay kaa caawin doonaan dariigada aad uga shageyn lahayd qoraalka laga rabo, inuu kaa kaaliyo borojekaaga. Si loo giimeeyo heerka aad ka joogto manhajka qaranka, waxaad u baahan tahay in aad muujiso caddeyn la xarriirta wax gabadkaaga. Lataliyahaaga iyo barayaasha way joogaan si ay kaaya caawiyaan hawshaada.

Hawshaad waa ina ku jiraan

1. *Jaldi/amase xashada dusha kaga sameysan.*

2. *Tusmada Bogga*
   (Boggan ma dhameyn kartid, ilaa inta aad hawsha aad soo gabagbeyneysid).

3. *Baadhitaan*
   Waa inay ku jiraan sharax waxyaalaha aad soo ururisay

   (a) Waxyaalaha aad heshay. (waxaanney ka mid noqon doonto xaashid jantuska, sawiraada lwm)

   (b) Halka aad waxyaalaha ka heshay (waxaanna ka mid noqon doona magacyada, cinwaanada meelaha aad booqtay, magacyada dadka aad la hadashay, iyo cinwaanada buugta aad isticmaashay).

4. *Hordhac*
   Tani waa inay sharax cad ka bixisaa su'aasha aad dooneyso in aad xal ugu hesho borojetkaa. (Waa in aad xalishaa, su'aal aad dareemayso in aad ka bixi karto, marka aad isticmaasha qalabka iyo waxyaalaha dugsiga aaga heli karo).

   (a) Sharax su'aasha aad dooratay
   (b) Sharax waxyaalaha la rajeynayo xalkaago keeno.

   Tussale: waa inay dadka ku caawisaa inay fahmi karaan.
   Tussale: waa inay dadka soo jiidataa si loo eego.
   Tussale: waa inay waxyaloo adag ka sameysnaataa.
   Tussale: waa in aad ka dhowrtaa inay wax ka dhacaan.

5. *Fikradaha Hore*
   Isticmaal sawir iyo xusuus, si aad u sharaxdo fikradaad aad ku xalileyso su'aasha. (marka ay fikradahaagu bataan marks ay ka sii fiican tahay). Asal (color) aad ayuu ugu fiican yahay sawirada aad sameyneysid. Go'aanso fikradda aad istimaalaysid, isla markaa sharax sababtan. (mar labaad aad uga fiirso xirfadahaaga iyo qalabka dugsiga aan ku haysano, waxaa haboon in aad barayaasha ka la tashato.)

6. *Xalkaaga*
   Halkaa waa ion ay jiraan sharax xalkaagu.
   Waxa uu ka sameysan yahay, waxa uu u eg yahay, ints uu leeg yahay iwm, (in aad isticmaasho qaabab sax ah, waxaa laga yaabaa, laakin loo ma baahna in aad sameyso qaab tuse markaad heerkan joogto)

7. *Jaangooyo*
   Waxaad talaabo talaabo u qortaa, waxyaalaha aad isticmaali doontid markaa aad xalileyso su'aashaad.

8. *Qaado Jaangoyadaad*

9. *Qiimeyn*
   Aaad u eeg waxyaalaha aad soo koobtay (marxalada afraad) sharax sida uu xalkaagu u barabr dhigmi lahaa. (waxaa laga yabaa in aad tijaabisid). wax ka qor waxyaalaha qaarkood ee aad dooneyso in aad ka bedheso.

Figure 15.2 'Technology portfolio' guidelines, Somali

Technology Portfolio

The following information is to help you work your way through the paperwork that is required to support your project. In order for you to be credited with a level in the National Curriculum you need to produce evidence of your work. Your Mentor and the other teachers are there to help you with your work.

Your work should contain:

1. *Cover Sheet*

2. *Contents Page*
   (You will not be able to complete this page until you have completed your project.)

3. *Investigation*
   This should contain details of the information you have gathered:

   (a) What you have found out (this can include surveys, leaflets, photos etc.).

   (b) Where your information came from (include names and addresses of places you have visited, names of people you talked to and the titles of any books used).

4. *Brief*
   This should be a clear description of the problem that you are going to tackle for your project. (Please think carefully about your choice of problem; you should consider your abilities and the materials and equipment that we have available in school.

   (a) Describe your chosen problem.
   (b) Explain what your solution should be expected to do!

   e.g. It should help people understand something.
   e.g. It should be attractive to look at.
   e.g. It should be made of a strong material
   e.g. It should prevent something happening.

5. *First Ideas*
   Use sketches and notes to explain your ideas for a solution to the problem (the more ideas the better). Colour is useful in your sketches.
   Decide which idea you are going to use and explain why. (Again think carefully about your skills and the equipment we have in school; perhaps you could discuss this with your teachers.

6. *Your Solution*
   This should contain all the details of your solution: what it is made of, what it looks like, how big it is, etc. (Accurate drawings should be used. You may, but do not have to, produce a model of it at this stage.)

7. *Planning*
   Write out a step by step list of all the things you will have to do to solve your problem.

8. *Carry Out Your Plan!*

9. *Evaluation*
   Look carefully at your brief (stage 4) and explain how your solution matches it (you may need to test it). Write about some of the things that could be changed to improve your design.

Figure 15.3 'Technology portfolio' guidelines, English

examination would be in English. This marks a departure from practices in Years 7–9 where, although the importance of learning English is recognized, the use of other languages is regarded as an important part of gaining access to the curriculum for many students. Assessment in technology at GCSE is also implicitly an assessment of English. Equal access to the curriculum and assessment leading to accreditation will only be possible if students are allowed to submit course work and take exams in the language of their choice.

Art

Kay Campbell explained to me how important the students' own language and culture is in their art and design work. Their projects express their individuality and culture, but the work they do also helps to develop their language skills in English.

An Ethiopian student explained a large tableau she had done as part of her GCSE course work: the theme was 'Myself'.

> 'This is my writing here – it is our script – Ethiopian script. And this is our cultural musical instrument. It is like a drum, but it is different from a modern drum. It is made from animal skin. I've put some records here and over here are some trainers. These are all the things I like. This here is the style of clothing worn by an artist in the group TLC. I am going to write more things in our script. For hobbies, I've put books because I read books about history and politics. I read a lot. I used to read in Amharic but now I can't find the books here so I have to read books in English. I like drawing and writing. In my school in Ethiopia I didn't do art. We have to go to a special school to learn art. This is an Ethiopian church. It is a very beautiful artistic place. I am a Christian – Greek Orthodox – and our church is like this.'

This student is drawing on her own culture, experience and interests in her art work. She includes the script of her mother tongue, her books, her trainers, the clothes worn by a favourite singer and her church back home in Ethiopia. In art and design, students are encouraged to speak about their work in a personal way and to develop a critical vocabulary with which to do so. Kay adopts an approach which helps students build up a vocabulary associated with different places, objects and experiences. Language is an integral part of their work in art and design.

English

English as a subject is part of the Communications Faculty for the purposes of working towards GCSE and A-level examinations. However, all parts of the curriculum are seen as potential areas for the teaching and learning of English. The way in which skills in English are taught in the Communications Faculty also includes an emphasis on the students' own experiences. One lesson I joined started with a reading from *Cider With Rosie* about a child's first experience of school. Students were encouraged to discuss and write about their own early school experiences. These had often been in their country of birth and brought out a variety of feelings and experiences. Discussion moved on to their first memories of school in England and the differences between education systems.

Eileen Sabur, principal teacher and responsible for the Communications Faculty, explained how the English curriculum taps into the students' own knowledge and experience:

'We see a link between capturing their experiences and helping them develop their linguistic skills. For example, when pupils arrive here they are given an opportunity to write in some meaningful way in an autobiographical manner. If we capture what they have to say on the word processor, then we can revisit those pieces as their own vocabulary improves or as they understand more about structure. They write in English but we also encourage pupils to write in their mother tongue because we have so many pupils in the school who can actually interpret and translate for us.'

This approach to the English curriculum is promoted and supported by Brent. It reflects, Eileen explained, 'the tradition in Brent of a commitment to the way in which ideas and beliefs can be translated into classroom practice'.

But didn't this approach to teaching English come into conflict with government policies on teaching and assessment for English?

'The sort of approach we are advocating will make more competent writers in the long run. Unfortunately time now has to be made to carry out the government assessments. It's an interruption in their progress. The proposed introduction of an examination with the balance between 30 per cent course work and 70 per cent examination is a massive change from 100 per cent course work. It is going to make a very big difference to those whose access to the written text in English is limited for whatever reason. We have had many young people who have been able to develop their writing skills in English without being dependent on an outside written stimulus because they have been using the stimulus of their own experience. They are going to be very disadvantaged by the introduction of assessment by examination.'

Pankaj Gulab, headteacher of Alperton, explained another aspect of the threat to course work in English:

'Much of the course work carried out at Alperton High School has not only greatly contributed to improving the students' English and language skills but has had an important role in helping students write about themselves and their experiences. Much of the counselling work with refugee students has occurred in the process of developing course work based on individual experience. When we go back to, say, thirty per cent course work, it's going to affect a lot of this work – 30 per cent course work has contributed to the counselling and socialization of students because they are able to discuss and write about their experiences. If there is greater focus on exam work and less on course work, this could be lost. We are going to have to acclimatize our students to straight exams which means we will have to take time out of the curriculum and focus on that.'

'Minority' or 'modern'?

English has the status of a *lingua franca* at Alperton. It is the only common language within the school and newcomers need to learn it. However, great importance is given to the learning of other languages.

Gujarati, Hindi, Urdu, French, German and English are all taught in the school. Hindi and Urdu are not formal options but are included as examination options for those who have one of these as a first language. In addition students have the opportunity of studying Tamil at the 'weekend school' run on the school premises by Tamil groups. Although Tamil and Arabic are not part of the taught curriculum, students are encouraged to develop these languages and take GCSEs and 'A' levels in them.

In a report of the study of a group of 3,000 children in twenty comprehensive schools carried out over a period of five years, Smith and Tomlinson (1989) argued that 'minority languages in Britain have long been regarded, along with their speakers, as being of low status. They seldom appear on the modern language curriculum for all pupils and are thereby implicitly devalued' (p.93).

The importance given to the study and use of mother-tongue language at Alperton is in sharp contrast to current practices in most schools which promote English as the only linguistic currency of value in school, with French and German as high-status 'modern' languages. The use of the term 'minority languages' for Asian languages in contrast to 'modern languages' is devaluing, marginalizing and white Eurocentric. In fact, the framework of the Education Reform Act 1988 allows for schools to offer Asian languages as foundation subjects and includes them in a list of acceptable 'modern' languages *if they also offer a 'modern' European language*. Students could therefore study an Asian language and literature as part of the 70 per cent of classroom time allocated for the study of the National Curriculum (Smith and Tomlinson 1989). There is no requirement, however, for this stipulation to be reversed and this must mean that in many schools some students are discriminated against. The lower status accorded to Asian and other non-European languages is therefore institutionally sanctioned.

A threat to equal opportunities?

The central position occupied by students' own language and culture is an integral part of the very explicit equal opportunities policy of the school. However, changing conditions in terms of curriculum, assessment and accreditation could have an impact on the balance of what is included in the curriculum. Mr Gulab explained that the exam boards are now cutting down on the syllabuses they are willing to offer or are changing syllabuses: 'Some examination boards are not offering subjects like Gujarati in which we get 70–100 per cent passes in the A–C grades, and languages like Tamil and Arabic are going to be even less supported by the exam boards. Last year we got 13 'A' grades out of 17 entries.'

SUPPORT

We have seen how students support each other in lessons and how the individual and broader cultural experiences of students are acknowledged, in lessons and in the broad curriculum of the school. This is in contrast with models of support (which also exist at Alperton) based on a teacher or learning support assistant being present in lessons or withdrawing from classrooms.

Brent Language Service

Other support comes from 'Section 11' teachers who work for the Brent Language Service. Section 11 funding was set up to provide language teaching and support for 'new commonwealth students' only. This meant that at Alperton High School many of the students who need support from this source have not been entitled to it because they come from Somalia, Zaire, Iran and other non-commonwealth countries. In fact recent legislation has slashed the government contribution to Section 11 funding from 75 per cent to 57 per cent but removed the restriction on its use for 'commonwealth' students only. The amount of teaching hours allocated under Section 11 funding falls far short of the true level of need. In practice at Alperton support teachers have worked with whoever needs their support. As one teacher explained:

> 'What happens is that overtly our records have shown that we are working with 'new commonwealth students' but covertly we are helping those with the greatest need and if that happens to have been students who come from non-commonwealth countries that is neither here nor

there and this is something that is just taken for granted because it is ridiculous and discriminatory to have that kind of label.'

The brief for teachers from the Brent Language Service is to enable students to gain access to the curriculum. The policy is to support students in ordinary lessons without withdrawing them, although there are occasions when newly arrived students with very little knowledge of English are given intensive help in small groups. The Language Service support teachers work across the curriculum. Anoma Siriwardena explained some of the issues:

'When we have assessed the needs of new students we work with the mainstream subject teachers inside the classroom. We may try and pre-pare material in advance which will help students understand the content of the lesson. We really focus on getting the concepts across. Conceptually new arrivals are at the same stage as their peers so they do have some frustrations if you simplify everything – because they are quite capable of understanding an idea – they just can't express it in English. So if the concept is got across you can actually work on putting that into English. I work in science, humanities and English in Years 10 and 11 and my colleague works in maths. We work on anything from terminology and all the different discourses necessary for those subjects, to exploring techniques in terms of what is required of you in terms of certain questions. Very often students understand the content of what is required but they don't understand how they should present that information. For example, they don't understand the words "discuss" and "compare". We have to work on the skills involved in actually breaking down infor-mation, reproducing it, understanding and responding . . . There is a lot more pride and an emphasis on the advantages of being bilingual rather than seeing it as a disadvantage or an obstacle. The idea that somehow a first language impeded your learning in a second language belongs to the early 1970s. Now being bilingual – certainly in Brent – is the norm.'

Anoma described how she supported students in their humanities lesson:

'They have been doing the Arab–Israeli conflict for GCSE. I have been sitting there with the students going through the maps and handouts the teacher has prepared for the whole class. I can adapt these materials for the class teacher to use. There is a lot of source material which is very difficult. The students need the same material but in a more simplified language. You can't simplify the idea but you can help them to under-stand the key words so you can give them a glossary. You have to remember that if these students were given the chance to answer the question in, say, Tamil they could probably do it brilliantly. In making the glossary for a particular unit of work we pick out groups of words relating to certain ideas: "conflict" and "peace", for example, which are the main themes of this whole unit. We talk about the Arab–Israeli conflict, conflict in South Africa and in Northern Ireland. We look at words to do with settlements, policies, decisions . . . and discuss synonyms and associated words such as "strife", "freedom" and "independence", "persecute", "tolerate".'

Changes in government funding may mean that students will lose the kind of language support they need in order to gain access to the curriculum. One support teacher explained:

'The government is cutting the funding and increasing the access, saying: "Right, you can help anybody you like now because we know you are doing it anyway, but at the same time we are going to cut the funding to the bone." This means that authorities like Brent will have to supplement the Section 11 funding – already very inadequate – and opted-out schools will have to hire a language support teacher.'

Support for learning

'If three people all stab someone at the same time how are we going to know whose blow actually killed the victim?'

This is how an English lesson on *Julius Caesar* begins for a small group of Year 9 students who are experiencing some difficulties in learning for a variety of reasons. It is a 'support' lesson but it is taking place in a separate classroom.

The lesson continues:

'He has killed an animal. No, not to eat. He is going to do something with it. Caesar has been disturbed by the storm and he has ordered the priests to make a sacrifice to the Gods.'

The next ten minutes are spent discussing the different meanings of the word 'sacrifice' and what forms it can take in the different religions represented around the table. The vocabulary is extended to include 'ritual', 'soothsayer', 'palm reading', 'omen', etc.

The group take turns to read parts from the play. Progress in actually getting through the text is slow because the main purpose of the lesson today is to discuss words and concepts and relate them to the students' own experience. Ms Katona, coordinator for learning support, explained that all students in Year 9 had to study *Julius Caesar* ready for the SATS in the summer even if they had only recently arrived from Somalia or some other part of the world. A Shakespeare play was obligatory and the choice was between *Romeo and Juliet*, *A Midsummer Night's Dream* and *Julius Caesar*. The students in this group studied the same texts as those in the ordinary lesson but they were withdrawn so that language and concepts could be discussed. In an ordinary lesson a reading of *Julius Caesar* would teach them very little. The pressure of SATS, Ms Katona explained, means that it is difficult to slow the pace of the lesson down sufficiently to meet the needs of all students.

At first this may appear to be just an example of students being withdrawn from ordinary lessons – and hence excluded from them – because they are experiencing difficulties in learning. The difference is that this kind of grouping is seen as a continuum of support in specific subject areas and one which is reluctantly adopted. There is a determination to cut class sizes so that the principles of in-class and collaborative support can be maintained and reasserted and the withdrawal of students the rare exception. Unfortunately the pressure imposed on staff and students by SATS at the end of Year 9 and the re-introduction of more formal assessment at GCSE may be endangering these principles.

The student perspective

Students I spoke to had the following comments to make about their experiences of learning and the kind of support they had received:

> 'My country is Sri Lanka. I've been here one year. I lived in Sri Lanka before. My friends help me when I don't understand.'

> 'I speak Tamil. I've been here one year and eight months. I like it here but the language is very difficult and the subjects are different. My friends help me. I feel I have enough help. No, I've never been in a special English class.'

> 'I am from Somalia. I came here eight months ago. Some of us here knew each other in Somalia. When I came to this school I felt very happy. Yes, the language is difficult. School is very different here. When I don't understand in the lesson, I speak in Somali or Arabic and other Somalis help me.'

DISCUSSION

In this chapter I have tried to show how one school recognizes and draws upon personal, linguistic and cultural differences through the ordinary curriculum as a means of developing students' language skills. At Alperton the importance of learning English is recognized, but the development of collaborative learning through the matter-of-course use of mother tongue languages is integral to the curriculum. The central position given to the different cultures and languages in the school community and the value system implicit in this position arise initially not out of some pedagogical decision about teaching 'language' but out of the raw necessity of meeting the needs of a culturally diverse community and the equal opportunities policies and practices of the school. A fundamental part of those practices is the way in which students are organized into inclusive groups for learning based on equality of value and opportunity. The way in which language is used by students working collaboratively and individually to gain access to the curriculum has developed out of these principles.

In spite of a commitment to an inclusive curriculum for all students at Alperton, inclusive practice is being challenged from outside by government policies. The introduction of SATS, assessment by examination in English and other subjects, the reduction in Section 11 funding and the publication of league tables could undermine equal opportunities policies at Alperton High School.

REFERENCES AND FURTHER READING

Donald, J. and Rattansi, A. (1992) *Race, Culture and Difference*, London: Sage Publications.

Hart, Susan (1992) 'Collaborative classrooms', in T. Booth, W. Swann, M. Masterton and P. Potts (eds) *Learning for All 1: Curricula for Diversity in Education*, London: Routledge.

Smith, D. and Tomlinson, S. (1989) *The School Effect*, London: Policy Studies Institute.

Troyna, B. and Siraj-Blatchford, I. (1993) 'Providing support or denying access? The experiences of students designated as "ESL" and "SN" in a multi-ethnic secondary school', *Educational Review*, 45 (1).

Chapter 16

YT? Youth Training in the visual arts

The Sam Morris Project

Petra Pryke

In this chapter Petra Pryke describes how she 'became a teacher' on the Sam Morris Project based in an old tabernacle hall at Shepherds Bush, London, and her experience of developing a BTEC course in Art and Design for young people on the Youth Training Scheme. Her account describes the constraints on creativity and imagination which can be imposed by such schemes, in contrast to the opportunities which have been made available to young people on the Sam Morris Project.

'If you don't work harder you'll end up on a youth training scheme.'

This is not an unusual threat to teenagers nearing the end of their school career. The idea of government training has a reputation which conjures up images of exploitation, futility and a dead end. Yet if you are 16, and leave school with few or no GCSE qualifications, you may be 'unemployable' but you cannot claim income support or any other benefit. You have to wait until you are 18. Meanwhile the government is obliged to offer you a place on a Youth Training Scheme. You may have to go on a waiting list to get on the course you want. In this case you are entitled to a bridging loan for up to eight weeks, though none of the trainees or prospective trainees I have spoken to knew of this entitlement and often the wait is much longer.

If you do get onto a scheme you will receive a weekly allowance of £35 (£29.50 if you are 16), plus travel if you live more than three miles away from the training centre. You will also get eighteen days' paid holiday a year plus statutory holidays and sick pay. You will become known as a trainee. This is a nebulous category but it means you do not have the rights of either the employed or the unemployed, or of students.

There are about 288,000 youth trainees in Britain today. Who are they, what are they given in their training and what happens to them?

YT is funded mainly by government. It operates through Training and Enterprise Councils (TEC's) and Local Enterprise Companies (LEC's). At a local level TEC's or LEC's organise the training or, more commonly, contract with YT providers to run the training programmes. YT providers may be Local Authorities, Chambers of Commerce, voluntary organisations, Colleges of Further Education, private employers, industrial training groups or private training providers.

THE SAM MORRIS PROJECT

Sam Morris was born in Grenada and received part of his education in Barbados. He came to England during the Second World War as Liaison Officer to Sir Leavy Constantine between the Caribbean and the British force. After the war he worked as private secretary to Kwame Nkrumah of Ghana. He encouraged and stressed the importance for black people to create their own libraries and exhibitions. There is a Sam Morris Centre in east London with a permanent exhibition about black history. He was Assistant High Commissioner in Grenada. In the 1960s Sam Morris was deputy chair of the Commission for Racial Equality. He lived in Hammersmith and was an active member of the Hammersmith and Fulham Council for Racial Equality.

The early days

The project is a youth training scheme set up by the Council for Racial Equality with the Manpower Services Commission under the Youth Opportunities Programme in 1979. It offered training in bag-making to about twelve 16 to 21-year-olds of mixed ability and race. The scheme followed the apprenticeship model of training, instructors and trainees working together to supply goods (bags, pencil cases and roly-poly bags) ordered by the Red Cross. My friend Carol was employed by the scheme in 1982 to start a new training programme in knitwear. She was later promoted to site manager as well. The following year training in photography, graphics/silkscreen printing and leather crafts were also on offer. Sales and services to outside organizations and companies decreased and more emphasis was given to training. In about 1984, following given criteria the trainers compiled currricular and assessment procedures which were validated by the Royal Society of Arts (RSA) and City & Guilds (C&G). The project could then award vocational training qualifications to trainees. Due to new strategies in funding within the Manpower Services Commission in 1986 the project became managed by Hammersmith and Fulham Training Services (the training branch of Hammersmith and Fulham Business Resources). Silkscreen printing became a department in its own right and training in leather crafts ended. In 1990 Hammersmith and Fulham Training Services merged with Hammersmith and Fulham Business Resources (HFBR).

Meanwhile, on a national level, the Youth Opportunities Programme (YOPs) became Youth Training Services (YTS) in 1986. Three years later this was changed to Youth Training (YT). And in 1990 the main government funding body for HFBR known as the Training Agency was superseded by CENTEC (Central London Training and Enterprise Council).

Recent history

The Sam Morris Project is one of three training centres within HFBR. The others offer training in information technology, floristry, hairdressing and retail. The organization has a hierarchichal managerial system consisting of managing director, site managers, work placement officers, administrative staff and trainers. Like Carol, site managers are also instructors. Over the last few years the amount of administrative workload increased for managers, which restricted their teaching time. They became involved in constructing detailed proposals for schemes that might bring in new funding. Cutbacks in 1992 saw the HFBR restructured. One of the training sites was relocated to head office and this involved the redundancy of a few instructors. Two managers/instructors, incuding Carol at Sam Morris, were made redundant. A 'floating manager' was employed to oversee all the YT work within the organization.

MY TIME AT SAM MORRIS

When I first knew the Sam Morris Project in 1989, it was offering training in graphic design, photography, silkscreen printing and knitwear design. The full-time graphics instructor was on holiday and I was asked to cover and was employed as a graphics consultant. I had not long become a self-employed graphic artist working mostly with a DTP Apple Mac system from home. I had no teaching experience or teaching qualifications. The project was well equipped and was soon to have its own Apple Mac and printer. The building was a converted tabernacle hall belonging to and situated behind the Baptist Church near Shepherds Bush Green. Photography and screen printing workshops were downstairs and a fire escape access led upstairs to the graphics and knitwear workshops. In those days trainees spent their first four months studying each subject for a month. They chose two areas in which they wanted to specialize. They would then alternate month by month in each subject area, working on projects, building a portfolio of work and achieving all that was necessary to complete their vocational qualifications. The different subjects complemented each other and this gave the trainees a wide base of skills and helped to determine visual understanding. We operated in a similar way to a foundation course at an art school.

Because Sam Morris's location was isolated from the other sites and because of Carol's ability to draw all the instructors together in the working of the project, we operated with a sense of autonomy and appeared more like a cooperative than a management organization. At the end of the day we had to answer to the main IIFBR office for funding, and meet all the criteria laid down by the government bodies, but as much as we could we would make decisions or put forward ideas which were either supported, or not interfered with, by head office.

THE INSTRUCTORS

Carol had studied knitwear design at Nottingham. There she met Simon, a fine art student who was to set up and run the photography department at Sam Morris. Marvena had joined the project in 1988 to help Carol in her administrative work. She also helped trainees to fill in forms and instructed in various office skills such as preparing CVs. Later, as Simon became involved with his own work in the film industry, he job-shared with Patrice, a professional photographer, and also with Andy, an MA photography student who had previously been teaching at a secondary school in Brixton. A young Chelsea Art School MA graduate in printmaking ran the screen printing course. Others joined – all friends and ex-art students and all commercially active in their particular subject. We were employed on a part-time/job-share basis or as freelance consultants. In 1990 I job-shared for a year with Henry, another practising graphic designer, when the full-time instructor took maternity leave. This continued when the instructor left for another job.

Looking back, I see myself involved and working with a bunch of (mostly) white middle-class ex-art school people in their late 20s. Some of us had been involved in the London art scenes of punk music, film making, designing and painting. More often than not these scenes were founded in and proliferated from a 'street-level' life style of pubs, drugs, politics, and bed-sits or short-let housing. We were all involved in various projects, or freelance work, but none of us had settled with a 'real' job. Some of us had been back to college or were following part-time postgraduate courses. Some had teaching or social work experience. I remember there being a sense of us having arrived at respectability when starting work at Sam Morris. We had expertise to pass on and a structure which gave us some power and status. Unconsciously, like children playing, we were constructing a mini art school and continuing the art education philosophy which we had known and which some of us (myself included) had once reacted against.

Need for teacher training

Although I was quickly gaining confidence in my ability to teach, it bothered me that I was unqualified. Until 1989 there was funding to register us all for a C&G direct training certificate. We were also given a three-day course in counselling. The C&G course was simple and unchallenging. Educational psychology was simplified to the point of naivety and in a way that prevented criticism or debate. So official guidance was given to me but I found it difficult to accept. Perhaps this arrogance illustrates the way I worked at the project – a bit overconfident and idealistic and from a background which was based on upsetting given structures in order to explore new ones.

TRAINEES

To get onto a YT course you have to be referred by a local careers officer. A school leaver may show an aptitude for art, but not have the qualifications to apply for art school. From what I have seen visual knowledge is given little priority in secondary education compared with other subjects. It is even separated from numeracy and literacy. This segregation is a great failing – language and numeracy rely a lot on visual understanding and vice versa. It amazes me that typography is not taught as part of learning to read. Understanding print and lettering and the technical possibilities in which they can be organized on a page must surely be an enormous benefit in understanding the process of reading. It seems common that pupils who find English and maths hard to deal with do well in their art class. And it seems that this ability is automatically labelled 'unacademic', 'slow learning' or 'vocational'. My own secondary school streamed those who didn't achieve results learning Latin into learning pottery. Taught as a subject that doesn't see itself as marginalized, pottery is a highly technical subject requiring a lot of scientific knowledge. But those who studied it at my school were already on the road to being categorized as low achievers. Things haven't changed and a YT scheme in design training is oversubscribed with young people caught in this tangle.

Recruitment and selection

Friday mornings at the project is a 'come in and look around' for career office referrals. Those who are interested then apply for a formal interview. For this they must complete a set project and present a portfolio of other work if they have any. They are also asked to write about two examples of graphic design, which they read aloud at the interview. The project requires them to go to the National Gallery, look around and make notes and sketches and produce a poster advertising the gallery, giving information about where it is, what it is and when it is open. Not all applicants come straight from school. Some have gone to FE college to retake GCSEs, but have got nowhere. Some have started art and design courses but are unhappy with the way these seem to be a continuation of art classes at school. It seems that such colleges have poor equipment and there is little or no evidence of computer training, technical processes or, as I have already mentioned, any knowledge of typography.

It is very rare for an applicant who has completed the required work to be rejected. But some just don't turn up. The work shown at interview varies enormously. It may consist of very classroom-guided drawings glued onto pieces of faded sugar paper with hand written labels giving the name, class and project title or it may be sophisticatedly executed compositions. Applicants often illustrate cult themes like graffiti (the most common), hiphop music, rave iconography and video game characters.

STANDARDIZATION, QUALIFICATION AND VALIDATION – NVQ AND BTEC

The government set up the National Council for Vocational Qualifications (NCVQ) in 1986. This was an attempt to standardize and validate awards as National Vocational Qualifications (NVQ). Much of the Council's success in implementing standardization depended on the Business and Technology Education Council (BTEC). This was a non-departmental public body, issuing awards with the Education Secretary acting as guarantor and the Department for Education having an influential say in decision making. BTEC pioneered the model of NVQ and after ten years of existence it has become a recognized qualification by FE colleges, universities, schools and employers. From October 1993 BTEC became independent with limited company and charity status, competing directly with the other two major vocational award bodies, C&G and RSA Examination Boards.

In the early 1990s CENTEC gave directives that all YT qualifications must be NVQ Level 1 and 2. We had to rush to find the courses which would give the relevant qualification to the training we offered. C&G in Graphic Design rated as a Level 1 and BTEC First Diploma was provisionally accepted as rating a Level 2. The C&G involved an immense amount of technical expertise and equipment (hands-on experience with electronic guillotines, off-set litho printing presses, photography and laboratory skills), some of which we could not offer. We taught the modules we could and relied on personal contacts in the printing world to take the trainees on for day training sessions to cover the other modules. In the circumstances we did well but at the time it all seemed a bit botched. HFBR paid Kingsway college a fee of £1,000 to use their accredited BTEC syllabus and the facility for final assessment and examination.

SPECIAL TRAINING NEEDS – CATEGORIES A, B, C

At the end of their initial interview with a careers officer a young person may be unendorsed or endorsed as being of A, B or C ability. An unendorsed person is known as a 'basic' and they are considered able to follow a NVQ Level 2 (or above) confidently without any extra support. The 'A', 'B' or 'C' endorsements are as follows:

> You are seen to have a 'special training need' in YT if you: 'have a training need arising from a disability or other disadvantage which will significantly impair your ability to undergo a successful course of training' (*TEC OA, Words and Expressions, p. 105*) This could include literacy and numeracy difficulties, physical or sensory impairment, mental illness, learning difficulties, chronic ill health, emotional and behavioural problems, difficult personal circumstances, problems associated with prolonged absence from work, problems associated with drug/solvent/ alcohol abuse and difficulties with English because it is not your first language (*TEC STN*).

> A: you require Preparatory Training before you join mainstream YT;
> B.   you have no realistic prospect of achieving an Approved Qualification at NVQ Level 2 standard;
> C: you could get an Approved Qualification at NVQ Level 2 if you had significant additional support and help (*TEC OA, para B37.3*).

If you have a literacy need and/or a numeracy need 'which significantly impairs' your opportunities in the labour market (*TEC OA, Words and Expressions*), you may be endorsed as belonging to (*TEC OA, para 36*):

Category L – you need foundation level literacy training; and/or
Category N – you need foundation level numeracy training

Rumour has it that these endorsements are the results of 5-minute aptitude tests. The careers officer I spoke to said they were a result of a 40-minute interview. He felt unhappy about the procedure: 'I am here to guide not to assess, but at the same time I have to give some fair report about the young person's ability. They are thinking about bringing in isometric tests for endorsement, which I am opposed to. Then I will be an assessor not an adviser.'

The careers officer supplies the YT scheme with an endorsement certificate often adding comments or additional information about the young person's training needs. Figure 16.1 is a copy of the Career Officers' YT Training Endorsement form. Figure 16.2 shows the CENTEC Training Endorsement notes for guidance for careers officers.

Training projects get extra funding for Bs and Cs, so they are not discouraged from YT schemes, but the fact that these endorsements determine what level a person is allowed (funded) to achieve can in my mind amount to discrimination. Furthermore the NVQ validation of design curricula which are Level 1 and Level 2 is as yet incomplete and muddled.

Mark was a category B who had been at the project for four years. He had opted to do graphics and was talented but found it impossibly difficult to

cènTEC

Endorsing
office copy

YT TRAINING ENDORSEMENT

TO: _____

ADDRESS: _____

_____

_____

_____

FROM: _____

_____

_____

_____

TEL: _____

Scheme Title _____

This form introduces/Thank you for contacting me about _____

_____

who is being considered for a place on your _____

_____ programme.

If this young person starts on the programme, you must retain this form as confirmation of my endorsement.

Additional information on the young person training needs.

_____

_____

_____

CATEGORY OF TRAINEE

Please tick box.

A. Level 1 Preparatory   □   N. Number power   □

B. Up to Level 1 Achiever   □   L. Wordpower   □

C. Level 2+ Achiever   □

Comments.

_____

_____

_____

Any enquiries regarding this endorsement should be directed

to _____ at this office.

Signature _____

Position _____

Date _____

ENDORSING OFFICE STAMP

Figure 16.1 CENTEC YT training endorsement

Source: Careers office

communicate to anybody and was easily confused by instructions. He was angry and bitter that after so many years at the project he was only allowed to achieve a Level 1 because of his endorsement. The BTEC only applied to graphics. There was no NVQ qualification for knitwear design so that area was closed down. Screen printing could only qualify as part of the C&G

cĕnTEC

TRAINING ENDORSEMENT NOTES

Programme details must be specific with the full course title, N/VQ level and reference number.

CATEGORY OF TRAINEE

LEVEL 1 PREPARATORY

This category includes trainees who need some preparatory training before entering a vocational programme leading to a N/VQ Level 1 (eg, Wordpower and Numberpower).

UP TO LEVEL 1 ACHIEVER

This category includes trainees who are working towards an N/VQ Level 1.

NCVQ LEVEL 1 DEFINITION.

* Competence in the performance of a range of varied work activities, most of which may be routine and predictable.

LEVEL 2+ ACHIEVERS

This category includes trainees who will achieve a Level 2 or above at the end of their prescribed training plan.

NCVQ LEVEL 2+ DEFINITION.

* Competence in a significant range of varied work activities, performed in a variety of contexts. Some of the activities are complex or non-routine and there is some individual responsibility or autonomy.

* These definitions of the NVQ Levels provide a general guide and are not intended to be definitive.

CenTEC will provide the Careers Services with a full portfolio of qualifications on offer at each YT provider in the cenTEC area.

Figure 16.2 CENTEC training endorsement notes

Source: Careers office

Graphic Design and Production certificate. The other B candidates apart from Mark had all opted for screen printing so they were happy about taking the C&G as there was no other choice. We put Mark through the Level 1 course and meanwhile set about re-endorsing him so he could be registered for BTEC. Mark passed both exams. Meanwhile the C&G course lost its NVQ validation and the HFBR organization was restructuring to meet huge cuts in funding. Consequently the screen printing section was closed down.

TEACHING BTEC

Once again ideas of qualification and value rear their contradictory heads. I feel (as I did when I originally 'became a teacher') as if what I am doing is more credible because it involves teaching a respected qualification. The trainees definitely see themselves as working towards something worth while – and this defeats the YT reputation. We had a big party when the first BTEC trainees completed their exam. All of them passed, some with merits and distinctions. At the party the certificates were presented to jubilant faces and amidst great cheers and screams of excitement. Mark was in tears with delight.

I am against systems that are preoccupied with the value of qualifications as they often operate at the expense of people's real activities and experiences. But here I could see those systems work in giving the young people a sense of worth. They were defying all those who had told them that they were too stupid to achieve anything. However a system with such strict and narrow structures of value can only give rise to problems.

In many ways following a defined curriculum makes teaching easier. However, with clearly stated projects and step-by-step handouts covering all the areas required by BTEC, teaching could become mechanical. A defined curriculum has the potential to usurp individual training plans. I often hear myself saying 'The BTEC examiner wants you to do this' or 'You must do this for your BTEC' but ironically this has allowed me to introduce some spontaneous and diverse ideas which I don't have to justify because they can be given in a BTEC context.

When we 'bought' the BTEC syllabus from a further education college, Henry (my job sharer) and I were surprised that syllabuses were so sacred and protected. We had assumed that all educators were happy to share their ideas and curricula. Perhaps because of the copyright mentality we encountered, we felt an atmosphere of competition between ourselves and Kingsway College, a sense that we had to prove ourselves. We also felt that our existing syllabus was better and more interesting than the one we were now obliged to take on. We rewrote the BTEC course, partly in order to redesign the layout, it looked so shabby and amateur, and partly to incorporate some of our own ideas. Sam Morris Project now had four Apple Macs and a scanner, so we added a new module with deliberately chosen high-tech descriptions of what the course would cover in desk top publishing training. The computers were our main strength and we knew that Kingsway gave their students little opportunity to learn desk top publishing. Our results for the following year (1993) were excellent.

Ever since I began teaching YT I have had in the back of my mind the question: what is the difference between 'education' and 'training'? During my first month at Sam Morris I was asked to teach a day seminar at another YT scheme in north-east London. The subject was women in graphic design, and I was talking to female trainees on the design training scheme and to girls about to leave school who were looking around to see what training was on offer. The place horrified me. The training site was a purpose built factory with clocking-in machines and alarm bells that sounded lunch and tea breaks. The Design Department gave basic skills to a bored bunch of young people. Not one element of their training involved teaching them to think critically, working on projects to build a portfolio, thinking about what graphic design was and its relation to art and commerce. Above all the course did not attempt to develop creativity and imagination. These words were contentious to me when I was at art school. They were associated with eighteenth- and nineteenth-century Romanticist notions of innate god-given artistic genius. These notions opposed, among other things, social and political contexts, skills, art criticism and art history. Now I felt I had gone full circle – this government scheme was in my opinion unable to give anyone a career in graphics. To be a graphic designer you need to be involved in a creative process and creativity is not a skill that can be trained, it is something that can be developed only through a process of looking, thinking, reading, discussing, writing, making – in short, education.

WORK PLACEMENT

'HFBR plays a significant role in providing employers with a first class training service', wrote Barbara Hamilton, Managing Director, in HFBR's 1991/2 annual report. YT and BTEC training can be received wholly or partly, while the trainee is working for an employer. This is called a work placement. The employer and trainee are continually monitored to make sure that the trainee is learning everything required for NVQ certification. If necessary the trainee comes back to the project once a week to obtain training that is not covered at the work placement. As a 'trainee status' employee the trainee gets £35 from the employer (i.e. their YT training allowance). The YT centre tops this up to about £50 and pays travel expenses. After about three months if all is going well, the trainee achieves 'employed status' and receives a minimum of £80 from the employer and nothing from the centre. The trainees retain YT status until they achieve their NVQ. While they are in 'trainee' or 'employed' status the training centre is funded the same amount for the trainee, so obviously it is profitable for the training centre to have as many trainees as possible in the work place. Most of the trainees are keen for work largely because they will get more money. We also take on 'real' jobs at the project. The project used to design and screen print publicity material for events organized by the Council for Racial Equality. The Shepherds Bush Homeless Families Project is local, and we have produced information leaflets and publicity material for them. Occasionally I will hand over a job that I have been given to one or two of the trainees. This often means more work for the instructor, but the trainees benefit, and it prepares them for work placement and looks good in their portfolio.

POST SAM MORRIS: EMPLOYMENT OR FURTHER EDUCATION

At the moment work placements in graphics are hard to find. Most employers do not have the time to train people. Often they want trained people for little money. I am against rushing trainees into employed status. After a year at the project most trainees are ready and would benefit from working in a real job. Those who have been placed usually become fully fledged employees. But over the last few years many trainees achieved full-time employment only to be made redundant later. Since the introduction of BTEC more trainees want to go on to further education and continue with BTEC Level 3. This year half of our BTEC candidates got places in colleges.

Once trainees are qualified and their two years of allocated time is complete, that's it, they are off our books. The time allocated used to be more flexible – we could apply for an extra year or more if we felt a trainee needed it. But trainees who did take longer were unhappily self-conscious about being 'behind' everyone else.

Over the years there has always been a fairly balanced racial and gender mix. From when the project started right up to the first few years when I began teaching, the group included students of all abilities. I recently talked to Carol about her time managing the project. She regrets the dissolution of all-ability: 'The trainees supported each other – the more able supported the less able'. The project sees fewer young people who need a lot of support as these are now referred to Initial Training Schemes as a result of the endorsement proceure. The introduction of NVQ qualifications dictated specialization. Carol saw how the demands of NVQs resulted in employing 'freelance consultants' to the project, which on one hand introduced a new wave of specialization and professionalism but on the other was killing the intimacy of catering for very individual needs. The project now only offers BTEC training in graphics and photography. Whenever possible I devise projects that involve both departments working together and learning from each other. But they are one-off events; the curriculum makes it impossible to sustain amalgamation. The trainees who studied all the subjects offered at the Sam Morris Project prior to NVQ achieved a far greater understanding of design and production.

Figure 16.3 Tom

TWO TRAINEES

Tom (18)

'I hated college. It was a waste of time, I could have gone straight into BTEC. Art was the best subject at school. I got an A, but no one told me what I could do with it. I didn't know what graphics was. I live at home. I've got two younger brothers and a younger sister. I've got an older sister. She's 22. My older sister, she's mentally handicapped. I've always known her like that, and looked after her. I want to get out of education and work. A small design company would be best, and earn money to buy records and clothes. Some of my mates are involved in burglaries and drugs. My mates reckon that YT is the last resort – for dossers, but I don't care. I want to get a good grade at BTEC, something to be recognized by an employer. I reckon I'm friendly and I'll talk to anyone. You lot have taught me a lot. I like the smallness of Sam Morris, it makes a good team.'

Tom came to Sam Morris from a college where he was retaking English and Maths GCSEs. He is quick and articulate. He is gregarious and street wise.

Figure 16.4 Jenny

Jenny (19)

'I didn't get GCSEs. I went to college, Kilburn College. Had a careers officer, looked to things in art training. I liked the art. Drawing. I was born at Park Royal, it's near Harlesden but now I live in Dalston, well, near Dalston. Monday, Wednesday and Saturday I work in Asda, in the evenings. In the evenings I look after my brother. I have two sisters. One is 18 at college. Last Saturday I went to dancing with some friends. Soul music . . . I would prefer to be at a college because of being with other people, not all the same people at the same time.'

Jenny was endorsed as a B by the careers officer but she said she knew nothing of this. This year she is the only girl in graphics and she doesn't like any of the boys. Because of this and because she is the oldest and has been at the project the longest she feels her confidence is undermined. She has literacy and numeracy problems and was not very satisfied with the extra tuition she was given at another site. She is shy and keeps things bottled up. She has a very sweet nature and seems younger than the others in the group. She had a few clashes with one of the girls on the course last year. The girl was suspended for a week for bullying Jenny.

Because Jenny is a category B she is only supposed to achieve a Level 1. There is no Level 1 NVQ in graphic design. She wants to become an illustrator, but is very unclear about employment. She has made slow but sure progress at Sam Morris. We will re-endorse her as a C so she can take the BTEC in June 1994. She wants to go to college and study for her Level 3.

With the NVQs came output-related funding – funding by results. Because BTEC examination requires the trainee to produce three written projects we had to introduce the essay-writing task in our interview procedure. We ask the interviewee to read the essay they have written aloud if they want to, not so much as a test of oral proficiency, but as a way of avoiding marking an essay. They bring the piece of graphics they describe – usually something they like, and the 'talk' usually gives rise to off-the-paper chat particularly when specific features about the design in question are being described. However, the interview procedure (copies of which most of the local careers officers will have) is not encouraging to anyone who a careers officer thinks will not achieve a NVQ Level 2.

Over the last year the young people who have applied have been predominantly white males – very different from the class of 1993 (Figure 16.5). Some have parents who are architects. I spoke to a careers adviser about this trend and he agreed that we were getting the art college rejects and that the NVQ regulations are making YT direct competitors with local colleges. What is happening to all those young people who aren't given immediate Level 2 endorsement? And where are all the girls? Several people I have spoken to within the YT organization have acknowledged that the NVQ system which works together with the endorsement system and performance related funding is effectively screening out the young people for whom YT was set up.

A recent CENTEC inspector reported that the Sam Morris Project was giving excellent training and he recommended that it took on NVQ Level 3 certification. However, CENTEC's new policy states that training can no longer take place in 'community centres or church halls'. They require high-profile glossy glass offices to house their training programmes, but will not offer extra funding. Our manager has told us that the local colleges who also offer BTEC qualifications are our main competitors and we are not getting enough applicants for photography (graphics has a waiting list, probably because there are fewer BTEC graphics courses on offer). Because of the NVQ criteria laid down by government, we now offer the same courses as a college and we have shown that we can succeed in achieving college status. But is this the point? As a result we can now *only* cater for young people who have not been endorsed or those who have been endorsed as a C. Maybe this is an attempt to raise the profile of YT, but what about all those school leavers who are not immediately ready to take on NVQ Level 2 training? In future shouldn't YT be offering everything that the colleges cannot, e.g. good equipment, small groups of instructor/trainees, a broader base of skills and subject areas, rather than competing with them?

Charles Brown. I live in Chiswick. I am 18 and I'm on a graphic design course because art and design is about the only thing I can do and enjoy. My interests are comic art (reading and drawing it) listening to various types of music, avoiding exercise, eating and sleeping.

Rodney W George

Paul Roberts. I am a person made up of many moods, dress, music is all decided on how I feel. Things that are of importance to me are jazz, Hip Hop, funk, soul, family, friends, health an peacefulness. Too many dislikes to write, need sense of direction, need direction of sense. LATER!

Roger Morgan

My interests are art, filming, graphics, music and my Super Nintendo. My favourite type of music is trance music such as Aphex Twin and the Orb etc. My ambition is to become a very successful film director and make music. I am addicted to my SNES and cigarettes. I enjoy saying I'm trying to give up.

Sandra Vega

Tim Conlon. Currently living in Isleworth which is a small town situated next to Hounslow. I am 17 and doing a course in Graphic design. I like computers, going out, eating and sleeping. I dislike having no money and cold weather.

Rodney W George

Shahid Islam. I live in a small flat in Holborn. I've been coming to the Sam Morris for over a year and have one year to go to do my BTEC portfolio. I enjoy sketching, using Freehand computer programme and reading horror boks in my spare time.

Donna Edwards

Steven Boyd. Im 18 years old and at Cleverly estate shepherds Bush. I'm 5'6" I take a size 6 shoe I have brown eyes and brown hair. My interests are football, murder ball, cadets, running, girls, art, talking too much and listening to music. I do not like drugs, sitting down doing nothing, thieving, swimming, John Major and eating too much.

Rodney W George

Jennifer Turner. I enjoy soul music and sport. I also like art. Magazines that I like are 'Black Beat', 'Fresh' and 'Word Up'. The tv programmes that I enjoy are 'The Cosby Show', 'Eastenders' and 'Brookside'. My favourite film is 'Made in America' I have a part timr job as a sales assistant.

Rodney W George

Thomas Galbraith. I have brown eyes, a size 8 foot, I am 5'10" in height and I am studying graphic design. I have interests in art, football, girls, music and living to the max. I would class myself as a Hip Hop junkie, so when the shit goes down you better be ready!

Rodney W George

Marvin Cyrus is my name. I'm 18 years old and interested in graphic design. That's a littlr bit about what I'm interested in career wise, now into the hard core stuff, Hip Hop, rap, soul, ragga and reggea along with family, friends, football and the world as a whole. Respect!

Rodney W George

PHOTOGRAPH
UNAVAILABLE

Tolu Salau. I am 17 and live in the messy part of London called Stockwell. I have a big interest in graphic design and music. I like racing and snooker. I loathe football, rugby and boxing. I listen to hip hop and soul music. My favourite films are Harlry Davidson and the 'Marlboro Man' and 'Harlem Night'. I am a fun loving person with an out going personality, (ask my mother).

Shane Lowes. 17 years old, lives in a tiny town that nobody's heard of called Bedfont. to give you a rough idea where it is, it's near Feltham detention centre. Likes almost any music, dosen't like cury. And wants to earn lots of money doing graphic design.

Rodney W George

Figure 16.5 The Sam Morris Project graphics class of 1993

In September 1993 HFBR was informed that CENTEC will cut our 1994 grant by 90 per cent. Photography is to be shut down and the Sam Morris Project is to move into the HFBR head office. The future is uncertain.

Chapter 17

An inclusive curriculum for teacher education

Hilary Bourdillon

Traditionally initial teacher training has ignored issues relating to equal opportunities or has done little more than pay lip service to them. In this chapter Hilary Bourdillon describes her early development as a teacher and her growing awareness that equal opportunities need to be firmly rooted in the curriculum and classroom practice. Her account leads into a discussion of the way in which Equal Opportunities have been made an integral and generic part of the Open University PGCE course.

In 1992, I joined the Open University PGCE team, with responsibility for the secondary history course. One of my main interests has been the development of equal opportunities in schools and the models of in-service training which most effectively support this. I have also been particularly interested in equal opportunities in relation to my subject specialism – history. Developing the new PGCE appeared to provide a unique opportunity to include these aspects of teaching in an initial teacher education programme. This chapter looks at how my experiences as a teacher, advisory teacher and LEA inspector informed my approach to introducing PGCE students to issues of equal opportunities.

DEVELOPING AN UNDERSTANDING

Like many graduates who trained to enter the teaching profession in the early 1970s, my PGCE course said nothing about equal opportunities. It was only when I began teaching in a split-site mixed comprehensive school behind Waterloo station that I began to develop any understanding of the ways in which a pupil's 'race', social background, gender and special educational needs influenced their attainment in school. ('Race' is used throughout in inverted commas to emphasize the problematic nature of the term.) The school was streamed, and so were the teachers! Newly qualified teachers, like me, were given the bottom-band forms. Whilst my head of department taught the then 'O'-level classes in the relative peace and quiet of the main school building, I taught the younger, and generally 'lower-band' classes in 'the annexe' – an enormous multi-layered 1876 Board School building. My tutor group, 3J (a Year 9 class), were the bottom stream. For many staff they provided the justification for the continued use of corporal punishment – the cane and the slipper! (Bourdillon 1987)

On probation

By the end of my probationary year, I had just about managed to survive 3J. I can't claim to have taught them much, but they taught me a lot. They taught me about how gender can influence the relationship between teachers and pupils. Many of my male colleagues who taught this class relied on the threat of physical punishment (of the boys), and loud voices to maintain order. Unable and unwilling to adopt this approach, I, along with other women teachers in the school, had to rely on interesting my pupils, grabbing their attention and teaching history which had an intrinsic interest, to motivate them. They also taught me how to keep a classroom quiet by giving pupils tasks they found easy and undemanding. I admit I was guilty of providing pupils with activities which had little to do with history. Colouring in pictures of Queen Elizabeth I was a favourite with the few girls in the class, doing word searches for the names of kings and queens went down well with the boys.

At the same time, 3J made me realize what a limited capacity I had as an individual teacher to provide them with appropriate learning experiences, and made me question the constraints of the wider school structures and systems. Why were the majority of the pupils in this bottom-stream third-year class black? Why were there more boys than girls? Why was absenteeism higher amongst the girls than the boys? Why did some of the pupils find school so difficult when it was quite obvious from my chance meetings with them down East Lane market on Saturday mornings, that they were adept and competent working on the fruit stalls? It was this early experience of teaching, rather than any formal course I attended, which led me to understand the effects of schooling on pupils – the teacher stereotyping and subsequent low expectations, the inappropriate curriculum content, the invisibility of black and women's history in the school textbooks, the effects of streaming on pupils' self-esteem and self-respect.

The development of this understanding was a struggle, and on reflection probably has less to do with 3J and more to do with the support and discussion with other teachers. There were several of us in our probationary year, and several other staff who, united by the shared political perspective that collective action could produce results, worked collaboratively to produce a supportive social and professional environment. We set up a discussion group for teachers, which was open to any teacher who wished to join us. We analysed the function of schooling and the curriculum; pupils' resistance to schooling; racism and sexism, and produced a termly magazine where we shared our collective thinking on these issues with the rest of the educational world.

Questioning practice

For me, this early experience of teaching has left me with an understanding that equal opportunities issues cannot be approached purely from the abstract, that is from reading about it, in the same way as one can introduce beginning teachers to lesson plans or schemes of work. Rather the starting point has to be an individual's experience – both of their personal life and of their interaction with the life experiences of the pupils they meet in school. This enables students to develop an understanding of the cultural values schools transmit, whether intentionally or unintentionally, and to understand what must be questioned in existing practice to create better learning opportunities for all pupils. In the light of this, the OU PGCE programme team has attempted to stress the importance of students reflecting on their own experiences both of school and of how equal opportunities has affected their lives personally. We also aim to stress reflection on the social and political context of teaching, and the assessment of classroom actions for their capacity to contribute towards greater equity and humane conditions in schooling and society. Prospective and practising teachers bring to the classroom implicit and unarticulated assumptions, beliefs and values about pupils and their potential. So, when discussing issues such as equal opportunities, where attitudes and values influence action and understanding, the social context of schooling and the relationships between gender, 'race' and social background on the one hand and access to school achievement and knowledge on the other, need to be explored. In other words, it is relevant here to stress an understanding of the social and political context of schooling and to assess classroom actions for their ability to contribute towards greater equality of opportunity.

Initial training and continuing development

Thinking about my own learning experiences as a beginning teacher has left me with an awareness that no matter how thorough and well thought out it is, a PGCE course is *initial* training – exactly that and nothing more. The PGCE course, in recognizing this, draws on Berliner's work (Berliner 1988), which points to the futility of attempting too much in the initial stage of training and of failing to articulate the progression from initial teacher education to the early years of teaching or the induction period. The course provides the opportunity to make the transition from initial teacher training to induction more significant. The school, for example, which employs the newly qualified teacher, can be formally presented with the newly qualified teacher's assessment portfolio which indicates strengths and weaknesses and makes explicit where the national course hands over responsibility to any school-based induction. Issues of Equal Opportunities and Learning for All will feature in this programme of continuing professional development. This is an area which all teachers need constantly to revisit and is a perennial component of all teachers' professional development requirements.

THE CONTEXT OF DEVELOPMENT

When the PGCE programme team began planning and writing the course (April 1992), we were well aware that the official reports on teacher education, those from the DFE and the Council for the Accreditation of Teachers (CATE) did not feature Equal Opportunities as a high priority. This is not to say that Equal Opportunities was absent from the guidance given to higher educational institutions on the content of initial teacher education courses. Since both the 1944 and the 1988 Education Acts claimed to provide greater equality for pupils, any initial training of teachers would have to take this into account. The Council for Accreditation of Teachers in the DES circular 3/84, *ITT: Approval of Courses* (DES 1984b), stated that student teachers should be made aware of equal opportunities legislation and that students should 'guard against preconceptions based on the race and sex of pupils'.

However, the context we were working in was changing. Initial teacher education was undergoing rapid reform with government policy showing an increased questioning of the extent of university and college departments of education's involvement in initial teacher training. The length of time allocated for mandatory school experience has been increased, and skills-based criteria (competences) against which student teachers are to be assessed have been issued. These new skills-based criteria (competences) (DES 1992) state that newly qualified secondary teachers should be able to, for example: 'employ a range of teaching strategies appropriate to the age, ability and attainment level of pupils' and have the foundation to develop:

> an awareness of individual differences, including social, psychological, developmental and cultural dimensions; the ability to recognize diversity of talent including that of gifted pupils;
> the ability to identify special educational needs or learning difficulties;
> a self-critical approach to diagnosing and evaluating pupils' learning, including a recognition of the effects on that learning of teachers' expectations.
>
> (DFE Circular No 9/92. June 1992)

No reference is made here to 'race' or gender.

For me this raises questions about the connection between the official criteria for initial teacher training as laid down by the DFE and CATE and the subsequent practice. Despite the emphasis on stating that student teachers should be made aware of equal opportunities legislation, etc. (DES 1984b), the practice has been shown to fail to do this. To some extent, this lack of interest and research into how best to prepare student teachers, and the corresponding lip service to equal opportunities and learning for all should not come as a surprise, the majority of teacher educators themselves being white, monolingual and male.

Equal opportunities and initial training

The 1988 equal opportunities investigation set up to 'ascertain the extent to which teacher training institutions included equal opportunities (gender) in their students' educational and professional courses' found that:

> on paper the prospects for equal opportunities practice in both curriculum content and the organisation and management of the institutions looked quite good. However, the reality of the situation was considerably less good, and so varied as to make generalisation difficult.
>
> (EOC 1989)

There was

> overall, an unsatisfactory situation of benign apathy towards equal opportunities. The issue was acknowledged, among the institutions without exception, as being a 'good thing', but in competition with 'other pressing demands' the approach of the majority of institutions was reactive and incoherent.
>
> (EOC 1989)

LEGISLATION AND SOCIAL CHANGE

Undoubtedly, official support for equal opportunities, in the form of policies and legislation, legitimates the work being done. It does not, however, necessarily produce changes in attitudes and practice. Such 'official' support contributes to changing attitudes towards the respectability and relevance of equal opportunities issues. This was a lesson which was made very clear to me whilst working as an advisory teacher for equal opportunities in ILEA from 1984 to 1986. The education authority had an equal opportunities policy and was working on the broadening of the idea of 'achievement' (ILEA 1984). When asked to visit schools to help with the development of equal opportunities, policy documents would be readily available. Classroom practice, however, often remained uninfluenced by these policies. Legislation and policies in themselves, then, are not instruments of ideological and social change. They exist *because* of changing attitudes and expectations, rather than the other way round.

If all educational institutions could only raise and develop equal opportunities issues because policy dictated, then very little would have been done in our schools or teacher training institutions. The prevailing influence of the right of centre groups such as the Centre for Policy Studies, which sees the emphasis given to equal opportunities in the form of LEA policies as being 'faddish concerns' of 'loony leftists' (Lawlor 1990) has to be challenged. At the same time we have to defend the autonomy of teachers, which has, with or without official support, changed equal opportunities practice in schools.

Whilst working as a history teacher and head of department in school, it was the influence of the wider social changes, heralded by the women's liberation movement and the civil rights movement of the 1960s and 1970s, rather than any piece of legislation, which involved me, working collaboratively with other colleagues, in developing women's history in school (Adams *et al.* 1983). This began long before such issues were considered important enough to include in HMI reports on the teaching of history (DES 1984a). Women's history and black history now have a place in school history. The History Statutory Orders require history to be taught from a variety of perspectives and that 'Pupils should be taught about the social, cultural, religious and ethnic diversity of the societies studied and the experiences of men and women in those societies' (OFSTED 1993). The centrality of these aspects of teaching history have their origins in classroom-based curriculum development by teachers. The fact that women's history and black history are still neglected in many schools (OFSTED 1993) is further evidence that curriculum change does not result simply from legislation and reminds us of the limitations of 'top-down' educational and curriculum change.

The relevance of this experience for writing the PGCE course lies in the fact that we considered this issue to be an important, indeed essential one to student teachers' understanding of pupils' achievement in school. Whilst deploring the absence of 'race' and gender as specific criteria in the teacher competences laid down by CATE, we have not allowed this lack of official recognition to minimize our coverage of equal opportunities issues.

THE OPEN UNIVERSITY PGCE COURSE

A key consideration in planning the PGCE course was to link the students' school experience and their exploration of educational issues through readings and the audio-visual material. The primary and all the secondary subject lines follow a 'common core' (see Figs 17.1 and 17.2). All the different course lines draw on the particular context of the students' schools to examine the general principles behind teaching and learning.

Since all aspects of school life, whether it be the schools' admissions

Month	Stage / Block	Content	Study time	School placements*
	STAGE I			
February	BLOCK 1	Introduction	20 hours	
March	BLOCK 2	Stage 1 cur.studies & application	55 hours	3 weeks full-time
	STAGE II			
April	BLOCK 3&4	Stage 2 cur.studies & application	180 hours	
May		Focus on:		
June		curriculum planning, organisation, management and assessment;		
July				
August		the development of teaching and learning within the primary classroom;		
September				
October		English, maths, science, RE and PE within the primary curriculum.		4 weeks full-time
November				
	STAGE III			
December	BLOCK 5	Part A Language and Learning	240 hours	
January		Part B Learning For All		
February		Part C Effective Schools		
March	BLOCK 6	Stage 3 cur.studies & application		
April		Focus on:		
May		further development of all aspects introduced in Stage 2;		8 weeks full-time
June		the teaching of national curriculum foundation subjects		
July	BLOCK 7	Preparation for induction and further professional development	10 hours	

Figure 17.1 PGCE course outline for primary courses

* Involvement in school-based activities across the 18 months (e.g. parents' evenings, drama, sports) – 3 weeks

Source: Open University PGCE /02A

Month	Stage / Block		Study time	School placements*
	STAGE I			
February	BLOCK 1	Introduction	20 hours	
March	BLOCK 2	Stage 1 cur.studies & application	40 hours	3 weeks full-time
	STAGE II			
April	BLOCK 3	Part A Planning	80 hours	
May		Part B Classroom methods		
June		Part C Classroom management		
July		Part D Assessment		
		Part E Whole curriculum		
August September October November	BLOCK 4	Stage 2 cur.studies & application	80 hours	4 weeks full-time
	STAGE III			
December	BLOCK 5	Part A Language and Learning	90 hours	
January		Part B Learning For All		
		Part C Effective Schools		
February March April May June	BLOCK 6	Stage 3 cur.studies & application	120 hours	8 weeks full-time
July	BLOCK 7	Preparation for induction and further professional development	10 hours	

Figure 17.2 PGCE course outline for secondary courses

* Involvement in school-based activities across the 18 months (e.g. parents' evenings, drama, music, sports) – 3 weeks

Source: Open University PGCE /02B

policy, the way in which pupils are grouped and interact in the classroom, the policy on discipline, what is taught in the classroom and teacher expectations etc., are affected by equal opportunities, pragmatic decisions had to be taken about covering this in the PGCE course. Whilst the PGCE team agreed that issues of Equal Opportunities needed to permeate the whole course, we were aware that this approach had its limits: 'A permeation model alone cannot be satisfactory unless equal opportunities has a very high profile of its own in the training programme, built on skills, knowledge and a positive attitude and an active approach to learning' (EOC 1989). We decided therefore to cover Equal Opportunities through the generic issues such as classroom method and management, lesson planning and assessment, but it was also considered important that these issues received some in-depth investigation and as such needed a dedicated block of study time. The positioning of this, at the beginning of Stage 3 of the course (see Fig 17.1 and 17.2), means that the course materials can draw together students' experience of these issues from earlier blocks of study as well as drawing on some evidence surrounding equal opportunities practice which students have been able to collect from their two school placements. This block also prepares students for their eight weeks' teaching practice at the end of the course.

We also decided that the subject- and phase-specific aspects of Equal Opportunities would be covered in the blocks of study which covered the teaching of history (or science, maths, modern languages, primary, etc.).

Equal Opportunities

In developing the course, the team recognized that whilst having considerable expertise amongst its own members in the area of Equal Opportunities and Learning for All, it was important to draw on the expertise of others from both within and outside the university. Teachers in school have contributed to and commented on all aspects of the course, and they will continue to contribute to its evaluation. Staff tutors with responsibility for the PGCE working in the different Open University regions have done likewise. A PGCE Equal Opportunities task group has been set up, including representatives from the Equal Opportunities Commission and the teacher unions as well as from the course team and the university's Equality Working Group, with the aim of sharing good practice in this area. It has also been able to draw on the course materials E242 'Learning for All' and the advice of colleagues who work on these materials.

These early discussions raised some tensions in the team about the discourse of equal opportunities and its 'political correctness'. One of the reasons why this area is low on the list of priorities on teacher education courses may well be the feeling that whatever materials are produced, they will be subjected to adverse scrutiny and criticism from the rapidly expanded industry of the so-called 'expert' on equal opportunities. Generally this criticism focuses on language and terminology. We were aware of the debates which surround the definition of equal opportunities, learning for all, gender, of racism, anti-racism, black perspectives and epistemologies and postmodern discourses of 'difference'. However, we were also aware that our materials, whilst introducing our students to these debates and encouraging then to view practice in schools critically, would have minimal impact on students' understanding if they were seen to be completely at odds with schools practice. Students are far more likely to accept what they experience in school as being the 'reality' rather than what they read in course materials. For this reason we have chosen to use the term 'special educational needs' as this is the phrase which has entered into the everyday language of teachers. At the same time, we point out the dangers of categorization and encourage students to see pupils' learning needs as part of the same continuum and introduce then to the concept of Learning for All.

As well as raising issues about language and the conceptual framework, our discussions on Equal Opportunities raised questions about how we could introduce students to the complex interactions of 'race', gender, ability and social background and to the ways in which Equal Opportunities are influenced by institutional structures. Block 5 of the course then explores the ways in which 'race', gender, social background and ability influence and are influenced by teacher expectations and institutional structures. Students are then introduced, through the printed and audio-visual materials, to approaches used in schools to mitigate these inequalities. This work draws on students' observations made in their stage 2 school placement and prepares them for their final eight-week school practice where they are asked to explore these issues in school.

Equal Opportunities and learning to teach history

All students on the PGCE course will be applying the educational issues they have explored generically in their subject- or phase-specific context. In writing the history materials then, I have attempted to emphasize the subject-specific (i.e. history) aspects of Equal Opportunities. This includes the discussion of the definition of school history and the ways in which this definition has been challenged by the pedagogy of the history classroom and the developments within the subject, particularly the emergence of publications on women's history and the histories of minority ethnic groups, over the past decade. It emphasizes the importance of understanding the ways in which pupils develop historical understanding and the relationship of talk and language, and teaching and learning styles to this development.

For example, it is often thought more fitting to give pupils with reading difficulties or special educational needs, pictures or oral history to work on. This approach assumes that oral history and pictorial evidence reduce the emphasis on writing and reading and are therefore accessible to pupils with a wide spread of attainment. Yet oral and visual sources are no less complex than written sources in the historical concepts they contain. Pupils learning history have to be taught to 'read' pictures – a conceptually complex task. There is no justification whatsoever in concluding that lower-attaining pupils can only profit from a different sort of history from that deemed appropriate for the average and high-attaining pupils. The PGCE history course attempts to introduce students to the idea that the aims and objectives of the history curriculum should be common across the ability range and to introduce them to ways of making this accessible to all pupils. Table 17.1 shows a brief summary of the coverage of Equal Opportunities issues in the history course.

The PGCE Assessment Model and Equal Opportunities

Finally, I need to say something here about how the students are assessed. As any experienced teacher knows, what is in the examination gives status to those particular aspects of the subject! As well as permeating the course content, equal opportunities needs to inform and permeate the course assessment model.

The assessment model is conceptualized in terms of two dimensions of assessment – areas of teaching competence and a consideration of professional qualities. The areas of competence have been identified as:

- curriculum/subject planning,
- classroom/subject method,
- classroom management,
- assessment, recording and reporting,
- the wider role of the teacher.

The professional qualities have been identified as:

- a commitment to professional values,
- effective communication,
- appropriate relationships,
- efficient management.

This assessment plan grew out of a parallel model which also sought to integrate a *values* dimension into the assessment of professional competence, in particular the ASSET model developed at the Anglia Polytechnic University (Winter 1992).

Students need to demonstrate evidence of reaching necessary levels of competence with each of the competence areas which have been disaggregated into competence statements. These statements include issues of equal opportunity and 'learning for all'. In parallel, however, students will be required to demonstrate *professional qualities* in the way that the competence is displayed. Students demonstrate these qualities by personal

Table 17.1 PGCE history course content – focus on Equal Opportunities and Learning for All

Stage 1 *Block 2*	Equal Opportunities and Learning for All focus
	Exploration of 'What is History?' – students introduced to rationale of school history including gender and history and what constitutes 'British' history
	Introduction to Learning for All – definition of terms and exploration of an increased awareness of and changes which have taken place in school with regard to disability, gender issues, minority ethnic groups, social background
	Introduction to resources for teaching history, including criteria for the evaluation of materials, including Equal Opportunities
Stage 2 *Block 4*	Exploration of these issues in planning and resourcing history lessons
	Activity on using historical documents including questioning on race and gender
	Key Questions in Teaching History – examples on Women Through Time
	Planning differentiated activities – focus on strategies for Learning for All
Stage 3 *Block 6*	In-depth consideration of race and gender, a central dynamic in planning history
	The development of historical thinking – strategies for teaching historical concepts to all pupils – differentiation
	The language of history and the development of historical understanding – ensuring access to all pupils
	Equal opportunities and Learning for All – considerations for teaching and learning history
	Classroom method and management
	Different interpretations of history

example and through their role in school. So, for example, they demonstrate a commitment to professional values by respecting and valuing pupils as individuals in order to promote their personal growth and autonomy, and understanding and implementing equal opportunities principles and practices, etc.

There are some important points to make here. First, the defined professional qualities are not assessed independently of the normal day-to-day tasks of the teacher. Professional qualities – such as a commitment to Equal Opportunities – cannot exist in a vacuum and must have some context for their realization. As students demonstrate increasing understanding within the defined areas of competence, they will simultaneously develop a foundation of evidence for their capability in relation to professional qualities.

Students are primarily responsible for developing an assessment portfolio within which they accumulate the varieties of evidence to support their progression through the course. Both the portfolio activities and the tutor-marked assignments include examples of work where students have to consider issues of Equal Opportunities and Learning for All in their planning, classroom method and management, resourcing and evaluation of lessons.

CONCLUSION

The Open University's PGCE course operates on a national scale, involving over 1,000 schools, teaching staff and students. This chapter is an attempt to share some of the developments which have taken place in producing the course, particularly the way in which the PGCE aims to develop student teachers' understanding of equal opportunities. I have focused here on the course structure, content and the assessment model, but am aware that Equal Opportunities is inclusive of many other aspects of the course – such as student recruitment, the implications of school-based training, and the influence and role of the mentor in initial teacher education. I am also aware that one important dimension is missing from this chapter – the experience of the PGCE students and their mentors in schools. How effective are the course materials in developing students' understanding of equal opportunities? Does being involved as a mentor with the PGCE provide continuing professional development for those teachers involved, and if so, does involvement with the course have any impact on their understanding of equal opportunities? All these aspects need careful evaluation and the practice described here may well need to be modified in the light of that evaluation. At some future date I hope to be able to report on both the strengths and the shortcomings of our PGCE in its attempts to contribute to quality provision for initial teacher education and to prepare its students to teach all pupils.

REFERENCES

Adams, C., Bartley, P. and Loxton, C. (eds) (1983) *Women in History Series*, Cambridge: Cambridge University Press.

Berliner, D. (1988) 'Implications of studies of expertise in pedagogy for teacher education and evaluation', in *New Directions for Teacher Assessment*, Proceedings of the 1988 ETS Invitation Conference, Princeton, NJ: Educational Testing Service.

Bourdillon, H. (1987) 'Lessons of history: beyond the male-stream classroom', in Gail Chester and Sigrid Nielsen (eds) *In Other Words – Writing as a Feminist*, Explorations in Feminism, London: Hutchinson.

Bourdillon, H. (ed.) (1994) *Teaching History Open University PGCE Reader*, London: Routledge.

Calderhead, J. (1989) 'Reflective teaching and teacher education', *Teaching and Teacher Education* 5(1): 43–51.

DES (1984a) *History in the Primary and Secondary Years: An HMI View*, London: HMSO.

DES (1984b) *ITT: Approval of Courses*, Circular 3/84, 13 April, London: HMSO.

DES (1989) '*Future Arrangements for the Accreditation of Courses of Initial Teacher Education: A Consultative Document*', Circular 24/82, London: HMSO.

DES (1992) *Reform of Initial Teacher Education: A Consultative Document*, 28 January, London: HMSO.

DFE (1992) *Initial Teacher Training (Secondary Phase)*, Circular 9/92, London, HMSO.

EOC (1989) *Formal Investigation Report on Initial Teacher Training in England and Wales*, Manchester: Equal Opportunities Commission.

ILEA (1984) *Improving Secondary Schools*, Report of the Committee on the Curriculum and Organisation of Secondary Schools chaired by David Hargreaves, London: ILEA.

Lawlor, S. (1990) *Teachers Mistaught: Training in Theories or Education in Subjects?*, London: Centre for Policy Studies.

Melnick, S. and Zeichner, K. (1993) 'Education for cultural diversity: overcoming cultural insularity in the education professorate'; Paper given at International Conference on Teacher Education, Tel Aviv.

Moon, R.E. (1992) 'A new route way into teaching', Paper given at the 1992 ATEE, Lahti, Finland, *Education Review* 6(2): 28–31.

OFSTED (1993) *History Key Stage 1, 2 and 3*, London: HMSO.

Shulman, L. (1987) 'Knowledge and teaching – foundations of the new reform', *Harvard Education Review* 57: 1–22.

Siraj-Blatchford, Iram (ed.) (1994) '*Race*', *Gender and the Education of Teachers*, Milton Keynes: Open University Press.

Winter, R. (1992) *The Asset Programme (Accreditation of Social Services Experience and Training)*, Chelmsford: Essex County Council Social Services Department/ Anglia Polytechnic University.

Part III

Managing education in the 1990s

Chapter 18

Competition between schools
Inclusion or exclusion?

Jim Conway and Mary Lawrence

Jim Conway and Mary Lawrence are committed to the raising of edu-cational standards and to the principle of an inclusive educational main-stream. In this chapter they discuss and illustrate how they try to achieve both in the context of a grant-maintained secondary school in the 1990s. They are aware of the tension between their twin commitments and the pressures which exist to adopt a selective approach. They argue that there is bound to be a limit to the tolerance of cultural diversity within a single school, but that a creative middle way can be taken so that all students are valued as well as supported to reach their varying potential. What is necessary is a notion of community.

We work in a comprehensive secondary school which has recently become grant maintained and was formerly voluntary aided. It is located in a metropolitan district and because of its denominational nature, attracts children from a very wide catchment area. This helps to ensure a balanced social and academic intake. We are aware of the potentially damaging aspects of recent government policy. We are also conscious of the dangers inherent in those approaches to educational policy which undervalue either academic achievement or the British tradition of 'the school as a community' which was so perceptively described by David Hargreaves (1982). Our experience in managing this school and in other senior positions within the education system leads us to argue that simple ideological solutions from either the political left or the right are unlikely to be met with overwhelming enthusi-asm by senior managers in education who have to deal, on a daily basis, with the complex social, economic and political issues facing schools. These ideological solutions are often political ideas which may have a populist appeal, for example 'market forces', but are not grounded in the experience of practitioners in the schools. As senior managers working within a popular and successful school we are concerned that a proper regard for academic success and achievement does not become an excuse for rejecting 'problem' pupils.

One of the most worrying implications of the move towards league tables and crude performance indicators is that children who are difficult to educate may become unwelcome in popular mainstream schools. There are few if any comprehensive schools which do not claim to attempt to treat all pupils equally. Indeed equality of opportunity is often at the cornerstone of a school's aims. It would be unthinkable to suggest that any school set out to create a sort of educational apartheid where the advantaged gained at the expense of the disadvantaged. However, equality of opportunity has been interpreted by many schools as the need to treat all their pupils in the same way.

One of the ways in which this was effected in schools in the 1970s and 1980s was through the organization of teaching in mixed-ability groups. Teachers listened to the evidence from researchers such as Jackson (1964) and Ferri (1971) on emotive issues such as the self-fulfilling prophecy, where children in the main live up to teacher expectation and so prove streaming 'right'. Mixed-ability teaching was seen as having the potential to improve our unfair society. The important question is 'does this approach improve childrens' learning?' The evidence is inconclusive in terms of pupil achievement but we do know that this approach does make considerable demands on the teacher in terms of the preparation of learning materials and in classroom management. What is clear too, is that while many teachers were prepared to defend, sometimes passionately, this approach in the 1980s, it has, in recent years, been subjected to closer scrutiny. Some may say that this is due to the introduction of the National Curriculum programmes of study and testing at Key Stages 3 and 4. Others may argue that publicizing data on the performance of pupils has forced schools to adopt pupil grouping policies which they hope will result in the greatest number of pupils achieving the highest possible examination grades.

Whilst these changes have certainly caused us to evaluate our approach to teaching and learning it is also the dissatisfaction of parents, pupils and their teachers with the organization of classes that has resulted in a review of our own arrangements for setting by ability. Differentiation in the classroom has always been an area of concern for conscientious teachers. It has required considerable preparation from the teacher, both in terms of the tasks set in class, and in the evaluation of the range of outcomes expected from the pupils. The demands of the National Curriculum have increased the classroom teacher's workload, particularly in terms of monitoring and assessment, and many have expressed a preference for a narrower range of ability so that they are better able to target learning materials and tasks in order to meet the needs of all pupils. Parents' knowledge and expectations have also been heightened by the high public profile of educational issues and pupils too have become increasingly aware of their own progress through the process of self-evaluation and regular feedback from their teachers. The result is that there is increased pressure on pupils to 'do well' and achieve and for the school to create an environment which ensures that effective learning can take place.

Within a secondary school it is inevitable that there will be staff in some subject areas who prefer to organize pupils by ability and others who feel that this is not necessary. Much will depend on the external demands made by the School Curriculum and Assessment Authority (SCAA) and internally on the departmental culture and expertise. In our own school we have sought, within the constraints of the timetable, to offer setting to those subject areas which require it while maintaining mixed-ability groups in other areas. We believe this reflects the true meaning of equality of opportunity in that each child now has a better opportunity to *access* the curriculum. Teachers are able to target classroom activities more appropriately. Pupils readily accept this approach and the range of groupings ensures a good social mix within the year group. The commitment of the subject staff to their preferred organizational structure is, we believe, the key to its success. The teachers believe that their chosen structure ensures the pupils have the best opportunity for success and that message is in turn conveyed to their pupils. We are monitoring the changes and will be concerned, not only with higher levels of achievement for pupils in the future, which is often cited as the main reason for setting pupils, but in increased motivation and a resulting improvement in pupil behaviour in the classroom.

Can we meet the needs of the most disadvantaged in a climate where the debate centres around 'league tables', 'parental choice and voice', and 'grant-maintained status'? The success of local management of schools is now recognized by many in the educational world. Perhaps the most pertinent issue in this debate is not self-management but the pupil-led formula funding which is the means by which a market was introduced into the education system. This is common both to locally managed and to grant-maintained schools. It has served to highlight differential funding and intensify competition between schools. It has heralded the introduction of the language of commercial competition such as 'image', 'customer', 'marketing', 'unit costs' and 'productivity'. A key question for those who believe in inclusive schools and who have experienced the significant managerial advantages of self-government has to be whether these gains are at the expense of the more vulnerable members of society. Media attention occasionally focuses on the increasing number of excluded pupils. It is assumed by some that this increase is a direct result of the pressures on schools of parental choice and this in turn encourages schools to exclude pupils who are difficult and can be expensive to educate. We believe that schools have a responsibility to all their pupils to provide an appropriate curriculum. There have always been pupils who have had difficulty in conforming to the social systems within a school. For some a move to another school is successful but for others the solution is more complex. We have accepted a number of students who were experiencing difficulties in other schools and who were midway through their secondary school careers. One such pupil adapted well. Away from friendship groups which had considerable influence on his behaviour in his previous school, he was able to move through our school with comparatively few problems. Another pupil was less successful and despite considerable support and counselling she was unable to settle. This did result in us adopting more formal assessment procedures as specified in the 1981 Education Act and subsequently she did leave our school. Will the future bring two types of school – the successful, oversubscribed, high-achieving school where there is little or no room for the non-conforming pupil, and those schools who are prepared to open their doors to any pupil who experiences difficulties and are prepared to accept that this may well be at the expense of academic achievement and success?

It should not be assumed that there is no middle way. Our own experience is that children respond well in situations which are unambiguous, well defined and yet can still allow them to express their individuality in a way that takes account of the needs and feelings of others within the community. This is an approach we are working towards. It is fundamental to our school's mission and is underpinned by a range of strategies outlined in our development plan. This includes the direct teaching of the Christian values on which the school is based and which form the core of our mission statement; for example,

> All persons are formed, sustained and strengthened by the quality of relationships with others.

It also means taking every opportunity to develop a sense of community within school through such diverse areas as school uniform, school newsletters and publications, public performance and creating opportunities for involving pupils in all areas of school life. Inevitably this approach is not successful with every pupil. Some schools have adopted policies which have prevented any pupil from being excluded, but is it realistic to suggest that all children within a school will successfully integrate into its community? We were unsuccessful with a Year 9 boy who appeared to be playing a key role in the misbehaviour of a small group within that year group. Despite our efforts to work intensively with parents and external support services, we made little progress and the boy transferred to a neighbouring school. So far this transfer seems to have been successful. It is likely that, in dealing with the diversity of human nature, some children will struggle to find their place in the fairly rigid structure of a school. Early recognition of difficulties and good support systems will help, but there will need to be a willingness amongst schools to allow pupils a place when they have experienced adjustment problems elsewhere. This may be more difficult in the more successful schools where places may be at a premium and ultimately could create the two-tiered system described earlier. Our own society has in recent times become less tolerant of those who fail to conform. The press now freely refer to disruptive pupils as 'undesirable elements', 'scum', etc. and this type of terminology seems to be used more openly by some teachers. Certainly, within the confines of school staffrooms, there has always been an acknowledgement of the difficulties in working with some pupils and this is often expressed as a desire not only for the pupil to be removed but as a way of providing a climate in which the other pupils in the class can progress. The extent to which these feelings prevail and are expressed often depends on the culture which prevails within the school and the attitude of the headteacher towards the exclusion of pupils. As a school working towards Christian values we believe in offering opportunities for forgiveness and reconciliation. We are a disciplined but tolerant community. However, short-term exclusion has been used as one of a range of sanctions for behaviour which endangers the pupil or another member of the school community. The imposition of clear sanctions often helps us to ensure that the rules and expectations of the school community are unambiguous and well defined.

None of this helps us address the cause of pupils' dissatisfaction with school. Our society does not support children in their quest for a set of clear values. They are continually frustrated by the materialistic expectations raised through the media and confused by the duplicity of values of those they see as being in authority. Examples abound of famous people in public arenas such as sport, television and politics who fail to tell the truth and are publicly 'found out'. Often these are the very people who proclaim loudly the need for a more moral society and the importance of holding onto basic family values. Continual discrediting of the education system and those who work within it, by government and individual political leaders, only serves to increase the general disillusionment that is apparent amongst members of the community, parents and pupils.

The recent emphasis on the need to improve standards in schools and the introduction of national targets have been an attempt to reassert the importance of educational achievement. However, when the government announced that examination results would be published there was an outcry from the educational professionals. Even more disquiet was expressed when it was proposed to place the schools in league tables. This was an attempt to give better information to parents on which they could base their choice of school. Interestingly, the recent appeal by parents against one city council's allocation of school places suggests that those parents who have used the information have still been unable to obtain places at what they obviously perceive to be more successful schools. Our own view, which we believe is shared by others, is that the more common criterion used by parents to select a school is the 'ethos' which prevails within it. However, there is no doubt that examination results have assumed a greater prominence in our own school in recent years. It would be oversimplistic and far from the truth to suggest that the reason for this is the threat of league tables. It would be far more accurate to claim that the real influence has come from HMI and educational researchers, the favourite targets of the political extreme right. The annual reports of HM Senior Chief Inspector of Schools, the illuminating reports produced by HMI on school systems in Japan (1991a), Europe and the United States (1991b), and freely available reports on individual schools, are amongst the wealth of material through which HMI were able to inform managers, such as ourselves, about the characteristics of successful schooling.

About the same time, the burgeoning school effectiveness research movement began to provide us with more insight into the question 'how do schools become more effective?' Until recently, the strongly held belief was that it was social, economic and cultural differences that were wholly responsible for differences in the achievement of the pupils. We now know that some schools are more successful in raising pupil achievement than others with similar catchment areas. International research suggests that to be effective, schools must show that they value learning and achievement. Other key factors which have been identified as encouraging school effectiveness include high levels of pupil involvement, curriculum-focused leadership, close parental and community links and reward-based control systems. In our own case it is the rapidly increasing awareness of the characteristics of successful schools and the fact that we have yet to meet a teacher who does not want the best for the children they teach, that form the real reasons for the extra emphasis we place on children achieving their academic potential.

So what of grant-maintained status and its implications for a school which wishes to continue to be inclusive and academically successful? We need to be an attractive choice for parents in the area and we have given careful thought as a community to the ethos and aims of the school. We have maintained the same admissions policy and have continued to cooperate and liaise with the local education authority where it is appropriate. The significant increase in funds available to support learning have meant that parents and pupils are aware of the importance we place on the work that goes on in classrooms. For too long we have had difficulties in ensuring access of all pupils to basic text books. Parents have complained about their children having to share text books and teachers have had difficulty setting appropriate homework. Departments were asked to discuss and set their resourcing priorities in line with their departmental development plans and there has been an increase in expenditure of 100 per cent on books and equipment. Many tasks which were being undertaken by teachers such as photocopying and the production of learning materials have been assigned to a team of curriculum support and secretarial staff, who have been appointed recently. This team's responsibility is to produce high-quality learning materials and we have invested in desk top publishing equipment to support this work. This has created the opportunity for teachers to concentrate a little more on teaching and a little less on administration.

Our awareness of the nature of market forces prevents us from becoming complacent. We recognize the need to celebrate publicly the achievements of members of our community. We know too that parents do have a choice in the school their child will attend and we seek to promote our school image in order that parents and children who value our ethos are informed and aware of what the school has to offer. We are conscious that high expectations in terms of pupil behaviour and achievement means that we put considerable emphasis on homework, punctuality, dress and attendance and this could be seen by some to be a recipe for alienating less successful pupils. There is no evidence of this happening and we feel pupils appreciate our clear values and caring ethos. We want to continue to attract pupils of all abilities. These are laudable and affordable aims for an oversubscribed school with a six-form intake. The uncomfortable question has to be: if we became less successful and attracted fewer pupils, would this tempt us to become more selective, remove disruptive pupils or even direct money away from the classroom to spend on marketing the school? We could no doubt justify these actions on the basis that it is worth sacrificing a few principles for the benefit of the majority of the pupils and the survival of the school! However, we are committed to meeting the needs of all children, irrespective of ability, and neither of us would wish to work in a school where children were selected on these grounds.

The introduction of market forces into the public education system is a high-risk ideological move. The success or otherwise of this will not be apparent for many years. We believe we have a commitment to an educational and management philosophy which will allow our school to reap the benefits of self-government without putting at risk our most vulnerable pupils. Will other senior managers share this view?

REFERENCES

Ferri, E. (1971) *Streaming: Two Years Later*, Slough: NFER.

Hargreaves, D. (1982) *The Challenge for the Comprehensive School*, London: Routledge & Kegan Paul.

HMI (1991a) *Aspects of Education in the USA*, London: HMSO.

HMI (1991b) *Aspects of Upper Secondary and Higher Education in Japan*, London: HMSO.

Jackson, B. (1964) *Streaming: an Education System in Miniature*, London: Routledge & Kegan Paul.

Chapter 19

Inspecting schools

Felicity Fletcher-Campbell

The new arrangements for the inspection of schools were introduced by the 1992 Education (Schools) Act. Felicity Fletcher-Campbell discusses how far they are appropriate for evaluating provision for disabled students and those who experience difficulties in learning or other kinds of difficulty. For example, if support services which are not based in a school are not therefore inspected, will they become marginalized? She also points out that the system of formal inspection as a whole cannot support schools to implement recommended developments. Felicity Fletcher-Campbell has tutored Open University students carrying out postgraduate projects and she has organized her chapter with their requirements in mind.

The Education (Schools) Act 1992 introduced significant changes to the way in which the external inspection of schools in England and Wales is conducted. Under the terms of the Act, all maintained schools in England are to be inspected on a four-year cycle by independent teams of inspectors regulated by the Office for Standards in Education (OFSTED) under the direction of Her Majesty's Chief Inspector (HMCI). The main features of the new procedures introduced are as follows:

- only teams trained and accredited by HMCI are eligible to tender for school inspections;
- LEA personnel can tender for school inspections (including those in non-LEA maintained schools) only if registered with HMCI;
- all inspection teams must include at least one person not involved in education – a 'lay inspector' (who receives training as the other inspectors);
- inspections are governed by a set of common procedures defined by OFSTED;
- all inspection reports are public documents and a summary of a school's inspection report is sent to the parent(s) of each child in the school.

Writing shortly after the announcement of the new procedures, Maychell and Keys remark

> The proposed changes came as a major setback to LEAs, since monitoring and evaluation were one of their principal remaining responsibilities after the 1988 Education Act. . . . There were also implications for team organisation and the provision of advisory services to schools, since inspectors who had a 'close relationship' with a school could not be involved in the inspection of that school.
>
> (Maychell and Keys 1993: 4)

It was interesting that in the first round of contracts, announced in July 1993, LEA teams were prominent, representing about 90 per cent of contracts (*TES*, 18 June 1993, p.1). A National Foundation for Educational Research survey of just over 800 headteacher (Maychell and Keys 1993) indicated that this might well be received ambivalently by schools. Generally, schools welcomed the idea of more regular inspections but did not find privatization acceptable and feared that they might no longer benefit from the customary follow-up to LEA inspections of support, advice and ideas for development and improvement. The prominence of LEA personnel may cause a degree of role conflict. Nixon and Ruddock (1993: 137) cite a common characterization of role among a sample of LEA advisers/inspectors that they studied. One of their interviewees remarked:

> Colleagues here did not take up jobs as advisers to monitor what was going on in schools, this wasn't one of their expectations. They came in to be specialist advisers – to give support and advice and to get heavily involved in in-service education and training.

A SPECIAL FOCUS

Provision for pupils with special educational needs represents a discrete element within the overall framework of inspection – which is common to both mainstream and special schools (OFSTED 1992). The regulations require that teams include members competent to inspect provision for pupils with special education needs. It will be interesting to see how this requirement is met and whether teams include a special needs specialist, for example, someone who has been an LEA special needs adviser or inspector, or the head of a learning support team, or whether all members of the team will consider provision for pupils with special needs. The latter, more general, approach was adopted by a number of LEA inspection and advice services following the introduction of the National Curriculum, successful implementation of which was, of course, dependent on the curriculum being accessible to all pupils regardless of ability. This generalist approach may accord more readily with whole-school policies for special needs. Arguably, every aspect of the inspection, including such things as class sizes and budgetary allocations, has implications for special needs. However, a considerable degree of specialism will have to be available for the low-incidence, highly intensive special provision such as in units, resourced schools or special schools for pupils with sensory impairments where there are discrete difficulties in implementing the National Curriculum. Will all 'generalist' inspectors have access to an interpreter when observing in a signing environment, for example? If not, what effect will this have on the quality of data collected?

The inspection framework does raise questions. For example, one of the four stated functions of the inspections is to report on 'the spiritual, moral, social and cultural development of pupils'. Can all students be expected to respond in the same way within these very complex areas? For example, is 'moral development' to be conceived of in cognitive or behavioural terms? Will the inspection framework and those who report within it, be sufficiently sensitive to the critical variables that affect what can be observed and measured?

THE LIMITATIONS OF FORMAL INSPECTIONS

Individual schools may like to reflect on the way in which the formal inspection process extends or limits their own ideas about provision for pupils with special needs. In some, the required data may be available via normal, well-established record-keeping systems. In others, its collection may be a new activity. And there will be other schools at various points along the continuum between these positions. All schools might usefully consider the degree to which the required information and documentation, together with the empirical data, help provide evidence that their aims and objectives with regard to pupils with special needs are being met.

The guidance for inspectors refers to outcomes achieved by pupils with special needs, the ways in which such pupils are identified and curricular access. Five questions are specified as representing 'useful enquiries'. Arguably, these are all tightly interrelated. They focus on:

- standards obtained by pupils with special needs;
- appropriate and effective whole-school policies;
- curricular provision for pupils with particular needs and disabilities;
- integration;
- the work of support staff.

The inspection teams are only in school for a relatively short and intensive time (the minimum number of inspection days required is calculated according to number on roll). This is similar to the much more sporadic and infrequent traditional HMI inspections which the present system replaced, though it is rather different from the way in which LEAs have often been accustomed to 'inspect' special needs provision. One-off, HMI-type LEA inspections have been a feature of some authorities (Maychell and Keys 1993) but, as regards special needs, many LEAs have monitored and evaluated schools' provision informally via their learning support teams whose members often enjoyed regular and extensive relationships with schools (Fletcher-Campbell 1993). One of the advantages of this model was that both formal and informal INSET could be grounded in the evidence gathered over time from this regular contact between specialist and classroom teachers. A further model is, of course, that of self-review (either departmental or institutional) linked to a development plan.

HARD DATA REQUIRED BY THE INSPECTION TEAM

It might be useful for schools to consider the degree to which the models replicate each other (for example, in the use of record-keeping) and/or complement each other (for example, in the different timescales involved or by way of prioritizing objectives and the setting of performance indicators). Can the hard data required by OFSTED be used for different purposes by different agencies? For example, there are clear differences between the following figures required for the pre-inspection forms. Schools are asked to give:

- the number of pupils about whom a statement of special educational needs has been made by the LEA;
- the number of pupils who are not already receiving additional support but whom the school considers would benefit from this;
- the number of pupils with special educational needs who are being withdrawn or supported in each year group (there is a breakdown for boys and girls in each of the categories of withdrawal and in-class support).

The first is, apparently, a clear, objective statement. But there are other levels to be explored. LEA policy and provision will be a determinant in the profile of pupils with statements in an area or a school. Once pupils have a statement, then there are statutory review procedures. What happens in the annual review? Is it merely a description of what has happened over the past year or is it an evaluation of progress made in that year, arising out of, and refining, a development plan? Does a statement carry additional resources? If it does, are these delegated to the school and, if so, how are they used? It can be argued that effective integration can only occur if resources are treated coherently (Hegarty 1993). Additional resources can be used creatively to the benefit of the whole school community. A study on integration (Fletcher-Campbell et al. 1992) reported the case of an integrated junior school where the decision was made to place all pupils with statements (and these included children with moderate and severe learning difficulties, and emotional and behavioural difficulties) in mainstream classes. This policy was supported by a resourcing policy in which the resources allocated for pupils with statements were used holistically throughout the school with the effect that mainstream classes were considerably smaller than usual within the primary sector (between sixteen and twenty-two pupils) and each class had a permanent full-time classroom assistant. These conditions not only made it possible to accommodate pupils with statements of special needs but also created a more favourable environment for other pupils. At this school, it would not make sense to 'inspect' special educational need provision discretely as it was an integral part of the school's total curriculum offer.

Unless the school is in an LEA which conducts a systematic and regular 'audit' or 'inventory' of special educational needs, the second piece of information required by OFSTED may be subjective and contextual. In a system with unlimited resources, all pupils might benefit from some form of teaching support. Within limited budgets, there are questions to be raised about the use of resources and alternative strategies (for example, the constitution of small groups, the use of classroom assistants). This requires an intimate knowledge of individual pupils, interactions between members of a class, the past history of teaching techniques used within a classroom and so forth. Again, the specific question can generate critical self-scrutiny. It is rather more than a way of explaining poor performance in league tables even if it could play a part here.

The third set of data raises questions about the appropriateness and quality of the response made. It may give information about what is done, but not about the reasons for strategies, the way these fit into the total curriculum experience of pupils or the effect of various arrangements on pupil progress.

OTHER PARTICIPANTS

Governors have the responsibility, with the headteacher, of both preparing data for the inspection team and considering the recommendations made in its report. They may have to be aware of issues wider than those accommodated by the framework of inspection and the resultant report. Nixon and Ruddock observe:

> It is important to ask whether the lists of criteria that new inspectors spend time in constructing are, at some level, a diversion from the profoundly complicated task of understanding the nature of professional judgement and applying it in a whole-school context.
>
> (Nixon and Ruddock 1993: 141)

The degree to which governors are aware of their responsibility towards pupils with special educational needs (established in the Education Act 1981) will, clearly, be critical. There are training challenges here: external training may be sufficient to alert governors to general issues of special education and the broad areas which they should pay attention to within the school but this will need to be complemented with a clear understanding of the particularities of the individual school with respect to its provision for pupils with special educational needs.

Parents, for the first time, are formally involved in inspections. The inspection team is required to hold an open meeting with parents and to ascertain their perceptions of the school. Is there any guarantee that parents of pupils with special educational needs will be adequately represented at these meetings? Will there be difficulties where a resourced school serves a wide area for a particular special need? It may be possible for a parent who lives nearby to attend but what about parents whose child travels in from a distance in order to benefit from particular facilities? As well as transport problems, the child's care needs may militate against parents' ability to attend such meetings.

THE CUMULATIVE EFFECTS OF THE NEW INSPECTION ARRANGEMENTS

It may, perhaps, be asked what the cumulative effects of the new inspection arrangements will be on special education provision. More regular and consistent inspection and the guarantee of reporting on provision for pupils with special educational needs in all types of schools are factors to be applauded. However, Fish (1993) points out that:

- the new arrangements do not allow for the inspection of LEA support services unless these are based in special schools; he fears that 'if they are not regularly inspected, like schools, they will cease to be regarded as important';
- no reference is made to the collaboration which often enhances special education provision and 'the ways in which clusters or pyramids of schools can share problems and make more efficient use of resources';
- HMI in OFSTED 'is unlikely to have time to build up a national picture by direct experience'; and
- inspection, however positive, is not sufficient for the professional development of special schools and units or of provision in primary and secondary schools.

Inspections may identify where integration is not working; this is to be welcomed. However, what is done to address the problem may improve mainstream provision or reduce it. For example, HMI (OFSTED 1993), having observed pupils with moderate learning difficulties in over 300 lessons in various settings, reported that more were of a satisfactory or better standard in special schools than in mainstream schools. They indicate criteria for pupils to be considered for integration in mainstream secondary schools at Year 7. These could be used as an excuse. Where adequate resources are used appropriately, practitioners might argue that these criteria are contingent.

As with so many other exercises, the *Framework for Inspection* is itself neutral as far as consideration of special education is concerned. Awareness of the management issues behind the hard data, the limitations of what can be observed within a short time and, most important, the development programme ensuring critical analysis of the inspection report will decide the sharpness of the instrument and its effectiveness in enhancing whole-school provision for pupils with special educational needs.

REFERENCES

Fish, J. (1993) 'A special approach to Inspection?' *British Journal of Special Education* 20 (2): 48–50.

Fletcher-Campbell, F. and Hall, C. (1993) *LEA Support for Special Educational Needs*, Slough: NFER.

Fletcher-Campbell, F., Hegarty, S., Allan, J., Munn, P. and Wells, I. (1992) *Report of the UK Case Studies for the OECD/CERI Project: Integration in the School*, Slough: NFER.

Hegarty, S. (1993) *Meeting Special Needs in Ordinary Schools*, 2nd edn, London: Cassell.

Maychell, K. and Keys, W. (1993) *Under Inspection: LEA Evaluation and Monitoring*, Slough: NFER.

Nixon, J. and Ruddock, J. (1993) 'The role of professional judgement in the local inspection of schools: a study of six local education authorities', *Research Papers in Education, Policy and Practice* 8(2): 135–48.

OFSTED (1992) *Framework for the Inspection of Schools*, London: OFSTED.

OFSTED (1993) *The Integration of Pupils with Moderate Learning Difficulties into Secondary Schools*, April 1991–March 1992, London: Ofsted.

Pyke, N. (1993) 'LEA Inspectors elbow out private operators' *Times Educational Supplement* 1 June 1993:7.

FURTHER READING

Archer, M. (1993) 'When the inspector calls', *Special Children*, January: 10–12.

Chorley, D. (1993) 'OFSTED prepares for special inspections', *British Journal of Special Education* 20(4): 127–8.

OFSTED (1993) *Brookside Special School*, ref. 416/93/55, London: OFSTED.

OFSTED (1993) *Heathlands School for the Deaf*, ref. 392/93/55, London: OFSTED.

Pyke, N. (1993) 'Inspection pledge broken', *The Times Educational Supplement*, 24 December: 1.

Stone, L. (1993) 'Inspecting special – a new approach', *Special* magazine, September: 33–7.

Visser, J., Davie, R., Hinson, M., Landy, M., McNicholas, J. and Gray, D. (1993) *Special Educational Needs and Legislation: A Guide to the Education Act 1993 and OFSTED Inspections*, Stafford: National Association for Special Educational Needs.

Chapter 20

Managing a non-maintained special school for deaf students

Tim Silvester

Debates about increasing the participation of deaf children and young people within the educational mainstream are complicated by these students' requirement for an appropriate linguistic and cultural environment; British Sign Language is rarely used in ordinary schools. The Royal School for the Deaf in Derby is developing such a linguistic and cultural environment in a specialized context. Issues facing students, parents, staff and governors in the 1990s include: uncertainties of enrolment, staffing and funding; changing relationships with LEAs; providing for 10- and 11-year-olds who arrive from mainstream primary schools with limited language and literacy skills and access to in-service training.

INTRODUCTION

One hundred years ago, Dr William Roe opened a school for deaf children in Friargate, Derby. For a number of years he had collected money from a variety of sources, persuading local nobility and businesses as well as the public, that this was much needed in the town. The original buildings served the children for eighty years and twenty years ago the school moved into purpose-built premises on the playing fields of the original school, about half a mile along the road.

In those hundred years, the school has catered for children and students of all abilities and with varying degrees of hearing loss. At present we provide for one hundred children aged 5–16, almost all of whom are profoundly deaf, and eighty students aged 16–19+ ranging from profoundly deaf to partially hearing. About half of the children live near enough to travel daily. The other children and all the post-16 students come from all over Great Britain and therefore live in.

The school was set up as a charity and administered by a board of trustees and paying members, who could vote at meetings. We are still a charity, but now also a Department of Education approved non-maintained special school, administered by a board of governors.

A range of issues affect non-maintained special schools in general and our school in particular. In this chapter I shall focus on four main themes and discuss them in the context of the management of the school. First, bilingual education; secondly, legislation and local authority support for a non-maintained school; thirdly, further education at the Royal School for the Deaf in Derby and lastly, local financial management and governing bodies. I shall conclude with some expectations and hopes for the immediate future.

BILINGUAL EDUCATION

There is no agreed definition of what constitutes a bilingual approach in the education of deaf children, but it will be useful to explain what we at Derby mean by it. British Sign Language (BSL) is the main language we use for communicating, teaching and discussion. It is a visual language which deaf children can easily acquire through contact and communication with deaf adults. It allows children to question, give answers, solve problems, enjoy stories, argue . . . in just the same way that hearing children use spoken English.

We approach English as a second language, important for reading, writing and communicating with hearing people. If children have a good grasp of BSL, we can use that language to help them to acquire English and understand its particular value and importance. Our approach, then, is to use two languages, BSL and English, in their full and proper forms.

Some years ago, the board of governors of the school took a decision that we would adopt this bilingual approach and made a commitment to give equal status within the school both to BSL and English and to deaf and hearing culture. However, at the time of that decision, there had been no plan which outlined what this would mean for the school – for existing children, for existing staff, for new intakes of children, new staff, for training, for the curriculum, for resources. There is often a significant additional cost when you want to make a radical change to the way you teach and it seems that the cost implications were not fully thought through.

That decision was made before I started at the school and it is interesting for me to speculate why and how the board of governors arrived at the decision. Most developments at schools come from government or LEA-imposed decisions, or ideas from staff. This decision does not appear to have happened like that.

The school had a communication centre that offered sign language classes to parents, staff and the public. The centre also became a focus for discussion about communication issues in the education of deaf children. From these discussions evolved the notion that the total communication approach of the school was not the best method of communication and that a bilingual approach would bring much greater educational and social benefits to the children. This view was pursued by some of those connected with the communication centre and the board of governors. Arguments were presented at board meetings and agreement was reached that it was, indeed, in the best interests of the children to follow a bilingual approach and that a definite commitment needed to be made to a bilingual philosophy. If carried out, this decision would have a significant, although possibly gradual, impact on all teachers and assistants working with the children. But the process of change is fraught with difficulties in any organization.

Teachers do not react favourably to externally imposed decisions that have a direct bearing on how and what they teach – recent experiences of the National Curriculum and associated Standard Assessment Tables (SATs) will testify to this. They are generally willing and able to accept change if they are involved in the decision, if the benefits are explained and they are told how they will be helped to make the transition. It is necessary to start this process before you implement the change. If this does not happen, but instead a board of governors' decision is made and the approach started, some resistance is almost inevitable.

Was there a fear that staff would not want to implement a new approach? Would the staff put obstacles in the way of the process? Is it too threatening to existing practices, or was it that the heart ruled the head – that this seemed a good idea and the sooner we started the better it would be for children? Change can be very painful when existing long practices are questioned, when fundamental notions of curriculum delivery and language development instilled during training and in the workplace are directly challenged; and the practical implications of implementing a different policy such as a bilingual approach become apparent.

Nevertheless, the approach has been implemented throughout the Primary School except for a group of children who are seen as experiencing difficulties in learning and who were expected to find working in collaborative groups very hard. Alison Wells, who is hearing, and Sandra Smith, who is deaf, researchers working with Susan Gregory in the Social Science Faculty of the Open University, have been monitoring the implementation and they have found that a bilingual approach is of significant benefit to the children.

Alison and Sandra have also made many suggestions about how we can make improvements and we are responding. For example, we are training our deaf classroom assistants to understand how a child's use of BSL develops so that they can support the teachers by correcting children's mistakes. Secondly, the researchers have advised us that we do not need to have a deaf adult present at all times in all lessons, but that we should have deaf 'consultants', perhaps one for sciences and one for humanities, to support curriculum development and teaching strategies. Thirdly, we have been made aware that the structure of our teaching should be revised to correspond more closely to the cognitive structure of BSL. At the moment, a typical lesson will begin with particulars and build up towards a general, overall picture of the topic under discussion. We are being encouraged to introduce the main topic or concepts of the lesson right at the beginning and then go on to the discussion of details.

We are committed and enthusiastic about our approach and remain optimistic that a bilingual method will give deaf children better access to the curriculum and will improve their literacy skills. However, with hindsight, there would have been undoubted advantages if the whole process had been properly discussed, planned and costed from the outset.

Employing deaf people as teachers

If a bilingual approach is to succeed, the children must have access to good models of BSL and this means employing deaf adults, especially among child contact staff. It says something about the education of deaf people that there are few of them who are 'appropriately qualified' to do these jobs.

We have to make some uncomfortable decisions. There is considerable pressure to employ 'qualified' people wherever possible. But what qualifications do we need from those providing BSL to the children? Ideally, the same standard as those providing English to the children. Few deaf people have been able to obtain these formal qualifications, as exams and training are almost always in their second language, English. There are exams and qualifications that recognize people's knowledge of and competence in BSL, but do not easily equate to other qualifications. We have taken the view that if deaf people can prove and demonstrate their competence in BSL and have a good general education, they have much to offer deaf children and we employ them as assistants in the classroom or as residential care workers.

In the classroom, these 'unqualified' assistants are asked to take on much more responsibility than should be expected, as they are the ones who reinforce the delivery of the curriculum in BSL.

Qualified teachers of the deaf, who are themselves deaf, are rare, but we are fortunate in having two of them on our staff. It is extremely difficult for deaf people to become qualified teachers as they have to spend some time teaching hearing children in mainstream schools and be assessed on this. So again, barriers exist to prevent schools having a wider choice of appropriate teachers for deaf children.

LEGISLATION AND LOCAL AUTHORITY SUPPORT FOR A NON-MAINTAINED SPECIAL SCHOOL

Over the past twenty years, more than half of the special schools for deaf children have closed. There have been a number of coincidental events that have led to this situation:

- Technology has led to significant improvements in personal and radio hearing aids. This has enabled many severely deaf children to have auditory access to the curriculum of mainstream schools.
- There has been a trend, supported by legislation, to place pupils identified as having 'special educational needs' into mainstream schools.
- Local education authorities have had their budgets cut and have needed to consider all the costs very carefully. Although not necessarily a cheaper option, integrating some pupils into mainstream could be seen as a way of saving money. This would be especially so if local mainstream placement could be provided instead of an out-of-county residential school.

The most recent Act to affect us is the 1993 Education Act, which was preceded by the White Paper 'Choice and Diversity'. One of the aims of the Act was to give parents of children seen to have 'special educational needs' the same rights as all other parents in their choice of school. In reality this choice extended to maintained and grant-maintained schools within the parents' LEA but not to non-maintained schools. Heads and governors of non-maintained schools as a body did lobby hard to allow parents to name a non-maintained special school as their choice of school for their children. Although they did not achieve this entirely, some concessions were made. Parents are now allowed to make a case for placement of their child in a non-maintained special school and LEAs must consider their views.

We depend on LEAs deciding to send children to us for their education. This may be because they do not have, or are not able to make, appropriate provision for a particular child at a particular age. It may also be because parents feel that we can better meet the child's educational needs than their LEA at a particular time. Often there is general agreement between parents and LEAs, but on occasions there is a dispute. Resolving these disputes can be unsettling for parents and may drag on for months, as, for example, it did for David and his parents.

David

David is profoundly deaf, has a high IQ measured on non-verbal tests and has been educated by means of oral methods in mainstream provision. He has had support in the classroom and his parents have had help from peripatetic teachers.

His parents felt that he was not progressing well in speech and language work nor in reading and writing. The authorities felt that reasonable progress was being made and that no change of provision was needed.

When he was 9, David's parents contacted the local social services for deaf people and explained their worries about David. The social services suggested that they look at provision which offered sign language so that David could make progress in his ability to communicate. It was explained that they were entitled to make a private visit to our school and look at the provision.

They made a visit when David was 10, thought that we could meet his needs and asked us to assess him with a view to his coming here. It was explained that we would make the assessment, but that it was the LEA who would decide if David could attend. We assessed David and felt that we could meet his needs.

The parents told the LEA what they felt and asked for reassessment. The process rambled on slowly and after several meetings and much lobbying by parents and social workers, the LEA did agree that David could come to us. The whole process of referral took nearly two years.

INCREASED REFERRAL OF 10- AND 11-YEAR-OLDS

There are a number of families involved in similar lengthy referral procedures. Sometimes, the parents and LEA fail to agree and the case has to go to appeal. Presently, there are two cases pending the result of an appeal; one is to the Secretary of State for Education.

One of the trends in recent years at our school has been the increased referrals of 10- and 11-year-olds. Parents and LEAs are aware that the mainstream provision has not been as successful for these children as they had hoped. Supporters of our bilingual approach will say that they are not really surprised as these children are unlikely to have been in an environment where they had easy access to a language they could understand from adults and peers.

Earlier, I stated that well over half of the schools for deaf children have closed in the past twenty years. Although many people do not like the idea of young children going to segregated special schools, they are nevertheless the places that can provide a natural environment for profoundly deaf children because they have contact with and learn from adults and children who use a common language, BSL, just as hearing children go to school and mix with adults and peers who use the common language English.

Authorities do vary greatly in their response to parents' requests for placements. The healthiest attitude is from a nearby LEA who will make a strong case for the placement they think will best meet the education needs of the child, despite what parents want. However, they do listen to parents and they have stated that they are reluctant to go as far as appeal since if the parents really do not support a placement, it is unlikely to succeed. Oh that all LEAs could be so enlightened!

Staffing

Delays in decisions about referrals also hinder us in making estimates of the number of children we are catering for each September. Class sizes are small, usually six to eight pupils, so numbers are critical when deciding staffing levels. If LEAs do not or cannot tell us before April or May if their children are coming to us it poses problems for staffing in September, because if we need to recruit a new teacher for September and they are currently employed in another school, they have to give in their notice by the end of May. Unfortunately, the reality is that it is usually in the summer term that we are notified of new entrants, which can also be the result of administrative hold-ups in the LEAs, as well as disputed decisions.

If there have been a large number of school leavers, we need a similar number to start the following September, just to maintain the existing staff levels – we are not able to redeploy as we are not part of the LEA. Consequently, late notice by LEAs can also force late, unpleasant decisions on us about possible redundancies.

FURTHER EDUCATION AT THE ROYAL SCHOOL FOR THE DEAF, DERBY

The 1992 Further and Higher Education Act took the financing and control of further education and tertiary colleges away from LEAs. Colleges were governed independently and financed by the Further Education Funding Council (FEFC). Within the overall structure of the Royal School for the Deaf in Derby, we have a post-16 department called the College for Deaf People (CDP). This was considered by the FEFC to be an 'independent institution providing education for students outside the sector'. This defi-nition is now causing some problems for us as the College for Deaf People is still part of the 'school'. The FEFC, under their rules, may not now support students who attend 'schools'. If the CDP were to have its own governing body and were financially independent, it might be considered as a college. If it does not have this independence, it may have to look to LEAs to pay for the students since it is the LEAs' responsibility to pay for places in schools that are needed for students or children with statements of special educa-tional needs.

LEAs tend to consider that it is the FEFC's responsibility to provide for students attending colleges, even if that college is technically part of a 'school'. If the FEFC will not fund a 'school', and LEAs have to make the provision, they may try to find an appropriate local course with support, rather than pay for the student to attend a residential institution like ours, even if that is the students' and parents' preferred option. So at present, the situation is unresolved and the future of CDP looks less secure than it did a year ago.

Although we are able to take certain actions ourselves, to improve and adapt to changing circumstances, much of our fate is often not in our own hands.

LOCAL FINANCIAL MANAGEMENT AND THE ROLE OF SCHOOL GOVERNORS

Over the past few years, most schools have had more direct control over the way they spend their budgets either from becoming grant maintained (GM) or through the Local Management of Schools (LMS) Scheme. LMS is now being extended to special schools. All of these schools are allocated a budget from either the Funding Agency for Schools (FAS) for GM schools or LEAs. The size of that budget is determined by a formula that takes account of many factors, including age of pupils, catchment area, rural or urban location, condition of buildings, special needs and, importantly, the number of pupils attending the school. It is this latter factor over which schools have most influence in determining the size of their budget. If the school is popular and successful and attracting a large number of pupils from a wide area (which it is permitted to do now under various Education Acts) it will increase the size of its budget. Thus, most schools now have considerable control over how they spend their budget and some influence over the size of that budget.

For non-maintained schools, the position has always been that they have total control over how they spend their budget and considerable control over the size of that budget. They do not have total control over the intake, and, therefore, the size of the budget for the reasons mentioned earlier in the section on legislation – i.e. however popular and successful the school or college may be, it is the LEAs and the FEFC who have the ultimate decision on who will attend.

Non-maintained schools have not had the back-up services of maintained schools – advisers, school meals service, buildings, grounds and maintenance departments, central purchasing facilities and a large administration that could advise on all financial, employment and educational issues, practices and regulations. Everything that we need, e.g. advice, information, resources and training, has to be provided and paid for by us.

All schools have a governing body. Before the advent of GM schools and LMS, these governing bodies had limited powers and responsibilities and much of what a school did was determined by the LEA. Although the powers and responsibilities have now been widened, they are still able to make reference to and have links with a larger organization (FAS or LEA) which can give advice and guidance on a range of issues and regulations.

Since governors are voluntary, they rarely have the time to become deeply involved in all the educational legislation that is appearing and to look at all the implications of this for the school. But for a non-maintained school this is crucial. Generally, the governing bodies of these schools rely on the headteacher to keep them informed and to carry out all the necessary requirements and directions. It could be argued that this puts these headteachers in a strong position with governors, but there is also a danger that there is no informed body to check and monitor that the school is being properly run in accordance with all the current regulations: educational, financial, health and safety, food hygiene.

The governing bodies of non-maintained schools are not eligible for local authority training and we have provided some training at the school itself. At the moment, most of the governors come from nearby areas and we are trying to extend membership to include representatives of more of the sponsoring LEAs.

As far as the monitoring of the work of the school as a whole is concerned, we are due to be inspected by Derbyshire Social Services Department in May 1994 under the terms of the Children Act (1989) and our provision for students over the age of 16 is due for inspection in June 1994 by a team from the FEFC. We shall also be inspected by the Office for Standards in Education (OFSTED) in due course.

THE IMMEDIATE FUTURE

Placement in a non-maintained special school has always been considered an expensive provision compared to the additional cost of supporting a child in the mainstream. Now that all elements of LEA provision have to be costed, it is emerging that schools like ours are not really so expensive after all. I know of two LEAs in the Midlands who charge other LEAs the same amount of money for a day place in one of their units for deaf children as we charge for a residential placement.

If our prices remain 'competitive' it will be interesting to see if this has an effect on LEAs when there is a dispute between themselves and parents over a child's placement. In making these decisions, LEAs have to make 'efficient use of their resources' and they have used this argument in the past to keep children in local provision. This should become less of a contentious issue as true costs of all provision are now emerging.

Under the 1993 Education Act, if a dispute over placement between parents and LEAs cannot be resolved, the case will be referred to a newly established tribunal. The decisions of the tribunals will be binding. Given that the arguments about cost should be less significant now, decisions can be made on more important, educational, grounds.

The majority of hearing impaired children cope well in mainstream schools and the provision there meets their educational needs. There is a minority of profoundly deaf children whose needs may best be met in a different environment – a school for deaf children. I have no disagreement with mainstream provision and I know that many of our pupils could benefit from well planned links with these schools. The 1993 Act was based on Choice and Diversity of Education. Let us hope that neither of these will be diminished any further for deaf children.

CONCLUSION

The current financial and administrative requirements of schools has meant that some staff have had to acquire new skills, or schools have had to bring in specialist staff. As they buy (and in some cases sell) services, they are realizing their true cost. It is a different situation from when most back-up services were provided by LEAs.

One of the interesting features of this for a school like ours is the realization that we are already where they are going – and indeed have been here all the time! We are used to working to a budget and adjusting our provision accordingly. In many ways, we are reasonably cost effective as well, as we have had to survive in the market place – we have not had a natural or automatic catchment area. We exist only so long as our services are valued and bought.

Chapter 21

Educating pupils who experience emotional and behavioural difficulties

A Northern Ireland perspective

Geraldine Bunting and David McConnell

Perhaps more than any other area of special education, provision for pupils who experience emotional and behavioural difficulties has been made in response to what teachers and administrators have seen as a crisis in mainstream schools. Children and young people are referred to special schools because of the need of teachers and other students to be free of them, rather than because of their own 'special need'. In this article, Geraldine Bunting and David McConnell begin with an overview of provision in Northern Ireland and set this in the context of the dual system, which is based on sectarian divisions. In Northern Ireland, 'integration' refers to the inclusion of Catholic and Protestant students in one school. Provision for students seen to have 'emotional and behavioural difficulties' is then discussed, in the context both of the introduction of the Northern Ireland Curriculum and local financial management and the 'troubles': what does it mean to be 'disruptive' in Belfast? The chapter concludes with an account of current debates about provision for students identified as having 'emotional and behavioural difficulties' (EBD).

OVERVIEW OF PROVISION IN NORTHERN IRELAND

In Northern Ireland much of the early provision for disabled children and those who experience difficulties in learning, or other kinds of difficulties mirrored that in England and Wales, with many of the schools founded by religious orders and charitable institutions. The period after the Second World War saw much growth in special education arising mainly from the development of charitable institutions whose original emphasis had been on care. The 1947 Education Act laid on the county and borough health committees the responsibility of catering for children who were deemed 'unsuitable for education' and, as schools for children with traditional types of 'handicap' were already in existence, the education committees concentrated on making provision for 'educationally subnormal' children, a category which had been defined for the first time in the 1947 Act. Remedial groups and classes were established in Northern Ireland in 1947 and special class allowances were paid to teachers from that date. Pupils who experienced emotional and behaviour problems were often placed in schools for children categorized as 'educationally subnormal' but in the 1970s several schools were opened specifically for 'maladjusted' children. No training was available at that time for teachers of maladjusted pupils but several teachers went to study 'the education of maladjusted children' in England where Manchester and Birmingham Universities offered courses.

Provision to meet 'Special Educational Needs'

The provisions of the 1981 Education Act in England and Wales were reflected in the Education Order (Northern Ireland) 1984. These provisions dealt specifically with special education services in the province and introduced the concept of special educational need.

Since April 1987, as a result of the Education Order (Northern Ireland) 1987, the Education and Library Boards have made provision for all children with special educational needs up to the age of 19. Subsequently the term 'maladjusted' was dropped and the pupils came under the special needs umbrella, although they are commonly known as 'EBD', pupils.

GEOGRAPHY AND THE CENTRALIZATION OF RESOURCES

It is important to look at the implications of the geography of Northern Ireland. Being a relatively small region with a total population of 1.5 million, it is possible to provide many specialist services serving the whole area, in one city. In the past children with serious disabilities came from all over Northern Ireland to Belfast, where one-third of the total population is concentrated, as weekly boarders. Children from rural districts, with relatively minor disabilities or with learning difficulties (including the 'maladjusted') attended mainstream schools, as there were insufficient numbers to constitute a special school in any one region. Integration has therefore been a feature of education for many years in Northern Ireland because of the geography of the region. Pupils with more obvious emotional and behavioural difficulties were often placed in Educationally Subnormal residential schools or if their problems were more severe they were referred to child psychiatry and then usually became resident in a hospital school.

Local government

In 1921 Northern Ireland had a similar structure of local government to Great Britain and the rest of Ireland, i.e. there were two county boroughs, Londonderry and Belfast, whose corporations were all-purpose authorities, and in the rest of Northern Ireland there was a top tier of six county councils, with a lower tier of twenty-four urban and thirty-one rural district councils. The system had been set up under the Local Government (Ireland) Act 1898. There had been a failure to reform the basic structure of local government which remained relatively unchanged from 1921 to the 1960s.

In 1966 a White Paper was published which stated that 'the present local government system stems from the nineteeneth century and is now in need of overhaul'. A review body, under the chairmanship of Patrick Macrory, was set up to study aspects of the reorganization of local government. It advised that Health and Personal Services, Education and Libraries be placed under an area board structure and this was accepted as the basis for local administration. This structure still exists today.

Education and library boards

There are at present five education and library boards (ELBs) but, in the mid-1990s, this is under review. They support pupils in nursery, primary, secondary, grammar and special schools. They are also responsible for public library services. Approximately 40 per cent of the members of each board are nominated by district councils, and 25 per cent represent bodies who either transferred their schools to the state or are responsible for voluntary schools with maintained status. There are also three teachers, three persons with a special interest in libraries and six or seven nominees of the minister (Minister of State for Education). The total membership of each board ranges from thirty-one to thirty-five. The majority of board members are appointed by the minister and do not have to account to the public through an electoral mechanism for their policies.

Funding of the education system

The whole system of reorganization had assumed the existence of a Regional government, but under direct rule, since 1974, the Northern Ireland Office ministers and the Westminister parliament now provide the only level of accountability. The boards have no power to levy rates or community charges to residents in their areas nor is any finance for education raised through district councils. The Department of Education for Northern Ireland funds the boards directly from the block grant which Westminster allocates to Northern Ireland.

A sectarian system

The major benefit which reorganization was expected to produce was the ending of claims and disputes about religious discrimination and sectarian bias in planning, employment and other matters. It was also hoped that people with the necessary experience would be appointed to the boards. It was hoped that people of all religious persuasions might be willing to serve on co-opted bodies, independent of party machines. This is more the case now than it was under a system of local elections, which often failed to attract appropriate representatives.

THE ORGANIZATION OF THE SCHOOL SYSTEM

The primary and secondary school system is organized broadly along religious lines with two main sectors; controlled and maintained.

Controlled schools

These schools are provided by the ELBs and are managed by boards of governors. They are attended mainly by pupils from the Protestant community. The running costs are met in full by the ELBs from grants paid by the Department of Education.

Maintained schools

The Council for Catholic Maintained Schools has responsibility for all maintained schools under Roman Catholic management which are under the auspices of the diocesan authorities and religious orders. In the past approved capital building costs were grant aided up to 85 per cent by the Department of Education and the running costs were met by the ELBs, but since 1990 all of their costs have been met externally by the Council for Catholic Maintained Schools.

Integrated schools

In recent years a number of schools have been established with the aim of providing education for Roman Catholic and Protestant children together. These are called 'integrated schools' (not to be confused with the integration of special needs pupils in mainstream!). The Education Reform (Northern Ireland) Order 1989 introduced new measures whereby new integrated schools receive public funding right from their beginnings, whereas in the past they received funding only when their viability was demonstrated.

BACKGROUNDS OF EBD PUPILS

The children in EBD special schools and units are not a homogeneous group. The expression 'emotional and behavioural difficulties' permits a very wide range of behaviours and needs to be gathered under its umbrella. As in Britain there are many more boys than girls in the special units and there tends to be a preponderance of those who have conduct disorders – aggressive young males. Consequently those who may be more emotionally vulnerable can find themselves swamped in the special unit and unable to receive the care and attention they need. Consider for example John, who is invariably quiet, works well and cooperates in class while most of his peers do not. Consequently as others regularly push their behaviour beyond the point where it can either be ignored or quietly sorted out, he receives less individual attention, the teachers get to know him less well and counselling time may be dominated by more demanding pupils. Despite his apparently good progress in school John appears to have a serious problem with solvent abuse, joyrides regularly and all of this is compounded by the poor mental health of one of his parents.

There is an ongoing debate in Northern Ireland concerning whether or not the number of disruptive pupils is increasing and whether or not the extent of their disturbance or distress is more profound. It has been illustrated by various pieces of research, however, that when teachers are under pressure (as they have been in recent years due to the unprecedented amount of externally directed change) they tolerate less deviation from the norm of acceptable behaviour.

Various attempts have also been made to assess the extent to which the 'troubles' may have contributed to difficulties. This is a complex issue, for while it is clearly possible to know whether families or individuals have had a direct experience (e.g. relative killed or injured, imprisoned, witnessed an incident), it is not possible to know the extent to which members of a family might be involved in secret organizations and how this could affect family relationships. Nor is it possible to know the extent to which a family may cooperate with or condone paramilitary activity carried out, in their own community or how this might influence a child.

We suspect that the children who come to special units will have backgrounds and experiences similar to those of their counterparts in Britain. It is unlikely that their emotional and behavioural difficulties are related to one specific incident (although this can happen) but rather to a series of interconnecting factors which often include marital breakdown (often with the mother left to shoulder an impossible burden), poverty, low self-esteem, difficulties with authority figures, aggression and poor peer relationships. The vast majority of pupils in EBD schools come from working-class backgrounds.

PROVISION OF EBD SCHOOLS AND UNITS IN NORTHERN IRELAND

At present there are five special schools in Northern Ireland which cater for the needs of EBD pupils and an increasing number of units which may be attached to controlled or maintained schools or operate on their own site.

Almost all EBD schools are in the controlled sector and pupils from both Catholic and Protestant communities attend these schools. Statemented pupils who attend mainstream schools may be enrolled in either a controlled or a maintained school.

The five ELBs in Northern Ireland have each produced their own response to pupils who experience emotional and behavioural difficulties:

- The North Eastern ELB has three guidance units with an educational psychologist in charge of each.
- The Western Board has one educational guidance unit and outreach support team with a teacher in charge.
- The Southern Board has the only residential school, which offers places, for boys from 11 to 16 years. It has recently extended its capacity from twenty to thirty.
- The South Eastern Education and Library Board has a primary unit which is located in an MLD school, a secondary school and another hospital school which takes pupils from 8 to 14 years. The hospital school is an in-patient facility of the Child Guidance Unit at the Royal Victoria Hospital.
- The Belfast Board has one school for secondary pupils, a unit for secondary pupils, a unit for primary pupils and a new middle school due to open in April 1994 which will cater for pupils in the 8–14 age range.

There are waiting lists for most of these schools and there is a further group of pupils who receive home tuition (also including pregnant teenagers).

Apart from the segregated provision, various schools have guidance units and most ELBs have teams of outreach teachers who offer support in mainstream schools, e.g. the SEELB has a team of six teachers who offer support to eighty secondary-age pupils spread around thirty-four schools.

In Belfast there is an intermediate treatment centre which operates a multiprofessional approach and also undertakes work with families.

There are also four training schools (Northern Ireland equivalent of 'community home with education') which operate within the juvenile justice system (i.e. not the education service) of the Northern Ireland Office. While these were originally for young offenders, they have found themselves dealing increasingly with children who are there for reasons of 'care', either on temporary orders or training school orders (now six months to two years). For example Sean, a 14-year-old boy, was placed in training school under a care order because he was endangering his life with severe solvent abuse. He lived alone with his mother who could no longer control him.

The training schools also receive children for 'educational' reasons (non-attendance) and a number of these are non-resident, attending only for schooling. This latter option will no longer apply when the Northern Ireland Children's Order is introduced, so there may be more children who need special provision within the education service, although some people have suggested other reasons may be readily available to ensure at least some of them enter the juvenile justice system. Three of the training schools are 'open' facilities, and one is a secure unit which presently has places for boys only (it also receives boys on remand as well as those who have repeatedly absconded from the more open units) but there are plans to open the facility for girls.

At present there is no residential provision within the education service for girls and the general absence of such facilities in Northern Ireland may be the result of a policy that residential provision should be the responsibility of health and social services and not the education service. A number of children's homes, however, have closed in recent years and there is a feeling that children being placed in care presently are those in most distress. Although it has been suggested that those homes were surplus to requirements, this seems unlikely as there is increasing difficulty in finding a place when it is considered necessary. As there is often pressure for places, those in most need are likely to be prioritized. All this creates more pressure for the care agencies and it is when such a placement breaks down that the children can be sent to training schools.

THE EDUCATION REFORM (NORTHERN IRELAND) ORDER 1989

The provisions of the Education Reform (Northern Ireland) Order 1989 apply to all schools (except training schools), with the Common Curriculum for Northern Ireland being introduced to special schools at the same time as mainstream schools. This Order came into effect on a basis of gradual introduction in 1990 and has introduced to Northern Ireland similar proposals to those contained in the Education Reform Act of England and Wales. The Department of Education in Northern Ireland provided extra financial resources to implement ERO in the areas of in-service training, extra resources, additional equipment and additional accommodation. The LBs also provided substantial support to schools at this time of immense change. There are of course difficulties for those of us in small special schools (eighteen to thirty pupils) as the resourcing for such areas as modern languages, technology and design and the provision of adequate facilities for science present immense difficulties.

THE EFFECTS OF LMS

Since April 1991 all post-primary schools and large primary schools have had fully delegated budgets. The Local Management of Schools (LMS) has not yet extended formula funding or delegated budgets to special schools but at present a working party is examining the possibility of such an extension.

Many teachers in Northern Ireland feel concerned about the effects of

LMS on pupils with special needs and find it difficult to comprehend how a relevant formula could be decided for demand-determined services. They fear the possibility of the re-introduction of the categorization of pupils and also have concerns regarding mainstream schools operating in competition with others in their area, unwilling to admit pupils who do not contribute positively to exam results.

The publication of league tables takes no account of the starting point of pupils and is unfair to many excellent, dedicated teachers.

LACK OF COORDINATION AMONG AGENCIES

As in Britain, the various professions are educated and trained separately, have little understanding of each other's role, often have different opinions about the priority of need in a particular case and consequently disagree about preferred outcomes. While there have been various attempts to organize some cross-professional contact and even training, this issue has not been seriously addressed at an official level.

Difficulties between mainstream teachers and other professionals are possibly greater than the difficulties experienced between them and special schools and units, which do have more regular contact. Informal networks can and do emerge. Even here, however, the contact is almost exclusively practical and problem solving and there is no official structure or forum to deal with broad issues or policy.

In fact the relationships between mainstream schools and special units can also be problematic. While it might be tempting to suggest that the core of their relationship stems from the fact that ordinary schools don't want difficult or disruptive pupils and would prefer that someone came and took them away, this fails to acknowledge the complexities of the situation.

REASONS FOR REFERRAL TO EBD SCHOOLS

Not surprisingly, teachers have always preferred to teach children who are ready and willing to learn and cooperate and follow the general class routine. Having said that, tolerance levels have always varied both between teachers in the same school and from one school to another. What provoked referral to a special unit in one school might not have done so in another. Schools vary also in their effectiveness in meeting the needs of children who experience emotional and behavioural difficulties.

In recent years the various changes in the education system with which schools have had to cope may have contributed to a general reduction in tolerance levels. The fact that more young children are exhibiting such behaviour could also be linked to social, economic and political factors which may have intensified the distress which some children experience. Certainly there are increasing demands for more provision outside the mainstream, and schools feel ill-equipped to deal with the behaviour of some of their pupils. Corporal punishment is still talked about nostalgically by many teachers and it would be fair to say that the general population in Northern Ireland has a traditional view of child-rearing with the abolition of corporal punishment being regretted by many parents as well as teachers. Some schools use 'rolling suspension' as a means of relieving them of their more difficult pupils who cannot be accommodated immediately in a special school or unit.

The failure of the special sector to provide an immediate answer can create its own tension, while at the opposite end of the process a request that a pupil be given an opportunity to return to mainstream can produce a response ranging from a not quite enthusiastic 'yes' to 'panic'.

LENGTH OF STAY IN EBD SCHOOLS/UNITS

Some of the guidance units, and the Belfast intermediate treatment centre, operate on fixed-term arrangements and the pupils remain on the register of the home school. The special schools tend to have the children for longer periods and most do not return to mainstream. When they do, the mainstream schools want an assurance that if it 'breaks down' the special school will take the pupil back. This means that a place must be held and therefore cannot be offered to someone else.

Some special schools now operate a system of shared care, i.e. initially the pupil spends four days in the special school and one in the home school (the particular day is usually carefully chosen by the outreach teacher) so that links are never completely broken. The days in the mainstream are gradually increased and in this way it is hoped that full return to the mainstream school will be much easier for both parties.

Difficulties can arise because teachers in the special schools tend to focus on the problems which the pupil is experiencing, while teachers in mainstream tend to focus on what it may mean for them and the rest of the class. It would seem too that many pupils, having experienced the atmosphere of the special schools and units (smaller, less pressure, more tolerance), do not wish to return to the mainstream. Ironically perhaps, it is often those who wish to return who are most definitely unwelcome, while those who might return don't wish to do so.

ISSUES OF CONCERN TO TEACHERS OF EBD PUPILS

As a result of the recent education reform, special schools and units are experiencing some confusion regarding their role. They were set up to address the emotional and behavioural needs of the children and when possible to return them to the mainstream school system. Since the introduction of the Education Reform Order, which ensures the entitlement of all children to the full Northern Ireland Curriculum (NIC), the focus is shifting to the curriculum.

Many of the units are small and will only be able to meet this obligation through links with further education colleges, shared appointments and peripatetic support. However some people question the appropriateness of the shift in emphasis. If these schools are to offer the pupils an experience which approximates more and more to that of the ordinary school, then are they reproducing the situation in which the children have failed before and setting them up for failure again?

The logic of this 'normalization' approach would suggest that their special needs are met through being in a smaller school with perhaps a greater degree of sympathy and tolerance in conjunction with well taught, interesting and well prepared lessons, geared to their current levels of attainment. No other modification of either the timetable or the length of time spent in class is necessary. Arguments that modifications are necessary deny these children their right to access all aspects of the curriculum. While no overall assessment has been made of schools and units in Northern Ireland, a DES survey of EBD schools and units covering the period 1983–8 (DES 1989) suggests that curriculum planning and delivery has been weaker in these schools and units than in mainstream.

Such an outlook, if implemented and carried to its logical conclusion, would suggest that there may be no need for separate schools or units, since such an environment can be created within any school. This is fully in accord with the commitment to integration which was made in the special needs legislation but runs contrary to the subsequent expansion of special provisions for pupils who experience emotional and behavioural problems.

Those who would question the logic of the above argument point out that the NIC was devised in the absence of consideration of children with special needs. To suggest that pupils undertake a normal timetable begs the question of why they are in a special school in the first place. Further, many pupils will already have been in small groups or withdrawal classes in mainstream schools but this has not solved the problem. Such an approach also fails to understand that those units must begin by addressing the most pressing needs of the children, whatever these may be. If there is a complete focus on the delivery of the curriculum this may increase the scope for conflict between teachers and children, lead to less tolerance and the removal of those who prevent the curriculum being taught. Since it is when these children are being intellectually challenged that conflict is more likely to arise, a twin focus on their special needs as well as the curriculum has implications not only for what is taught and how it is taught, but more generally for the organization of the school. If one expects such schools and units to be like ordinary schools, a contradiction is obvious when one examines the rationale for their establishment. It shows no real insight or understanding of the extent of the special needs of the pupils.

It would appear that DENI (Department of Education Northern Ireland) inspectors are promoting the 'normalization' viewpoint. The ELBs have not expressed a view either individually or collectively, but as this issue has only recently arisen this is not surprising. Unless it is acknowledged that there is an issue here regarding how schools and units should address the special needs of pupils, while at the same time meeting curricular responsibilities, two possibilities emerge: either the schools and units comply with the normalization model or some administrative compromise is sought. Another possible option, that of parent power, seems unlikely, for while there are parental pressure groups in other areas of education, none has been developed in the EBD sector.

It has been suggested that one way of resolving the problem is through the statementing process (i.e. statementing out). There are, however, a number of difficulties with this view. Educational psychologists may consider such an approach unprofessional and may not wish to comply with it. In any case, many of the pupils who attend special schools (EBD) are not statemented and the temporary exclusion procedure is complex (deliberately so, perhaps) and relatively untried.

Clearly, therefore, we are at something of a crossroads for EBD provision in Northern Ireland. There is a concern that these children should retain their unqualified right of access to a full education. The NIC is not the full curriculum but it is only when the NIC has been fully put in place that other 'value added' factors can be undertaken. However there is also concern that this approach begins not from the needs of the children but from the curriculum, that it flies in the face of reality and that some compromise has to be achieved. When it was recognized that the NIC was inappropriate for children with severe learning difficulties, 'Stepping Stones' was produced. The question remains as to what extent the special needs of pupils who experience emotional and behavioural difficulties should be acknowledged and reflected in the organization and curriculum of the school or unit.

REFERENCE

DES (1989) Report of HMI on *A Survey of Provision for Pupils with Emotional and Behavioural Difficulties in Mainstream, Special Schools and Units 1983–1988*, London: HMSO.

Chapter 22

Governing secondary schools

Margaret Bethell

Margaret Bethell is a school governor and governor trainer in Norfolk. In this chapter she begins by outlining the composition and statutory duties of school governing bodies. Governors have extensive responsibilities with regard to their school's curriculum and its provision to meet the educational requirements of all its students. Margaret sometimes uses a wheelchair and sometimes crutches, so she is aware that access is crucial to the participation in mainstream education of disabled students and adults. She concludes by describing her county's approach to governor training and argues that it might be sensible to make training compulsory.

THE COMPOSITION AND DUTIES OF SCHOOL GOVERNING BODIES

Prior to the Education Act 1980, there was no place for parents or teaching staff on a school's board of managers; indeed not all schools had managers. The 1980 Act changed the name to governors, brought in parent and teacher governors and gave every school a governing body. It was not until the 1986 Act that the numbers of governors was prescribed by law. The *Guide to the Law*, issued by the Department for Education (DFE 1993) to every governor, is the school governor's 'bible'. This document states, 'A school governing body is a combination of appointed, elected, and "co-opted" governors.' This statement shows the attempt made to ensure that schools are governed democratically.

The law says that there must be a stipulated number of elected parent governors, elected teacher governors, and governors appointed by the local education authority (LEA). Other governors are co-opted by the elected and appointed governors. The headteacher can choose to be a governor or not. There are also foundation and first governors in certain schools, and minor authority governors in county and controlled schools. The number of pupils on the school roll dictates the number of governors.

Grant-maintained schools have slightly different arrangements although they still have the same categories. In particular, in grant-maintained schools the headteacher *must* be a governor.

Parent governors, whilst not being delegates, will represent the parents' interests. Teacher governors will reflect the staff aspect of school life.

LEA governors are slightly more obscure in that while they officially represent the local authority they may be very remote from the authority unless they are council officials or employees. They are often nominated by a local representative of the main political parties, and the nominee's only qualification may be membership of that party. This can lead to appointees who have no interest in schools or education but simply fill a position. Minor authority governors, and foundation/first governors represent a particular body: the district or parish council, church authority, or other voluntary organization, or the previous governing body in the case of a newly accepted grant-maintained school.

Co-opted governors will be appointed to balance the interests of the governing body with special emphasis on representation of the local business community. Co-options are especially important in secondary schools where good links with local industries and businesses are essential.

All governors much be committed to the school. The main commitment is at governors' meetings. These are held at least once a term, and good attendance is vital. A primary school meeting may be fairly informal and discussion is likely to centre on easily understood items of low-key management, for example, the state of the playground fence or the age of the next intake.

THE ROLE OF GOVERNOR IN A SECONDARY SCHOOL

A secondary school is like a small business! The governors' meeting will be formal, involve large amounts of paperwork, and some governors may find difficulty understanding the complexities of a very large school. A typical agenda might include awarding of contracts worth thousands of pounds, development of new curricular subjects, examination results, and monitoring a budget of close on 3 million!

I overcome this by reading all pre-circulated document and querying any I don't understand with the sender. I'm then quite willing to ask questions during the meeting if I need to. A good Chair will encourage this as it is essential that all governors are fully involved.

In practice, the actual amount of involvement will depend on their role. The role of the governor varies from school to school. It is something which must be negotiated with the headteacher. Governors are often seen as 'lay people', even as interfering busybodies! This is very sad and is usually due to unfortunate incidents in the past when governors have overstepped the mark. The role of a governor should be as a supportive friend. The make-up of the governing body is such that there should be all types of skills available to the school. A headteacher who is 'lost when it comes to book-keeping' will welcome the help of a governor who works as an accountant. A doctor who is a governor will be invaluable when formulating the health and safety policy. A parent governor is often the best person to see the effect on the school community of a change in admissions policy.

Although every governor is equal on the governing body, sometimes parent governors see themselves as not as useful as, perhaps, an LEA governor who has been a governor for years. This is where negotiating roles can increase the confidence of certain governors. It also increases their effectiveness and therefore the effectiveness of the governing body as a whole. Governors are responsible for the conduct of the school. This means the ethos and image of the school, in particular within the local community.

Governors must agree policies on admissions, charging for activities, discipline, health and safety, and complaints procedures.

By 1996, all LEA schools will be working under a scheme of Local Management of Schools (LMS). Currently special schools and some primary schools are still managed by the LEA. In LMS schools, governors are responsible for managing the budget and have control over numbers of staff employed. They must also have a policy for grievance and disciplinary procedures for staff.

GOVERNORS AND CURRICULUM DEVELOPMENT

In all schools, governors share, with the headteacher and LEA, a responsibility for special educational needs, and the curriculum. These are the areas that many governors find most daunting.

The law states that 'responsibility for the curriculum is shared between the head, teachers, governors, the LEA and the Secretary of State'. There is a National Curriculum which covers ten foundation subjects (nine in primary schools). The governors, with the headteacher and the LEA, must make sure the National Curriculum is taught. Governors are responsible for deciding if sex education is taught and its content (this differs slightly in some types of school).

The governors share responsibility with the headteacher and the LEA for making sure that the requirements on religious education are met. In special agreement schools, those set up by a trust for a particular denomination or faith, the headteacher and the governors are responsible for the religious education provided. Governors share responsibility for ensuring that the requirements on collective worship are met. It is the responsibility of the governors to make sure that all parents know of their right to withdraw their children from religious education and collective worship. Currently this is the only part of the curriculum where parents have this right although this is in the process of changing to include sex education in some cases. The headteacher is able to make temporary exceptions from the National

Curriculum for an individual pupil in circumstances of special need. This may be a short-term need possibly due to emotional problems or illness, or may be linked to special educational needs.

RESPONSIBILITIES FOR MEETING SPECIAL EDUCATIONAL NEEDS

The LEA has a responsibility to formally assess all children with special educational needs in its area. This may lead to a statement of special educational need which can stipulate areas of the National Curriculum from which the children can be withdrawn. The LEA will also have a policy on special educational needs. It has a duty to educate a child in a normal school if possible, as long as the child receives the special education needed and resources are still used efficiently for other pupils. This may mean using extra equipment to facilitate learning such as a wordprocessor or adapted furniture. However, the funding for this must not create shortages for the rest of the children.

Under the 1981 Act every school must name a 'responsible person' who makes sure that all those who are likely to teach a child with a statement are told about the statement. This person is usually the headteacher but it can be the chair of governors or another governor.

The governors have a duty to make sure that all teachers in the school are aware of the importance of identifying pupils who have special educational needs and providing for them. The governors must make every effort to see that the necessary special arrangements are made for any pupil who has special educational needs. The governors must make sure that the 'responsible person' tells staff who are to teach the pupil in question about their special needs. See Figure 22.1.

The *Guide to the Law* states that 'governing bodies or staff must make arrangements to allow pupils with special needs to join in the normal activities of the school'. This is an area where governors can find that financial restraints come between their desire to do their moral best for pupils with special needs and the financial needs of the whole school. For example, a child with arthritis who becomes incapacitated and needs to use a wheelchair, will need wide doorways and possibly a lift. It is very unclear who, at the end of the day, is responsible for providing them. Governors (or staff!) have a duty to *try* to make sure all parts of the school are accessible. The LEA may argue that to spend money on this one project would mean the 'resources will not be used efficiently for other pupils'!

Clearly, governors must have a policy on special educational needs in their school. This should have regard to *all* special needs, including those with above-average ability; one school I know calls them the 'Turbo-charged group'.

Duties of governing body etc. in relation to pupils with special educational needs.

161.—(1) The governing body, in the case of a county, voluntary or grant-maintained school, and the local education authority, in the case of a maintained nursery school, shall—

(a) use their best endeavours, in exercising their functions in relation to the school, to secure that if any registered pupil has special educational needs the special educational provision which his learning difficulty calls for is made,

(b) secure that, where the responsible person has been informed by the local education authority that a registered pupil has special educational needs, those needs are made known to all who are likely to teach him, and

(c) secure that the teachers in the school are aware of the importance of identifying, and providing for, those registered pupils who have special educational needs.

(2) In subsection (1)(b) above, "the responsible person" means—

(a) in the case of a county, voluntary or grant-maintained school, the head teacher or the appropriate governor (that is, the chairman of the governing body or, where the governing body have designated another governor for the purposes of this paragraph, that other governor), and

(b) in the case of a nursery school, the head teacher.

(3) To the extent that it appears necessary or desirable for the purpose of co-ordinating provision for children with special educational needs—

(a) the governing bodies of county, voluntary and grant-maintained schools shall, in exercising functions relating to the provision for such children, consult the local education authority, the funding authority and the governing bodies of other such schools, and

(b) in relation to maintained nursery schools, the local education authority shall, in exercising those functions, consult the funding authority and the governing bodies of county, voluntary and grant-maintained schools.

(4) Where a child who has special educational needs is being educated in a county, voluntary or grant-maintained school or a maintained nursery school, those concerned with making special educational provision for the child shall secure, so far as is reasonably practicable and is compatible with—

(a) the child receiving the special educational provision which his learning difficulty calls for,

(b) the provision of efficient education for the children with whom he will be educated, and

(c) the efficient use of resources,

that the child engages in the activities of the school together with children who do not have special educational needs.

(5) The annual report for each county, voluntary, maintained special or grant-maintained school shall include a report containing such information as may be prescribed about the implementation of the governing body's policy for pupils with special educational needs; and in this subsection "annual report" means the report prepared under the articles of government for the school in accordance with section 30 of the Education (No. 2) Act 1986 or, as the case may be, paragraph 8 of Schedule 6 to this Act.

Figure 22.1 Statutory duties of governing bodies

Source: Education Act 1993, Part III, para. 161, pp. 102–3

ALLOCATING RESOURCES TO MEET THE EDUCATIONAL NEEDS OF ALL STUDENTS

In order to include all children in the normal curriculum, as we must, it is often necessary to put extra resources into this area. Schemes of local management will already be putting extra money into a schools budget to help integrate children with special needs. Some children will already have a statement of special educational need. This statement will bring special funding. This money will be retained centrally and targeted to meet the needs of the individual pupil. This can mean a school is funded for a teacher and/or support for that pupil, but not necessarily full time. The school will have money in the budget for 'non-statutory special needs' which is for the support of pupils who are seen as needing some extra help but who do not necessarily have a statement. The way this amount is worked out can be quite arbitrary, ranging from the number of children receiving free school meals to the standard of reading in the school based on reading tests. In some schemes this amount is not always easily identifiable.

Governors will have to agree how to organize special education and can put money in from the main school budget to supplement support and staff provided by the LEA for special needs. This is sometimes used to increase staff hours so that they work full time with special needs pupils. This can still be in mainstream classes and may include both statemented and non-statemented pupils.

ACCREDITING COURSES FOR STUDENTS WHO EXPERIENCE DIFFICULTIES IN LEARNING

One secondary school which has done this, has also devised a special course in history and geography for children with special educational needs. The course takes in aspects of the National Curriculum, tailoring it to the needs of children who would be unable to reach GCSE standard. It is followed by children with learning difficulties and in particular those for whom lack of fluency in the literary skills inhibits success in history and geography as well as other subjects.

The course, entitled Local Geography and History, covers only basic geographical and historical aspects of the immediate area, and leads to a school-based certificate. This may be the only paper qualification that some children leave school with and is highly prized by these children. The pupils may also be entered for the Associated Examination Board tests in Lifeskills and Basic Geography.

The pupils learn to work as a group, utilize research and reporting skills, and learn how to behave when out in the community. It also means that the children don't have to be excluded from this part of the curriculum.

The children are chosen for the course in consultation with the geography and history teachers and the special needs staff. It is by 'invitation only' and therefore gives the children the feeling they are exclusive. A welcome boost for their ego in a learning situation which may be seen by other pupils as one of lower regard, however hard we try to teach equality!

The course involves weekly off-site visits to places in Norfolk and this coupled with the higher pupil/teacher ratio leads to increased costs. Funding for this would be supported by the governors.

ACCESS TO SCHOOLS FOR DISABLED CHILDREN AND ADULTS

As well as being aware of learning difficulties experienced by students, governors should ensure equality in access. I know of very few disabled governors or teachers, especially in secondary schools. One of the main reasons, I'm sure, is the sheer inaccessibility of the buildings.

Our own training unit, supposedly dedicated to equal opportunities, recently took on a new venue for training sessions. It is in a large hotel with steps up to a revolving door. Although the hotel staff offered to carry me in, this is hardly equality. Working as I do from a wheelchair or on crutches, I soon realized how many secondary schools are on more than one level. Even those areas in a single-story building invariably have steps. The increasing use of mobiles, standing several feet above ground level, is not improving the situation. On one occasion my disability was a barrier on Prize Day. I could not be on the platform party because I couldn't get up onto the stage!

Potential pupils with mobility problems are usually steered towards a more accessible school. However, in rural areas this may not be possible. The governors may then be faced with a request to provide suitable arrangements for that child to be educated at that school. This could involve financing ramps or even stairlifts. Rearranging an individual timetable to accommodate the child in a more suitable environment, e.g. ground-floor rooms only, could be seen as against equal opportunities policy. This is another reason why policies must take into account all possible scenarios.

In grant-maintained schools and special agreement schools the governors are more responsible for admissions. A committee of governors hears appeals from parents of children refused a place. Could this be another area where the governors' concern for the financial position of the school as a whole is weighed against the needs of one less able child?

With open enrolment a school must admit a child if there is space unless:

1 admitting the child would push the number of pupils admitted above the limit agreed for the school; or
2 in grammar or secondary modern schools, the child has been assessed as not suitable for the education offered.

If a school is oversubscribed, the numbers of children applying being greater than the number a school can admit, these 'spaces' may be used for pupils who will have lower costs. Conversely, it has been said that since the introduction of LMS, requests by schools for statementing to be carried out have increased due to the extra staffing allocations. Could we also have a situation where a school, in an area where the scheme of LMS bases non-statutory special needs allowance on reading standards, deliberately reduces standards to get a higher allowance? I sincerely hope not!

LEAGUE TABLES AND PERFORMANCE INDICATORS

Funding is central to all decisions. This is no less true in schools than it is in home life. Income is generated largely by pupil numbers. From April 1993, at least 80 per cent of the aggregated schools budget is pupil led. This means 80 per cent of the general schools budget, minus certain specific items paid centrally by the local authority, is based on the number of pupils on a school roll. The comment that every potential pupil is a round £1,000 on legs can be very true!

This generates tremendous pressures on a school, and its governors in particular, to keep pupil numbers up to maximum allowed. A school which has a positive approach to special needs will be seen as a caring school. A school which gives its special needs department a low priority may give the impression of a school which does not see all pupils as of equal importance. If a school has a high number of children with special educational needs, could this lower the image of a school as a high-powered, dynamic educational establishment in the eyes of prospective parents? Human nature can be very cruel.

One criterion used by parents looking for a secondary place is the examination results: the 'league tables'. As with any statistics or results, the way in which the information is produced can alter the overall impression. We saw earlier that children could be withdrawn from the National Curriculum. This also applies to testing, the Standard Assessment Tests (SATs) and GCSEs.

In the reporting of examination results at GCSE level, this would raise the percentage of passes but would raise the number of pupils with no GCSE results. At A/AS level, the results are only published on those pupils who have entered one or more A/AS examinations. A school that has a policy of encouraging all pupils to try for an examination may compare unfavourably with a similar school which only allows the children who are sure of success to enter. Governors may even take into account the actual cost of examination fees when determining the policy.

Another indicator which measures the 'success' of a school is the destination of leavers list. This document records the intended destination of school leavers using four categories:

1 school/sixth form college/further education
2 higher education
3 employment
4 others

Will less able children have more difficulty in getting jobs, or placements on further/higher education? How will this reflect on the school in the destination tables?

Will governors in the future when formulating their policies on admissions and special needs, be encouraged or discouraged to welcome with open arms those less able pupils?

Indeed, are governors qualified to make these judgements?

GOVERNOR TRAINING

Training is available for governors. The LEA must provide the training it thinks necessary for governors to carry out their duties effectively. In practice this varies considerably from county to county.

In Norfolk, where I am a governor, there is everything from a four-session course for new governors to a two-hour seminar on the use of grounds. Most aspects of governing are covered and special subjects can be requested. Training is held in the evenings and during the day. Venues are all over the country. Training sessions are run by qualified governor and headteacher tutors with expert help and advice brought in.

A typical session in Norfolk will be held in convivial surroundings: a teacher training centre, hotel or (our latest venue) the executive suite of a local sports club. Refreshments are always provided and transport can be arranged. A session will accommodate form ten to fifty or sixty governors and will be staffed by several tutors as well as relevant experts. People from all walks of life and all ages attend the training sessions. The majority of participants join in with discussions and workshops, and evaluation shows that most governors leave satisfied that it has been a worthwhile learning situation.

Even with these excellent arrangements and selection on offer there are still many governors who do not attend training sessions, either due to lack of time or enthusiasm. Training is not compulsory to be a governor!

Perhaps, with all the extra responsibilities, it should be.

MONITORING AND INSPECTION

Finally, there is one aspect of the system of governors which worries me. There is no real check on whether schools and governors are working to the regulations as laid down.

I know of governing bodies who meet three times a year (the minimum), are told very briefly any major changes since last time, and go away feeling 'why am I here?' Governing schools is a partnership, an equal one, and will only work as it was designed if it is allowed to be that partnership.

I hope that inspection, with its overall view of a school, will highlight these bad examples of governing. Inspectors will be able to see from governing body documentation, or lack of it, how much or little real involvement there is. Bad practices can then be eradicated and the way forward will be as it was designed, together.

REFERENCE

Department for Education (1993) *Guide to the Law*, London: DFE Information Branch.

Chapter 23

Securing an appropriate education for Kirsty

Liz and David Arrondelle

Kirsty's schooling has been shaped by the active involvement of her parents in every educational decision. Kirsty is now in the sixth form and Liz and David are delighted with her courses. In this chapter, they describe Kirsty's previous experiences, what led up to her enrolment at Barnwell School and her wide range of current educational and recreational activities.

Kirsty commenced her secondary education at the local Catholic comprehensive school at the age of 12½ years, having stayed in a reception class for an extra year at the beginning of her formal education. She also repeated her final year in the junior school before transferring to St Mary's.

Kirsty's arrival here had been preceded by many months of preparation. Initially we visited three local secondary schools during her last year at Richard Whittington School. We had received excellent support from both the LEA and the school itself. The one thing we had learned so far was that the success of Kirsty's inclusion was due to a combination of factors. The attitude of the school and the staff was absolutely crucial – in conjunction with appropriate additional support from the LEA. We went through the statementing procedure with two different authorities as we moved from Berkshire to Hertfordshire when Kirsty was 8 years old. The statement in Berkshire was not complete, but it had been made absolutely clear to us that the only placement considered would be in a special school. Kirsty had attended the local infants' school very successfully, with the benefit of additional support, but with the advent of the 1981 Education Act the headteacher knew that the only way to get an allocation of appropriate resources was to go through the 'multiprofessional assessment'. We were fortunate, as a family, to have the support of Mark Vaughan, who had just set up the Centre for Studies on Integration in Education (CSIE) to help us through the minefield of the statementing process, which at that time was new to everyone. We took the opportunity to move when it was apparent that Berkshire LEA would not support Kirsty in a continued mainstream placement.

The attitude of Hertfordshire LEA was much more encouraging and as the local primary school agreed to include Kirsty on their roll the authority gave immediate maximum welfare support (non-teaching assistant 'NTA', no qualification required – anyone can apply) as the statementing procedure began again – there had been so many delays with the original that all the reports were totally out of date, so it was scrapped completely; the fact that Kirsty had been attending a mainstream school was the guiding factor to her continued mainstream education. All the support services were involved and the balance of a qualified teacher and a welfare assistant was quickly established in the classroom. This proved to be very successful, not only for Kirsty but all the pupils at the school and the team-teaching staff.

Kirsty was popular with the children in her class and was a frequent visitor to their homes and birthday parties. She formed good relationships with her welfare helpers and probably gave them quite a challenge as she has a strong stubborn streak which needs to be dealt with effectively. She joined the local Brownie pack which brought her into contact with another aspect of life and a different group of people – as well as some of her school friends.

As Kirsty's final year at Richard Whittington commenced we turned our thoughts to secondary education and a series of visits were planned.

The first of the three secondary schools we visited was in a delightful rural setting, with places for a few boarders for those pupils living in the more remote country areas. There was a pleasant calm atmosphere and we were warmly welcomed by the headteacher – a place could be offered, but the school was under threat of closure and we all agreed that a major disruption during her secondary career was not a good idea. The next school was an all-girls school which was due for amalgamation with a mixed school in the near future. The headteacher was not available at the time of our appointment, so we were interviewed by the games mistress who had responsibility for special needs. Frankly, we could not get out quickly enough – all she could see were assumed problems for the school and artificially created barriers for Kirsty's inclusion – definitely an 'over my dead body' prospect. The attitude of the headteacher at the third school was completely different: 'if we can't make it work here – where can it work?' Yes, they had a special needs department, a new and progressive special needs coordinator was due to start in September – we came away feeling like walking on air! It was suggested that Kirsty and I should go to school for two days, so that we could see exactly what went on in a normal school day (very different from visits on open days) to experience the hurly burly that Kirsty would encounter and the constant changing from one classroom to another. One day was not enough – a minimum of two days was agreed.

We soon realized that school days had changed quite a lot since we went to school! There was far more opportunity for independence and a more flexible regime. We felt that Kirsty would be able to adapt to the changes in the same way that all children experience on transfer to secondary school. During her last term at Richard Whittington, Kirsty and her welfare helper visited St Mary's regularly so that when she started in September, she would be more familiar with the layout of the school and also know some of the pupils as very few from Richard Whittington would be going there.

Kirsty remained at St Mary's for the next four years, although on reflection, many aspects were not as good as we had hoped, largely due to the very mixed attitude of the staff to a pupil with complex learning difficulties, some of whom were not prepared to make the effort to adapt to meet her needs – in sharp contrast to others who would do everything possible to allow Kirsty to take an active part at every opportunity.

The welfare support varied with the different personalities and their own attitudes to Kirsty's needs, but overriding all this was the fact that she had the benefit of the very best and most experienced Home Tutor (qualified teaching support) that we could have had, and it is thanks to her expertise and understanding that Kirsty achieved the success of gaining the Hertfordshire Achievement Project Award and remained a happy and well-adjusted youngster. She made many friends and the support from the pupils was magnificent. It is an indisputable fact that all the pupils that have come into contact with Kirsty have benefited from the experience and hopefully they will have gained a greater natural understanding of the needs of people with difficulties. The friendships made at St Mary's have continued and it looks as if this communication is as valuable to her friends as it is to Kirsty. She joined in after-school activities – the Gym Club and the Dance Group and took part in the displays given by the groups at the end of term with great enthusiasm and enjoyment. She also gained her IBM 10 Step Sports Award, thanks to the enthusiastic support of the sports staff and their determination to include her at every opportunity; they were equally delighted with her success.

Other activities at St Mary's included an annual sponsored six-mile walk. Kirsty decided she would like to take part, so her friends rallied round and gained an enormous number of sponsors and also joined her on the walk. We went along too with a couple of our dogs, across the fields, through the villages. Kirsty began to drop back a bit, unfortunately David had the haversack with the cold drinks which was rapidly disappearing into the distance! As we struggled on, various groups joined us. We forged ahead but with only about half a mile to go Kirsty got a 'stitch'. After a brief rest she was joined by a couple of the boys in her form, they really encouraged and helped her to finish the course, which she did in great style.

As Kirsty's sixteenth birthday approached we were told at her annual review that St Mary's would not be able to support her any longer. We had to agree that she would have become very isolated, as her year group were about to start on their GCSE syllabus. Although pupils can remain until they are 18, Kirsty's days at St Mary's were to finish. We feel the success achieved was due to a few teachers dedicated to the idea of inclusion, but a much greater degree of success would have resulted if the whole-school approach had been adopted.

The immediate alternative on offer was to attend the special school on a full-time basis. She had already been attending two days a week against our wishes, we could see no advantage in this arrangement and an increase to full time was totally inappropriate to her needs. We felt very strongly that she still needed more time in school before she would be ready for further education in college.

We were contacted by a careers officer from the LEA who understood our philosophy and set off to try and establish a continuation of mainstream schooling. She fully accepted that a full-time placement in a special school was not appropriate to Kirsty's needs. Locally there was nothing available, but in a different division of Hertfordshire was the 'Southern Consortium' – a group of three schools within walking distance of each other, a mainstream school, another mainstream school adapted for wheelchair access and a special school, which as a whole offered a fantastic range of educational opportunities. We took Kirsty to Barnwell – the mainstream school – at their invitation to see if Kirsty would like to go there.

The success of this venture has been brilliant, she is in the sixth form and her own self-esteem and confidence have blossomed. Since being there from September 1992 she has had two weeks' work experience in an hotel in Bishops Stortford (this was arranged by the school as it was more practical for this to take place near our own home). She has also attended a two-day conference in Stevenage, this was part of a programme arranged by the school with local businesses – we understand that she stood up and con-tributed her own views to the discussion – to everyone's delight. She has a stimulating timetable including a Diploma Course on Travel, and she visits the special school a couple of times a week to reinforce her written work. There have been many out-of-school activities including visits to the Science Museum, the Travel Exhibition, fishing in the local river, and numerous others. Barnwell also offers facilities for hearing impaired pupils and specialist teaching help to dyslexic students, which is a clear indication that this school recognizes the difficulties that many pupils experience and has addressed the issue by providing support from its budget plan! The staff have a very lively and imaginative approach to all pupils. To quote from their prospectus they have a commitment to:

- Maximizing individual achievement within a caring community;
- Developing respect and responsibility in all relationships;
- Promoting friendship, fair play and equality;
- Creating personal opportunities in a world of challenge and change;
- A better future for all.

Table 23.1 Timetable for Kirsty Arrondelle 1993–4

	P1	P2	P3	P4	P5	P6	P7	P8
Monday	Barnwell Diploma with Barnwell and Greenside pupils, including languages (French)				Music with Margaret Hughes			
Tuesday	As Monday, including science				Greenside Drama & Dance			
Wednesday	North Herts College with Greenside pupils Collect at 1.30pm from Greenside						(Very often) Library with Margaret Hughes	
Thursday	Diploma with Barnwell pupils				Art with Barbara Plester		With Margaret Hughes	
Friday	Speech therapy at Greenside		Collected from Greenside at 10.30am by Barbara Plester				Diploma with Barnwell pupils	

Notes:

Kirsty is in the second year of a two-year City & Guilds Diploma of Vocational Education course.

In the Monday and Tuesday morning sessions at Barnwell she has the support of a teacher from Greenside School. The area of study is Providing Goods and Services and she has worked on the following modules: Geography of Tourism, Reception Duties and Travel Agency Services. The Diploma course includes taking part in work experience and being involved in the sixth form conference.

On Thursday morning and Friday afternoon Kirsty works on the core element of the Diploma or continues the work of Tuesday.

The college course on Wednesday is a second-year course for Greenside students, aimed at involving them in the community, with appropriate visits out and speakers invited in.

The speech therapy group on Friday morning is led by one of our speech therapists and concentrates on the specific requirements of group members.

Margaret Hughes is a non-teaching assistant; Barbara Plester is a qualified teacher, a school-based Home Tutor.

These ideas are more than just a philosophy, they are real and they have enabled Kirsty to be included in her own right – to make friendships with students of all ages and abilities, form good relationships with the teaching staff, her helpers – even the taxi driver has been a tremendous support in many ways by liaison with the school staff and ourselves – a great messenger.

Kirsty's timetable is shown in Table 23.1. Other activities which she has developed outside school hours include our involvement with dogs (we breed Golden Retrievers and show them as a hobby). Kirsty has competed on equal terms in Junior Handling Competitions up and down the country with considerable success – in fact for three years running she qualified to compete at the Richmond Championship show semi-finals of the Junior

Handler of the Year Competition, which she did with considerable style and was well considered for a place in the final.

Her other great love is swimming. We used to take her into the swimming pool from the age of about three months – she now swims with the Bishops Stortford Swimming Club and has gained her ASA Silver Badge. She has medals galore from Special Olympics competitions but she swims because she enjoys it! She has not yet mastered a tumble turn but spends a lot of time under water in trying to achieve this manoeuvre; with her determination she will succeed one day. She is now a Ranger and is about to tackle some aspects of the Duke of Edinburgh Award Scheme.

Kirsty has just started her second year in the sixth form – still supported by the LEA, her needs now focusing more clearly upon the transition for after school, she will continue to work with pupils of her own age and ability to develop and enjoy skills of social interaction, assistance to develop speech and a programme to assist transition beyond school, careers advice and work experience. She has a wonderful opportunity in her grasp and she genuinely loves going to school; she has 100 per cent attendance and punctuality records and has made many friends.

Kirsty has Down's Syndrome.

Chapter 24

Barnwell School
A mainstream experience

Richard Westergreen-Thorne

Richard is a deputy headteacher at Barnwell School and has been closely involved in the provision of appropriate support for Kirsty Arrondelle. In this chapter he describes the features of the school and its local consortium partners that have enabled them to welcome Kirsty. These include funding, collaborative teaching and a commitment to equality between students. Richard is aware that there are disagreements between members of staff and that resourcing is always a problem, but he sees the inclusion of Kirsty and other students who require innovative approaches as a natural extension of his view of what constitutes an educational community.

Barnwell School is one of eight 11–18 comprehensive schools in Stevenage, Hertfordshire. It has 720 pupils with approximately 100 in the sixth form.

Stevenage was chosen in 1985 to be one of the pilot Technical and Vocational Education Initiative (TVEI) schemes in the country. As with many other TVEI schemes the introduction of TVEI forced mainstream secondary and special schools and their staff to work together with common agendas.

The Stevenage TVEI consortium consisted of all the 11–18 schools in the town and in addition those special schools with pupils aged 11 and over. Much of the work of the TVEI consortium took place through management and coordinator groups set up to establish joint policies and INSET using TVEI funding. This meant that groups of headteachers, deputy headteachers and subject teachers were brought together on a regular basis to work with common goals, on common activities. As a consequence of these developments a dialogue was established between teachers and institutions within the mainstream and special school sectors. Such working groups as were established included Post-16 Entitlement, Equal Opportunities and Work Experience as well as numerous curriculum groupings.

Within Stevenage the Town Consortium, as it became known, was split into three mini-consortia for post-16 links. These were the North, East and

South. Barnwell and Heathcote Schools formed the Southern Consortium. This arrangement proved relatively easy in the case of the South as the two schools are only 400 metres apart at their closest point. The Southern Consortium developed within a short space of time a consortium sixth form with a common timetable that operated as a single unit, thus allowing pupils access to a wider range of provision than would otherwise have been the case.

Special Schools in the town were left free to make curriculum links as appropriate. In practice geographical considerations were, and remain, a major consideration.

In particular, there soon became apparent a common interest in 16–18 provision between Mainstream and special schools. The TVEI initiative started in Stevenage at a time when the Mainstream schools were looking closely at their post-16 provision. Until this point the typical diet in school sixth forms were A-levels or, as an alternative, O-level resits. Stevenage schools reflected closely the national concern and debate during the 1980s as to the appropriate curriculum for those 16-year-olds not deemed suitable for A-level courses. All of the Stevenage Mainstream schools set up City & Guilds Certificate of Pre-Vocational Education (CPVE) schemes during the late 1980s. These were courses specifically designed for 16 to 18-year-olds with achievement credited through continuous assessment and a record of achievement rather than by exam. Designed by City & Guilds to be suitable for all 16 to 18-year-olds – and marketed as such – they nonetheless tended almost entirely to be entered upon across the country by non-A-level students. The way the CPVE was set out, students followed prevocational interests to varying levels of detail. Their progress was recorded and they achieved a record of achievement that matched what they had achieved regardless of ability.

CPVE had the potential to provide a sixth-form course for students interested in a very wide range of vocational areas. In order to maximise the range of choice and provide a more efficient allocation of their resources the mainstream schools in Stevenage joined together in a variety of ways to provide a wide-ranging vocational diet for students. For three years this took the form of a Town CPVE scheme that was based around the three mini-consortia but allowed students to move to other sites for specific vocational experiences. While it lasted this system also involved the local college of further education.

During the same period all the Stevenage schools were also developing their Post-16 compensatory education provision in order to match TVEI requirements. It was a prerequisite of TVEI funding that schools fulfilled a range of requirements. These ranged through equal opportunities policies, industrial links, development of new courses and a range of other related commitments. One such was the establishment of Post-16 compensatory education including such aspects as general studies, guidance, personal and social education (PSE), work experience and careers schemes to cater for sixth-formers and widen their post-16 experiences. Examples of this in practice included one and two-week work experience blocks for sixth-formers; timetabled guidance and counselling sessions with tutors; and the opportunity to continue Science and technology in the sixth form via general studies programmes if studying three A-level arts subjects.

As a consequence of the introduction of CPVE and compensatory programmes the sixth forms in Stevenage evolved into larger organizations offering courses that, for the first time, catered for all abilities and provided a more varied and vocationally oriented curriculum. It was this new context of mainstream post-16 provision that interested the special schools. They could see the potential for linkage where very little existed before such developments took place.

The Southern Consortium developed links with two special schools in particular: Lonsdale School that caters for 2 to 18-year-olds with physical disabilities, and Greenside School, which takes pupils aged 3–18 identified as having severe learning difficulties. Both schools wished to link post-16 with the Southern Consortium.

Lonsdale was particularly interested in the compensatory programme. It provided an opportunity for their pupils to mix with consortium students and also access a much wider range of general studies-type courses than they themselves could provide. Examples of their participation included students attending drama, communications, technology and science courses joining the other students of the Southern Consortium in the programmes of study.

In the case of Greenside School their particular interest was the CPVE, as by joining with the Southern Consortium their sixth-formers were able to work alongside mainstream students and access a wider range of prevocational courses, examples of their participation being students joining groups studying business studies, leisure and tourism, and manufacturing and design. The link with Greenside in particular is now very well established. Each year sixth-formers join integrated courses. As the CPVE has been replaced firstly by the Diploma of Vocational Education, and more recently, by General National Vocational Qualifications at Intermediate Level (GNVQ Intermediate), Greenside has continued to work with the Southern Consortium. Sixth-formers from Greenside taking these courses attend sessions at Barnwell three half-days a week. On each day they attend with a member of staff from their school. They are full members of the teaching group and follow the same programme of study as the others in the class. They continue their vocational programme back at their own school one day a week on a complementary programme.

In 1992 the link with Barnwell was extended as Greenside began to send pupils to join Diploma of Vocational Education courses at foundation level, that is, 14 to 16-year-olds. They joined prevocational caring and arts media courses and attended lessons at Barnwell along with one of their teachers.

On these courses they spend just over two hours a week at Barnwell. They follow a modular programme, topic based, including such areas as (in the caring courses) a look at local health services and (on the arts media programme) newspaper design and analysis.

For a mainstream school such as Barnwell such links raise important issues that are fundamental to the culture of the institution. Hertfordshire, as an education authority, has a policy of placing 'bases' in schools. Barnwell has for many years had a base for pupils with hearing and visual impairments with usually six to eight pupils on roll at any one time. The policy of this base has always been to have the pupils in the classroom with their peers whenever possible. Pupils are rarely withdrawn from normal lessons.

In 1991 a pupil with physical and learning difficulties joined Year 7 to follow a mainstream timetable within a tutor group of his peers. The pupil received welfare assistance and operated within a normal classroom environment.

In 1991 the staff and governors of the school developed a mission statement that attempted to encapsulate what Barnwell stood and strived for as an institution. The mission produced after considerable discussion and consultation was as follows:

At Barnwell, we are committed to:
Maximizing individual achievement within a caring community
Developing respect and responsibility in all relationships
Promoting friendship, fair play and equality
Creating personal opportunities in a world of challenge and change
A better future for all

Part of the process of evolving the school mission statement was a series of training opportunities developed with a leading national training organization – Time Management International (TMI). Under the headline Putting People First, a number of sessions took place that involved all the staff at the school, teaching, clerical, ancillary, catering, etc. as well as governors, local employers and members of the local authority. The intention of the training was to develop a clear school ethos and to assist in agreeing a common mission. One that reflected a genuine understanding of the issues involved in working in a complex organization.

Since the publication of the school mission the attempt has been made to both promote and act according to the statement. It is used with staff, pupils, parents and governors. It is a key component of the life of the school and is used as a basis for discussion and action. It is a feature of the school brochure and is referred to in many publications. It is used as a focus in preparing assemblies and is reflected in many dealings with pupils both as individuals and as groups.

This is not to say that all staff always have common perceptions. As in all staff rooms there are diverse opinions on such matters as excellence, streaming, discipline systems and the correct relationships between teachers and pupils. What the mission statement has provided is a framework within which such discussion and argument takes place. It has also informed discussion amongst governors and been an influence when appointing new staff to the school.

It is within this context that a number of other initiatives have developed. Firstly, the school was asked by the local authority to establish the first Specific Learning Difficulties Base in a Hertfordshire secondary school. This was designed to be the first such base in Hertfordshire and, when funds permitted, to provide the model for bases in other parts of the authority. The base was established with a complement of twelve pupils on the principle that its staff would work with base pupils in normal lessons wherever possible. It was also set up on the understanding that the base would act as an outreach agency for other schools.

Secondly, the school agreed in 1992 to accept a student, Kirsty Arrondelle, with Downs Syndrome to the sixth form for two years. The timetable agreed was a mixture of work in Diploma of Vocational Education classes, links with and lessons at Greenside School and individual tuition and support. The principle behind the arrangement was that Kirsty would be fully involved in the life of the sixth form, attending a range of classes with her peers and following a full timetable.

Barnwell has therefore pursued a policy of openness and flexibility in its approach to the local community and its provision of educational opportunity for pupils. Such a policy, supported as it is by the schools mission statement, raises important issues for the effective management of the school. There are a number of implications of such a policy, some of which may be viewed as positive – others raise serious issues and concerns. They include the real worry of appearing in the local community as specializing in the provision for certain groups of pupils and hence affecting the school's role and intake.

One important issue is the implications of such a whole-school philosophy for the individual staff at the school. As in many other institutions, individuals may become cautious and uncertain when faced with change. Staff need to be flexible, they need to feel confident, they need to feel supported. How will they react when four pupils from a special school and their teacher join their class on a regular basis?

In particular, what such a policy highlights is a concern expressed effectively by staff when asking each other the questions 'Are we getting it right?' 'Who can tell us if what we are providing is right for the pupils?' 'What about the quality of the materials we use and produce?' These and similar questions reflect an ongoing need for meetings, INSET and support for the staff of the school to enable them to have the confidence and flexibility that effective teaching in such an environment requires.

Teachers in considering their own classroom practice and expertise have needs and worries. Such worries can at times be generated by a school policy that widens the range of opportunities that exist for pupils within the school. Setting out to work in the manner described sets challenges within a school context that will not always be easily achieved by individual teachers working in isolation. It presents significant challenges to the individual teacher and hence major school management implications.

Another issue surrounds that of staff availability. In a mainstream school much of the activity is based around large groups of pupils being in one place together. If a teacher is absent then the class is 'covered' by a colleague. If you operate the school in such a way as to make provision for pupils who may require individual attention at times, it needs much thought, care and use of scarce resources when certain staff are absent. Such arrangements are not often the norm in mainstream schools and contingencies need careful consideration.

Also requiring much time and care is the planning for out of the ordinary events such as Activities Week, sixth form conferences and the like. These involve logistical issues, in particular if the events are off site such as the annual Industrial Society Conference for Sixth Formers held at a local conference centre.

Changes in accountability and funding of schools raise other issues. Governors are increasingly accountable for the schools that they govern. If a mainstream school is visited by an OFSTED inspection team how is its provision to be judged? If its philosophy is such that it accepts a wide range of pupils into its community will its diversity fall inside the experience and expertise of the inspectors? How should they report the activities of the school and the quality of its provision? Against what criteria should an inspector judge, for example, the success of a Year 10 arts media class that includes a number of pupils from Greenside?

How should the school be funded? The relevant sections of the 1993 Education Act are based around entitlement, not resource provision. How should resources be allocated? On what basis should governors make internal resource decisions? How should special and mainstream schools make funding decisions when they provide joint courses and they staff pupil groups together? Who should pay for resources used? Should you include the fixed costs of running a school, and is depreciation an issue when allocating costs? By way of example of this complex issue the following points could be considered. Should Barnwell charge Greenside for allowing its pupil's access to its courses? If so on what basis should such a claim be justified and costed? Should Barnwell's Governing Body allocate extra resources to certain areas? Should Greenside charge Barnwell for its support of Kirsty Arrondelle?

Within both the post-16 and 14–16 areas there is concern by teachers as to what is the appropriate curriculum for pupils. The National Curriculum is not very accessible to many 14 to 16-year-olds whose attainment levels are at the bottom end of the assessment scales. At the post-16 level the end of CPVE has seen the introduction of new courses such as GNVQ Intermediate with far higher expectations of pupil attainment. These new courses do not use a Record of Achievement to note success but rather are based upon exams and tests comparable to GCSE grade C standard.

Finding suitable post-16 provision was a major issue in the early 1980s. It has returned to many schools in the 1990s as they seek to provide for the full range of abilities.

Another issue is that of cooperation and competition. Barnwell and Heathcote Schools compete vigorously for pupils at age 11. Yet at age 16 they are asking pupils and parents to accept them working together as if one institution, an issue clouded further if you include the involvement of the special schools in the equation.

There are many very positive benefits to Barnwell from attempting to provide a relevant curriculum that operates within the framework of its mission statement. The experience of the policy to date is that it has proved very clearly that staff have gained considerable expertise from such work. For example, there is a very clear overlap in the abilities and talents of pupils from all the schools and backgrounds referred to above. Many pupils in mainstream schools have similar needs and aspirations to their colleagues from special schools. Teachers gain new skills from the experience of working with colleagues from other schools.

The issue of differentiation is a key one in education. It is an important aspect of successful schools. Such links as outlined provide an interchange for staff with colleagues who offer a wide range of expertise. They also provide contact with pupils with varied talents and needs and help keep the focus clearly upon effective teaching styles and appropriate resources.

Much debate has taken place in recent years over the provision for those beyond the 2 per cent of the pupil population generally given statemented support – the so-called 20 per cent of pupils within mainstream education with special educational needs. The two bases at Barnwell for Hearing and Visual Impairments and Specific Learning Difficulties have proved a marvellous resource for the school in this regard. They provide experienced teachers with skills valued by their colleagues. They bring to the school extra staff of quality. They bring to lessons when the base staff work in the room an extra resource upon which the whole class and the teacher may draw. They provide a fund of expertise drawn upon by colleagues from across the curriculum range. They have both led and coordinated staff development programmes and their presence enriches discussion in curriculum teams.

For pupils and staff at Barnwell the school's approach enables them as a community to live closer to the commitment of the mission statement. Taking the first line of the mission as an example ('maximizing individual achievement within a caring community') the developments, initiatives and cooperation with other schools as outlined are brought closer to reality.

Pupils can see themselves in a community that is striving to enable all to achieve. It assists pupils to develop respect for each other and widens their range of experience. Finally, it places the school firmly within the local community. A school is physically within a community, but does it truly reflect that community? A policy that is open and involving is much more likely to do so. A policy of inclusion will also lead to the school more accurately reflecting the local community to which it belongs.

In summary, the work that takes place at Barnwell School does so within a framework that is underpinned by its mission statement. Such words are easy to set down. They are much harder to achieve. By being prepared to widen and enhance its provision Barnwell can bring its mission statement closer to reality. This causes the potential for anxiety for staff. It raises issues of accountability and funding. It implies significant staff development needs. It will not always prove easy to achieve the desired results.

At the same time it brings benefits to teaching and learning styles. It provides a vehicle for improving the appropriateness of curriculum provision for all pupils. It enables staff to work more closely with colleagues both within and outside the school. Above all it enables the school to move closer to the community of which it is a part and allows the pupils to be involved in that operation.

Index